THE *Smart Women* SERIES™

Smart Women *Live* Their Why

How Women Entrepreneurs Are Living On Purpose and In Passion

Sheri McConnell
CEO of Smart Women's Institute of Entrepreneurial Learning

www.smartwomeninstitute.com

Smart Women *Live* Their Why
by Sheri McConnell

Smart Women's Institute of Entrepreneurial Learning

ISBN 978-1-936214-58-7

Additional copies of this book are available at www.smartwomeninstitute.com

Presented by Sheri McConnell Companies, Inc.
24165 IH-10 W, Ste. 217-637
San Antonio, TX 78257 USA
866-821-5829

Smart Women's Institute of Entrepreneurial Learning
PUBLISHING PROGRAM
in collaboration with

Dedicated to all Smart Women

Laura
May you lead your
change to a
bright future!
[illegible signature]

Table of Contents

Section Two
Transformational Transitions

Section Three
Living in Daily Discovery

Section Four
Brilliance is in the Balance

Section Five
Big WHYs Lead to Big Growth

SECTION SIX
Resources

Sheri McConnell

Sheri McConnell is fast becoming the voice of Smart Women Entrepreneurs all over the world. Her current company, the Smart Women's Institute of Entrepreneurial Learning, focuses on teaching various wealth-building business models, such as information publishing, membership-based companies, and real estate. Her company also teaches its members how to market online, create a magnetic brand, and most importantly, do this while maintaining down-to-earth balance in their lives.

As a consultant, Sheri is considered the only resource in the world specializing in creating thriving membership-based businesses like associations, institutes, and alliances. Sheri has consulted with hundreds of these networks across the Internet, and considers herself lucky to have helped birthed so many powerful and successful brands over the last decade.

Under the Smart Women Institute umbrella, women entrepreneurs can enroll in annual programs ranging from $197 starter memberships to a $50,000 six month long one-on-one mentorship. Sheri's goal of building a company where women truly inspire each other and hold each other accountable in a graceful manner is exactly what has set her company a part. "Money is power," she explains. "Power to create positive change."

Sheri is also the author of the series of Smart Women books, including *Smart Women Know Their Why*, *Smart Women Create Membership-Based Businesses* and *The Smart Women's Book of Powerful Quotations*. Sheri plans to catapult the success of over 100,000 women-owned businesses in the next decade through the continuation of the Smart Women Book Series™.

Sheri lives in San Antonio, Texas with her husband, their four children, and two adorable "weenie" dogs.

Connect with Sheri at:
Website: www.smartwomeninstitute.com
Twitter: twitter.com/SheriMcConnell
Facebook: tinyurl.com/swifanpage

Section One

Transforming Into a New Way of Being

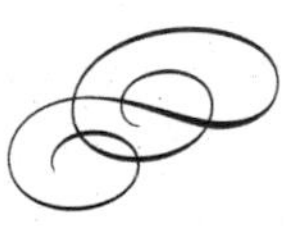

CHAPTER 1

The Journey Continues

by Sheri McConnell

Welcome once again to another powerful book in the Smart Women Series™. If you were lucky enough to have already read the prior book in the series, *Smart Women Know Their Why*, then you are aware that the discovery and knowing of your WHY is really just the tip of the iceberg isn't it?

Living your WHY…now that is a tall order and really the foundation of the iceberg. I decided to dig deeper for you and call on the many brilliant and soul-filled women I am blessed to know so that they could share not only what it is like to live their WHY each day, but what was the catalyst that led them to the discovery of their WHY.

As you will read in the pages that follow, these women practice awareness as they relate to the world around them (their families, their customers, their environments…) and they continue to shift into their purpose more each day.

The fact that these women are entrepreneurs and leaders as we move forward in the new age of commerce is even more exciting!

In the last book, I shared my own journey, and now I share it again here just in case you and I haven't "met" before.

My Journey

Every woman's journey starts somewhere. In the humble spirit of let's just get it all out on the table, I thought I'd share some of the key details of mine up front. By unwrapping the most challenging aspects of my life for you now, I hope you'll feel even more empowered as you delve further into both my story and your own.

In sharing my prior hardships and false hopes, I offer up positive energy for whichever path you currently find yourself on. I imagine that the same angels that once stood by my side throughout my childhood and then again during my divorce, flank me on either side for you. I ask that they hold us all steady as we face the winds of change, individually and together.

I invite you to step into the light with me. Isn't it time to bring more joy and power to your world?

The best way I know how to do this is to take one step at a time, concentrating on moving past fear into power. Please forgive the Jerry Springer-esque texture to my story. What can I say? It's where I come from. But it's been my policy through the years that once I heal from something, I leave it behind and move on. I only stop to relive the drama now (for the first time) so you'll know that where a person comes from (maybe you?) needn't have any bearing on where they're going.

I offer you a key here, hoping that it will help unlock a door to a magical place for you.

Or maybe with this book, you'll simply find yourself making more good choices, more often. That's the real key to success, isn't it? Good choices. This key unlocks many an abundant door. "Make good choices!" I always tell my children whenever we part—as I drop them off at school or to daycare or at a friend's for a sleepover. I wish my mom had known to share that wisdom with me. Or maybe she did? In her own roundabout way…

My Not-So-Happy Childhood

Don't many unhappy childhood stories start with something about mom? Beginning with mine is perfect because she taught me countless priceless lessons at an early age.

That sounds sort of peachy, but believe me, it wasn't. Let's just say that I learned what not to do from my mother if I wanted a happy life. I watched her suffer because of her endless bad choices, which never eased up until the day I let her go. Once I grew into adulthood, I learned the truth: mom was bipolar. But as a kid, all I knew was that I couldn't trust her to brush the knots out of my hair or make me a PBJ for school, much less provide any stability whatsoever. And unfortunately, she was all I had.

My mother was an orphan who had married six times by the time I left home at 17 to put myself through college. My father was her first husband; they divorced when I was an infant. I wouldn't see him again or "meet him" until I was 21.

Mom was a stripper or exotic dancer (I dare say semi-prostitute, if I'm to be completely honest), which made my life even worse because of the environment in which she met her suitors.

All of my "stepdads" were questionable at best, dangerous at worst. Together, their alcohol and drug abuse multiplied exponentially, immersing me in a toxic soup in which I struggled every day to grow.

My version of my traumatic, unstable, and chaotic childhood meant that for years at a time, I experienced a great deal of mental, physical, and sexual abuse. I say "years" only because during a few of her marriages, mom stopped beating me. She was either too busy with her new husband, and thus ignored me—for which I was grateful—or because one of my stepsiblings was on the receiving end of the beatings instead.

Although my mother didn't participate in the sexual abuse, she never saved me from it either. When I finally asked her to protect me from the last unsavory man she'd trotted into my life, she blamed the abuse on me. She said, "It's your fault because of the way you dress." My mother made countless bad choices.

Let me pause to say that today I'm deeply grateful for my childhood. I understand now that my mom never healed from what must have been her own childhood traumas. Then, each time she veered off the cliff to make yet another rotten decision, she became that much more disgusted with herself. After spending my 20s seething with anger towards her, and my 30s letting go and forgiving her, I now feel sadness for the woman who gave me life. Although my 20s were hard, chocked-full of mistakes from my own monkey-see cruddy behaviors, I survived with my heart and sense of humor intact. And, more importantly, I learned a lifetime of lessons in a mere few decades! If life's a school…I got a double PhD.

I've come to terms with the fact that while we all deserve healthy parents, we don't always get them. I have to believe I was given my mom for a reason, and thus I'm extremely grateful to have lived through those years, able now to talk about them while holding a larger perspective. Our experiences, negative or positive, are gifts when we choose to see them as such. For instance:

A few of the many wonderful lessons of my tortured childhood:

- How to adapt to change quickly
- How to relate to different cultures
- How to rely on myself to make good things happen
- How to trust my intuition and sense danger in a split second
- How to move away from unhealthy situations and people
- How to be financially independent
- How to set boundaries
- How to forgive
- How to forgive some more

My experience is that a person can live his/her whole life and not learn some of these priceless lessons. The human spirit is resilient and seeks validation and love. These lessons helped me to make better choices. And everything begins with choice.

From "I Do" to "I Don't"

"If you are going through hell, then keep going."
—Winston Churchill

I mentioned some bad choices during my 20s. One of the biggest ones was marrying the first man that asked. We hadn't even finished unwrapping our wedding presents when he began treating me as my mother did—abusively. In retrospect, it makes sense that I would seek this familiar feeling of "love." It makes sense that I'd ignored the red flags. I had never had a real example of lasting love and I did not think

I was worthy of it, either. Yet, he was good for me in many ways, too.

First of all, I had two beautiful children with him within two years. The verbal and physical abuse increased with the stress of two young children and it didn't take me long to decide that I wouldn't allow my children to grow up like I did and if I didn't leave the abusive marriage when they were young, it would only get harder on them and on me.

I remember my therapist saying that some women who were chronically abused as children, later experience an awakening after having children. He said, "We would take the abuse ourselves, but we wouldn't let our children take it." Bingo. That is what happened to me. An Awakening. I didn't survive my childhood to only end right back in chaos. I was desperate not to turn out like my mother. Getting a divorce didn't help; it made me feel like I was repeating her mistakes.

Yet on the other hand, if I didn't save my children from this life of domestic abuse, I really would be perpetuating the insanity. Either way, I was at the crossroads of the hardest decision of my life.

I chose to file for divorce at 26 years old. I remember the feeling when I finally knew I was on the right path. I had left him and was sitting on the floor of a one-bedroom apartment: I had saved up enough to pay one month's rent. I had no money, no job, no furniture, and no family to help me (my mom had moved to New Mexico with husband number six). But I felt happy for the first time in ages. At a time when I should have been terrified, not knowing if I'd get to keep my kids or even be able to feed them, I still knew deep down there was hope for a better life. My soul and my children were finally in a safe place. I would go on to fight a nine-month legal battle. My ex-husband and his family had filed for full custody and were trying to take the children away from me as punishment for leaving him. I was scared, knowing that money had been known to sway people within the legal system. And, my ex and his family had far more money than I did.

This part of the journey is where I found my inner strength. You know in *Eat, Pray, Love* when author Elizabeth Gilbert discusses how her divorce was like having a car wreck every day for two years? I totally agree with that description, except that mine was a smash up every day for only nine months, but with two infants along for the ride! I went to multiple court dates alone while his large Catholic family told lies on his behalf to ensure they'd get custody of the children. In the end, one document, his psychological evaluation, helped me win my case. I wish the legal system would have allowed the psychological evaluation to be done in the first few months, saving my children and me a lot of heartache. But instead of being angry at the system, I chose to be grateful for the results of the evaluation.

It was the first time I could show in black and white that my truth was indeed the truth. And even though an entire family said one thing, the actual facts, in black and white, were undeniable.

In this instance, the court made the right decision and awarded me full custody. I am very aware that not everyone is so lucky. Of course they only ordered him to pay $450 a month in total child support. I remember at the time, though, thinking it was much easier for me to support them on my own than it was trying to fight a broken man and a broken system. I can't tell you how good it feels to be financially self-sufficient (a millionaire over and over again actually!) 16 years later. There were times during the nine months, however, I thought I would lose my children. The reality was that I had no money, a brand new job which his lawyer (the most expensive lawyer in Fort Worth) was forcing me to leave, sometimes multiple times a week, to attend depositions (a tactic to try to cause me to lose my job), and no family support whatsoever to help me with two young daughters under the age of two. I am aware I had angels during this time.

And I am saddened by how often the story doesn't turn out as well as mine did. I owe my success to the growth I experienced during that year. In the beginning, I went through a deep depression and I would cry and shake during the depositions while my soon-to-be-ex-husband would just laugh. This is not an exaggeration. I'd made a very bad choice in a husband. But by the end of the fight for my kids, I literally turned inside out in who I was (like Neo at the end of the Matrix movie) and I moved forward with more wisdom and strength and love for myself; love I'd pass on to my children.

To me, running a successful business is a piece of cake in comparison to living through my divorce and raising my daughters by myself for the next four years. I process the bumps along the entrepreneur path much more easily because I know what my lowest point is, and nothing has even come close to it again.

They (my mother and my ex-husband) taught me this one valuable lesson. If you can't have honesty and integrity in a relationship, then the relationship isn't worth having.

The space we hold here on this earth is to be treasured, and we should all be vigilant gatekeepers when choosing who we let occupy our time. And in my opinion, we have to be even more careful when it is family. They do not get a free pass to mess with your destiny. It doesn't serve them and it doesn't serve you when you allow toxic behavior to go on around you.

Years later, I married a much nicer man who I'd known from high school. We had two more children—a girl and a boy—and we're going on 12 years now. Like any couple, we've had our ups and downs, but nothing marriage counseling and lots of world-class nagging can't fix! Contrary to what my ex-husband predicted umpteen times during our time together, I didn't turn out just like my mother after all.

My husband is my calm sea. I am eternally grateful he's in my life. He was the first person who ever allowed me to put up boundaries in my life when my mother or my ex-husband would abuse me. I would feel guilt because I was still an abused soul each time my mother or my ex-husband would abuse me and I would try to process what I did to cause each situation.

One day, my current husband looked at me and said, "You don't deserve this." This one sentence allowed me to start creating boundaries where the abusers were concerned. I eventually was able to not react to my ex-husband's words, to take a breath, and hang up the phone. And then I made one of the hardest decisions ever when I was 30 (ten years ago) to stop all contact with my mother. If you have ever had experience with someone who is bipolar and doesn't take medication for it, then you know how unhealthy it was to have her around my children and in my life. I let her go so that I could grow. And I have been healing ever since.

For me, I had to let go of our relationship because the mother I deserved and needed did not exist. She never had. I used to joke that it was hard "raising my mother." Once I let go of her, I could become a good mother myself and try to be the mother I never had. Once I let go of her, I could stop being mean. Have you ever noticed that being around mean people makes you mean? Around both my mother and my ex-husband, I felt the lower-based need to fight for survival. Once I let go of them, I could begin to love and forgive them. I'll be honest and tell you it is much harder with the ex-husband because his choices still affect my children, and I get frustrated because they deserve better. But I do my best to point out what I think is good about him. Additionally, I'm proud of myself for giving them the opportunity to see what a healthy marriage can look like. It isn't perfect, but we continue to try to love each other at a deeper level as the years go by. I never had that example, and my hope for them is that they will be able to make better choices.

In an effort to support each other during our journeys, I want to also recognize how difficult it is to have a blended family. As a mother, you feel stuck in the middle between your children from a previous marriage and everyone else in the current family. This was another major area of growth for me in my second marriage. It still is. Because I grew up as "the stepchild" my whole life, I was painfully aware when my daughters felt like they didn't belong. I continually have to work hard to not let my own past pain be their pain. It's hard to tell the difference sometimes.

I'm learning to focus on healing my previous wounds or inevitably I'll miss out on the opportunities and love from the new people that come into my life.

It's All Good

No matter what you've gone through, you can heal from it. I think being an entrepreneur is undeniably what saved me in adulthood. I'm convinced I was able to learn and grow infinitely more during the last 11 years because I owned a business.

For me, having this place to go and spend my time in helped me not focus on the bad stuff as much. It gave me a place to shine rather than be reminded of my mistakes. I just have to be careful about balance like we all do so that my life doesn't veer off the road again while I am running a successful business. We women are resilient souls. All of the bad stuff eventually melts away when you replace it with enough good stuff. And having a global Internet company continues to allow me to see how we're all connected, all one, here on this planet. We get to see how common our experiences are and be inspired by each other's brilliance.

Chapter 2

Did the Dalai Lama Mean YOU?

by Linda Rivero

"Où est ta mère?" I asked the stunning girl child clinging to my hand as we walked through the dusty path to the rice field. "Where is your mother?" Little Khady pointed with her tiny right hand to a woman just ahead of us…and then to a woman to our left…and then to another behind me; and she turned around to point to yet another planting seedlings behind a tree. Khady looked up at me with her big, coal-dark eyes and smiled. "Elles sont ma mère," she said, happily. "They are my mother."

Here in Senegal, women know their feminine power. A mother is one who gives birth, yes, of course; and a mother is also one who cares for the child. She's the sister. The auntie. The elder. The mother next door. The caregiver.

Women here are in touch with each other, and with their power as feminine creatures, and they transmit this power to their daughters. It is straightforward, organic, and simply the way things are.

It's time we learned from them.

We women in the West are living on the cusp of a glorious groundswell of change. Something is happening within and among us women, something very big. We don't know exactly what it is, but we know it's coming. We feel the earth-deep tremblings of a seismic shift resonating in our very beings.

This new age of feminine consciousness and awareness is an enormously powerful—and natural—evolution of the work we women did in the 60s and 70s during the feminist 'Women's Lib' movement—which I remember with great fondness and of which I am proud to have been a part. Following the initial, post-war high of the 50s, we young kids got the ball rolling in terms of awareness and protest; and the brilliant leaders and writers of our day—Bella Abzug, Gloria Steinem, Betty Friedan, and others—devoted their talents, time and lives to the progress and equal rights of women.

Now it's all coming 'round again, bigger and better. Because now we have communicative power! We can easily and instantly find and connect with each other, thanks to technology. Without the Internet, would we feel this global tidal wave swelling in our souls? (Without satellite phone connections, would women farmers in Africa feel the economic control of paying their bills by cell phone?) The answer is, of course, no.

Yet within all this glorious and exhilarating movement forward, I see a troubling tendency to overlook some of the essentials: core pieces I am profoundly and viscerally reminded of when I travel to Senegal or Uganda or Kenya to work with rural women.

Whether I am organizing a project to build a first-ever well for farming women or a first-ever literacy center for 40-year-old women who want nothing more than to learn to read with their children, I am reminded of the power each one of us has to make our world a better place.

Unfortunately, though, not enough of us are doing that.

"The world will be saved by the Western Woman." Thus proclaimed the Dalai Lama, as you no doubt have heard many times. An inspiring pronouncement. And one filled with the weight of thought, intelligence…and profound responsibility.

For better or worse, we now see his words everywhere. In fact, sad to say, they have become almost trite—not for lack of their depth, but for lack of the understanding of their depth. His words are now tossed blithely about by marketers and in casual conversation, evading the power of what this wise and learned man no doubt intended.

Let's look at the essence of his prediction.

First, who is this Western Woman?

I believe she is the woman who is educated, living a comfortable, middle class life, and enjoying the luxury of living in a country with a solid infrastructure. There are many educated, comfortable women—two of those three qualities—in developing countries. Mexico, Argentina, Brazil, Nigeria, South Africa: they all have their share, as do others.

But I do not believe these women are in that group—not because they are not capable, but because their world is so different due to lack of the third quality: societal infrastructure. Without that, one must rely heavily on one's own personal resourcefulness, connections, and creative collaborations. Life is simply a lot harder.

So the Western Woman, in this context, is the woman who is educated, comfortable, and living in a country with a stable infrastructure. She lives in a developed country with roads. Sewage. Plumbing. Electricity. Clean water. Schools. Medical care. All these essential life services are in place and are reliable.

This Western Woman, then, lives in the United States or Canada in the Western Hemisphere or Australia, New Zealand, Western Europe or Japan in the Eastern Hemisphere.

Now, how is she expected to save the world? That's a tall order. What is she supposed to do?

This is what "going global" is all about: feeling, being, and remaining connected to our wider world, and nurturing that sense of connectedness. This is our responsibility.

And what does that mean?

It means waking up to our feminine core…and putting it to use for the betterment of our global community.

We women today have the glorious opportunity and astounding luxury of choosing to heighten our awareness of and connection to our own light, our own innate, feminine luminescence.

Harmony, compassion, understanding, listening are cornerstones of our character as women, our feminine character. And this is the foundation of life! In English and in Latin-derived languages (and perhaps many others), we refer to our planet as our Mother Earth. She is feminine: La Tierra, La Terre, La Terra. She is our home, our magnet, our belonging for us and all who share this home with us.

Openness is who we are. We are open: to life, to the birth of life, to our souls, to the people we love. We are open to their problems, to their suffering, to their wholeness, to their heartache, and to their giving. We are the receivers. We are open to our other half, our counterpart. The world lives in us...and on a deep, psychic and spiritual level, we know this. We are open.

Yet as we know, light has its counterpart. Suffering is also inevitable in our home, our Mother Earth. No matter how much we may try to ignore it, or pretend we do not see it or actually avoid it...it is there. A glimpse of the headlines or a glance at the mail from the non-profit organization we care about quickly reminds us. Suffering is part of our path, part of our experience.

The beauty in all this, the good news, is that we women have a special connection to this suffering, to this understanding. While we may fear it, we also feel it, viscerally.

Maybe we don't go around talking about it every day, but we feel it.

We relate to hardship and to internal struggle. We feel and appreciate another's need to psychically and physically survive. We are women.

So it is up to us to change the world. Who is better suited than we?

But in reality, most of us do nothing. This isn't what we want to hear, but it's true. Most of us do nothing. And why is that?

I see four reasons why we do not take consistent, serious action.

First, there is fear. Then there is our busyness. And our overwhelm, and of course, our not knowing where to start.

Our fear is, first, fear of ourselves. Fear of what we will find if we look as deeply as we could into ourselves—fear of our own "shadow." Fear of what we really long for, fear of presenting our true selves to the world: fear of our own light, our own capability and influence. Fear of our own power.

We also fear the "other," the unknown: the battered woman seeking shelter; the terrifyingly harsh, sex-trafficked girl; the mutilated rape victim; the desperately unappealing homeless woman. While our compassion for this person may be deep, how do we begin to relate to her?

Second, we are unrelentingly busy with our own lives. We get up, go to work, stop at the cleaner's, rush home, pick up the kids, make dinner, clean up the kitchen, say, "Oh, hi," to our husband, watch a little TV, and go to bed. And we check email, read email, delete email, call our friend we've been meaning to call for weeks now, and....

Then there's the problem of overwhelm with the problems of the world, our feeling of utter helplessness. Hundreds of thousands of women raped in the DRC? Over a billion women living on less than $1 USD a day? How can you, little ol' you, do anything to help that kind of problem?

...Which leads us directly to the obstacle of not knowing where to start. Even if you are desperately eager to help, where do you begin? The problems are so big, and your own daily concerns are so pressing....

So what happens, realistically, is that maybe during the course of the day you read an inspiring quote by the Dalai Lama, or an inspiring article in *O, The Oprah Magazine*, and you feel great for a while and maybe even discuss it with your girlfriends or in your women's group. But then it's time to get back to your life...and that's the end of that.

And nothing changes.

Now I want to know: why does nothing change? Something must change.

It is our job to make the world change. For if not us, then who?

The truth is that it is not hard to pitch in, to do your part, to actually help save the world.

It's all about "going global," and going global is an inside job. It's internal. It's not even just a mindset. It's mindset plus heart-set. It's a sensitivity and, above all, a receptivity that resonates in your core.

When you begin to feel your own skin vibrate with connection to another outside your realm, outside your everyday world, then you are beginning to feel the stirrings of going global.

Developing a global identity is not simply a matter of traveling everywhere you can think of or having a business that serves customers in 30 countries. Those things don't make you global. Those things simply mean you've traveled everywhere you can think of and have customers in 30 countries.

Fortunately, however, going global does take on many forms. Because this is an internal process, an awakening, it may be expressed in as many ways as there are people doing it.

The constant is the deep, inner orientation toward and caring for the "other." To me, personally, going global means literally going global. It means engaging the whole world because that's been the trajectory of my life. I began navigating my way through cultures and languages from the day I was born. I've continued to live simultaneously in multiple cultures and worlds ever since.

But my world may be very different from yours. Your world may be your local world. That may be your globe. Wonderful! Then you have the opportunity—and the responsibility—to use your own innate feminine gifts of compassion, nurturance, listening, serving, and collaborating to heal that world that is your globe.

Going global means expanding and reaching beyond yourself.

Whatever that means to you. If you are drawn to helping battered women in your town, or in your adjacent city, that's global. It's a different kind of global from mine, but it's global. Going global means, essentially, getting out of your self: waking up to and deeply connecting with the humanness of another, one who is outside your comfortable and predictable circle.

So how do you, Western Woman, fulfill the Dalai Lama's prophecy and save the world?

You do the work that connects you to the human community. You do the "global" work of connecting and contributing, whether that means around the corner or around the world. You do whatever it is that makes you feel your connection to those with whom you share the Universal Spirit.

Do you want to help rural African women learn to read, and sing and dance with them?

Then travel with me. Do you want to work at your local food bank and never travel?

Then do that. But do something. Bless yourself with the gift of feeling you're part of the human race. You do that by giving…of yourself. Not just your money. You must give of yourself.

When I am with the women I work with in Senegal, together with my Western travelers, we are desperately limited in our actual tribal language ability. But we connect. How do you explain that?

We connect because we all have hearts…children…mothers…brothers…sisters… families…communities…those we love and care for. And these connections that drive us also bridge our linguistic divide.

You, too, are part of this community: You are a woman. You are beauty. You are kindness, compassion, and intelligence. Your soul beats with the stirring of the wind and soars with the flight of birds. Your heart breaks with the lilt of a melody and throbs with the beat of the drum. This is your essence. You are a woman. You already are connected.

Yesterday, perhaps we were not in touch with this ability we have—our ability to connect, to resonate, to feel our soul in the breeze, or our pulse in the hand of a child.

But today we are in touch. At last we are waking up: to our loved ones, to our children, to each other, to those we have never met…and most importantly, to ourselves. Never before have we felt the potential we feel today—our planetary potential, our power of united feminine force.

This is our time. Together, we can save the world. We must be strong, and pliable. Fierce, and soft. Determined, and flexible. Above all, we must feel our deepest feminine core and our universal feminine bond. And this is, of course, our human bond.

In the end, it is this awareness and our chosen, deliberate actions that will save us all.

This is your cue. Make your entrance.

You are the woman we've been waiting for.

Linda Rivero, Founder of the Global Action Network of Entrepreneurial Women, describes herself as being in love with the fascination and richness of cross-cultural communication and travel, and forever inspired by the universal bond shared by all women, regardless of culture, religion, or national origin. Born in New York City to a multi-national and multi-lingual family, Linda learned as a toddler to navigate her way through languages and cultures, right in her own family.

Her interests and professional activities have been diverse, ranging from corporate training and language instruction to international travel consulting, film exhibition, bilingual counseling, and professional photography. She has written and performed a one-woman play on the life of her immigrant grandmother, and she has also been singing in various languages since she was a child. Yet all her activities have two common threads: Linda's passion for communication and connection through culture, language and travel, paired with her dedication to helping those in need of support. And she has explored all these activities through her own businesses.

Linda's love for personal expression through business combined with her passion for culture and caring for women in need has led her to found the Global Action Network of Entrepreneurial Women (ga'NEW), a membership-based network serving women entrepreneurs in both the industrialized and developing worlds. ga'NEW is the evolution of Women Travel for Peace, Linda's travel company offering female travelers life-changing, women-helping-women travel adventures to rural Africa as well as spiritual retreats in rural Italy. Linda lives in Metro Washington, D.C. with her husband—and sons, when they visit home. You can reach her at lrivero@ganew-connect.com. Visit Linda on the web at www.ganew-connect.com.

Chapter 3

How to Enter Your Purpose A Non-Woo-Woo Guide for the Passionate Entrepreneur

by Christine Kane

Confession: I never discovered my purpose.

I never did a workshop to find my purpose. I never read a book about my purpose. In fact, I didn't even know I *had* a purpose until I was already reveling in it and making lots of money from it.

So no, I didn't DISCOVER my purpose.

I did, however, ENTER it. I didn't even know it at the time.

It happened one morning when I was crammed in a car of Metro's Orange Line on my way to my cubicle job that I despised. As I clutched the bar above my head and bumped into the tired people wobbling around me, I silently uttered a simple prayer to myself. It went like this:

"You have GOT to be freakin' kidding me if you think I can live like this day after day for the rest of my life."

Yeah. I know. Not much of a prayer. But the Universe understood me just fine.

Does that mean I woke up the next morning to UPS delivering me a box containing my shiny new purpose, complete with treasure map, golden key and parchment scroll of commandments?

Not even.

It means that the next week, I wandered into a small bookstore where I found and bought a book that became kind of a catalyst for me through the coming years.

It means that when I got promoted at my cubicle job the next month, I chose instead to leave.

It means that I moved away from the expensive city to a small town where the rent was crazy cheap and I could start up slowly.

It means that I reached out, asked for help, hired mentors and stayed curious.

It means that I moved through fear and discomfort more times than I can count so that I could at first survive in my own business and then thrive.

You get the idea.

My prayer was answered by an ongoing series of nudges, half-open doors, and an odd mix of unlikely gurus (or their books) showing up—and my job was to simply begin listening, moving forward and stepping into a greater passion and purpose in my life.

The non-woo-woo truth is this: I never "discovered" anything. I simply kept entering.

I've now mentored, taught and coached hundreds of purpose-driven people—from entrepreneurs to artists to business owners of all kinds. Their success was built by taking the next steps available to them and by listening to their curious delights. This is what ultimately reveals the depth and nature of purpose. Not—as so many people would have you believe—a one-time discovery.

Here are my 4 big arguments against DISCOVERING your purpose:

1—Discovery is a "big deal." Big deals hardly ever require any action on your part. That's because when something's a big deal, it's so easy to convince yourself that you don't yet have the right tools or you won't ever be quite ready. Your ego likes big deals for these very reasons. It's a convenient way to keep you from taking even the first imperfect action step.

2—Discovery implies that your purpose is outside of you. It's not. Your purpose is here now. It's already within you, speaking to you at every level of your being each day.

3—A Discovery is an event, a moment. It's a one-time "Ta-Dah!" occurrence that comes fully equipped with all the mystical special effects. Your purpose is NOT an event. Your purpose is an unfolding. It is dynamic. As you continue to enter and move forward, your purpose becomes bigger and more impactful. At the very beginning, however, you might not be ready for that level of awareness about your purpose. This is why it almost always begins with small imperfect steps.

4—Discovery requires waiting. Waiting is often what we do when we're scared. If you are waiting to discover your purpose, then you are probably not fully embracing your life and all of its signs and signals now. Whatever life situation you find yourself in now, it is every bit a part of your purpose as my moment on the Orange Line so many years ago is now a part of my purpose and my story. Waiting negates the truth of the present moment. Stop it.

Here are my 4 simple steps for ENTERING your purpose:

1—Settle for nothing.

Wanna hit the purpose-finding fast-track?

The first place to start is to notice where you settle for stuff in your life.

Why?

Because purpose doesn't "settle." Purpose isn't about "Oh well, I guess I'll just get this crappy job because hey, it's a bad economy." Purpose is the opposite of settling. Each time I probe a little deeper in conversations with people who tell me they can't find their purpose, I often discover that they have spent so many years "settling" that they've lost touch with even their smallest desires.

If this sounds like you, then begin by moving anything *unlike* purpose out of the way.

Answer the following questions. How much physical crap in my life am I completely "non-purposeful" about? How much time do I spend doing non-purposeful stuff that doesn't fill me up in the least? How many non-purposeful people are around me each day?

It's almost impossible to recognize your own purpose when the bulk of your life is about settling for things.

2—Honor your delight.

While you are cleaning up your world-view and no longer settling for stuff, begin mining your life by asking the following question:

"What do I kinda like to do?"

Don't start with finding your purpose. Start instead with language that feels more playful.

What makes me happy? What delights me? What floats my boat?

Why start with these kinds of questions? Because there's a slight problem with the word "purpose."

It's high pressure.

Hey, I'm all about purpose, playing big, upleveling in a big way.

However, if you haven't been clear or if you've settled for many things in your life for many years—and suddenly you start demanding that you FIND YOUR PURPOSE, your creative, happy, powerful muse is going to hide in a dark corner. It's too much pressure for a starting point.

At first, you need to start with delight. Begin with fun. Or "What makes me smile?" Give yourself that treat. And give yourself permission for the answer to be anything.

3—Fire your ego.

What comes after you begin finding delight?

The ego voices, of course!

Nothing kills purpose faster than the statement "Yeah, but you'll never be able to make money at it." (The ego is brilliant at bringing money into the equation first thing!)

My theory is that many people can't "find their purpose" because no sooner have they discovered something they love than the ego chimes in. Often unconsciously. The voices of the ego work 24/7—and their job is to *have* a job. They are very into job security. Ideas like "purpose" have nothing to do with job security. So these voices will work hard to convince you that you have no purpose. It's much safer that way.

Face it. For every idea that "can't make money," there's someone out there who proved that it can. They let themselves get creative and they stopped letting the ego run the show.

4—Take the very next step.

The opposite of a "big deal" is a simple action step. Simple action steps create discoveries and big deals when you add them up. But for now, all you need to do is this:

Take your very next step. This is the ultimate non-woo-woo truth of entering your purpose.

Start each day by asking yourself, "What is the very next step I will take today?" Sometimes it will be to read a book you've meant to read. Sometimes it will be about creating something. Sometimes it will be about sending a note to your circle requesting referrals. It doesn't matter what it is. It matters that each day you take the very next step.

Don't get me wrong. Living with purpose IS a big deal. It's an amazing choice to make and phenomenal path to follow. And you are meant to follow this path now. Allowing yourself to begin is the most important piece. The rest will unfold. Your job is to enter.

Christine Kane is known as the Mentor to Women Who are Changing the World. She is the President and Founder of Uplevel YOU™, a million dollar company committed to the growth and empowerment of entrepreneurs around the globe through teaching not only high-level cutting-edge authentic marketing and business strategies—but also transformational techniques to shift mindsets and wealth.

Christine has now worked with over a thousand people in her *Uplevel Your Life®* Mastery Program and *Uplevel Your Business™* Program & Blueprint, in addition to her popular events, workshops and retreats—where she teaches students how to create successful businesses based in their passion, attract an ongoing stream of customers, clients and income—while creating a life of meaning and purpose.

After 15 years in a successful career as a popular songwriter and performer, Christine shifted her focus so that she could provide a deeper level of service to other creative and entrepreneurial types. "Yeah," she laughs. "I went from being a rock star on the stage to helping people be rock stars in their lives and businesses! I love it! This is my dream come true!"

Christine provides upleveling advice, breakthrough techniques and other resources to over 22,000 subscribers from around the world via her Uplevel YOU™ eZine and other offerings at www.christinekane.com.

CHAPTER 4

Inspired Women Succeed

by Diane Cunningham

I have built a company around this concept—but before that, my life. Being a Smart Woman means living my WHY daily, hourly, and especially when it scares me to death. The more I live my WHY, the more "successful" I get on my own terms. I understand that the WHY is the foundation, both the question and the answer. My WHY is my faith in God and my mission is "to inspire women to dream big, catch on fire, and change the world."

My WHY is helping women learn to connect, create, and collaborate from all across the country as they build their businesses. God loves to nudge me into new and scary places with my business. Each new "be brave" step is a part of the beautiful masterpiece that He is creating. This is how I had the courage to launch the National Association of Christian Women Entrepreneurs in May of 2010.

Let me give you a sneak peek into my journey, my WHY. I want to share with you the secret struggles that you often don't hear from the successful women who you're following. I want to take off my mask and share my truth with you.

Many times, looking from a distance, all we can see is the victory and then we begin to compare ourselves. Well my friends, it is a long and winding road to get to that day full of victory. We mistakenly think that we have to hide the defeat, public and private failures, and many long days of endless work.

I started my career as a Master's Level Mental Health Counselor. I loved helping people find new solutions and create new ways of thinking about their situation. I was young, smart, and passionate about helping people. I worked full-time at a hospital in the Employee Assistance Program and it was a great fit for me as I began my "real career." It was at this same hospital that I met my future husband and we began dating. Things were moving along and I was happy as I looked into my future.

Not long into our courtship, one of my counseling clients took his own life. This suicide changed the course of my life, my career, and ultimately my marriage. I journeyed through a lawsuit and licensure issues for a four-year period. During this time, I married (2001) and was laid off from my job at the hospital due to the closing of my department. My husband also decided that it was time for him to make a career move from the Air Force Reserves into an Active Duty military assignment. So I became a military spouse and moved across the country to Texas. Both of these are what I call "never-say-never" experiences. The weekend before we loaded up the Uhaul, I received the final news on my lawsuit and license, and was devastated. I found out that my counseling license, which I had worked so hard to earn and had spent thousands of dollars to receive, was being suspended.

I was lost. I felt that my purpose had been robbed from me and that I had nowhere to turn. I cried out to God, seeking clarity. It was 2003, and I was in a new city, still newly married, with no family or friends nearby. I began seeking a job in the counseling field and there was nothing. I applied for 60 jobs, but was limited by my suspended license and the type of job I could have. One of my lowest days was when I sat at my local Target and filled out an application for employment. I just couldn't understand what I was supposed to do with my life.

Finally, the clarity came. I was going to hire myself. I became an entrepreneur. I found a book on purpose and life coaching. This book changed my life as I began training to become a "life purpose coach." I was intimately aware of the deep pain of purposelessness. I had worn those shoes and understood the heart cry and longing for significance.

I was ready and willing to help other women to seek their own purpose and passion. I jumped in and God began sending women for me to work with. This led to my first website, my first speaking events, my first info product, one baby step at a time. I trusted God as He opened doors.

It wasn't easy. At first, I didn't make the income that I was used to in my prior career. There were many years of just making enough to get by. I dove into learning, training, reading, and gleaning all of the information that I could. My penchant for moving fast served me well as I forged ahead, trying new things.

I helped hundreds of women through the coaching, speaking, and training that I offered. I was living my purpose and it felt good. I kept busy with my entrepreneur life during my husband's deployments to Iraq and to Afghanistan. I kept hoping that my deep desire to have a family would someday be fulfilled as we began the lonely and dark walk through infertility.

Then it was time for another military move, and I packed up my laptop and started over with him in a new city in 2006. I continued my life purpose coaching, rented an office and networked like crazy. Life was moving in the right direction.

And then it felt like I hit another wall. The year 2009 was one of failure. Nothing I tried worked. My mentor "dumped" me, my next business joint venture didn't work, and I was again looking at classified ads. The challenges in my marriage grew bigger and eventually led to the ending of my marriage in 2011. Yet during this time, the dream of NACWE became a whisper from God. I wanted to connect with other like-minded women in a safe environment to ask questions, to find support, and to gain clarity. I found these women through the power of social media. This led me to Sheri McConnell, through my "stalking" of Ali Brown's Facebook page. I wanted to learn as much as I could by connecting with ("friending") every woman who was in Ali's mastermind group.

It worked. I soaked it all in. I dove into the free preview calls, the teleclasses, and the $5 book from Sheri McConnell, *Smart Women Create Membership-Based Businesses*. I was on my way. The foundation was laid, my new mentor had presented herself, and my desire to help other women just like me was HUGE.

No time to waste on this God-given dream, I attended Sheri's one day *Create Your Network* event on April 20th. NACWE opened 22 days later on May 11th, 2010. My motto is to "act fast now" and that is what I did.

In the first year of NACWE, we were busy. We added 165 new members from all over the U.S. and Canada. We hosted our first annual conference in April 2011, the *Inspired Women's Event*, with 45 women attending from all over the U.S. and Sheri McConnell as our keynote speaker. We learned from experts, gathered on monthly Q&A calls, celebrated a virtual Christmas party, and much more. We invited 40 women to write a book with us called *Inspired Women Succeed*. It has been a wild ride, full of blessings, challenges and miracles.

I believe that living out our WHY includes three crucial ingredients: Passion, Persistence and People, what I love to call the "Inspired Women Succeed recipe."

Passion: As women, our passions run deep. We must be passionate about our WHY. It gives us a reason to get up in the morning and to stay up late at night. My passion gave me the courage to start over again and again as I kept looking for the right entrepreneurial fit for me. My passion to help other entrepreneurial women like me to connect gave me the courage to step out and create NACWE.

Persistence: To reach our WHY takes much more than a quick fix or an "overnight" success plan. It takes day after of day of consistent actions. It takes trying new things and setting new goals. It takes faithfully showing up, trusting in God's timing. My persistence gave me the fortitude to write the last chapter of the *Inspired Women Succeed* book after surviving a plane crash in March 2011. It gave me the willingness to trust that God's timing was perfect for my dreams of a business.

People: A WHY is nothing without the people we love. And we can't reach our WHY without people along the way who teach, train, and mentor us, and who hand us Kleenex when we need to cry. My people have been my "bridge" to each new goal and I know that it is my calling to teach others everything that I know. I want to reach forward and reach back at all times.

My desire is to help every woman that I can to succeed with the God-given business in front of her. That might be a million dollar company or a few ideas written on a napkin.

When I attended my most recent training with my mentor Sheri McConnell, I wrote these words:

> *We inspire women to connect, create, and collaborate to build and expand their God-given business. We teach them to "act fast now," to be brave, and to chase their dreams while supporting each other and trusting the process. We strive for excellence while allowing ourselves to make mistakes, in private and public, knowing that a spirit of love and acceptance will be waiting for us.*

This is my WHY. This is my heart. This is why I am overjoyed each day to go to work and get busy. So yes...I know that Inspired Women Succeed.

Diane Cunningham, M.Ed. is the President and Founder of the National Association of Christian Women Entrepreneurs.

Since 2005, Diane has worked under the DianeCunningham.com umbrella as a coach, speaker, facilitator, and entrepreneur. She founded the National Association of Christian Women Entrepreneurs in May of 2010 to help women connect, create, and collaborate. Under Diane's leadership, NACWE grew from 0 to 165 members in the first year and hosted the first annual conference, the *Inspired Women's Event* with 45 women in attendance.

She is a Certified Mastermind Executive Coach. Her training and background is in the mental health field. She worked for many years in a hospital Employee Assistance Program. Prior to that, she spent time working with domestic violence and addictions. She has a Master's Degree in Education (Guidance and Counseling) from Whitworth College in Spokane, Washington and a Bachelors Degree from the same school in Interpersonal Communications.

Diane is an author of "Dear Female Entrepreneur, My Friend" and co-author of *Inspired Women Succeed* just released in May, 2011. See www.inspiredwomensucceed.com. She is an avid volunteer and currently serves as the Regional Advocate for the Small Business Development Center for North Texas. She is active in her church, local community events, and non-profit organizations that fit with her life mission. She was named as one of the Top 2o Leaders Under the Age of 40 in her community in January, 2011 and chosen as the Inspirational Women of the Month for April for *Inspirational Woman Magazine*.

Diane loves people, shopping, Starbucks, reading, and spending time with friends. She has run four marathons with the Leukemia & Lymphoma Society's Team in Training program and loves to go to Zumba classes. She is passionate about God and is basking in the amazing journey that He has her on!

"My mission is to inspire women to dream big, catch on fire, and change the world."

Please contact NACWE with your request or see Diane's other website for more information at www.nacwe.org or www.dianecunningham.com.

CHAPTER 5

Taking the Leap

by Constance DeWitt

In 2005, I was busy running my real estate office and interior design consulting business in the beautiful hills of Vermont and living a life that had structure and purpose, but was lacking in passion. I had spent the previous decades finding jobs I could do (i.e. use the education I had) or creating positions that would allow me to focus on married life: husband and family first, job second, career a distant third. I had a growing sense that the self-expression I so longed for might elude me and that the purpose and contribution I wanted to make to society in some vague way, was being diminished the closer I got to "retirement." The usual list of volunteer positions peppered my life: baking pies for the community suppers, helping out at Church, helping with elections, serving on town boards and as an official. I was searching for a clue to what the next chapter in my life would hold because I could *see* life changing around me.

I had become increasingly involved with my elderly parents' well-being, a circumstance so many baby boomers face, and decided with my parents to move them from Florida to Vermont. We believed proximity to family and advanced medical care was better for them, and additionally I could assist with important decisions without spending valuable time and resources traveling to them; a circumstance that was becoming more frequent with each passing year.

Over the previous years, I had all of my senses tuned for something better; the next phase of my life, or you might say, I had been going through life with the expectation that there *was* more to it than what I was seeing and experiencing at the moment. I had worked as a delineator, an assistant to a surveyor, an interior designer, an appraiser. I had been a treasurer and had served as a trustee. I had worked for others in countless occupations, had co-owned and operated a restaurant, a second-hand shop, and apartments. Nothing seemed to be fulfilling or lasting. I could not find the passion: the situations did not last: I did not feel that I was making a difference.

Then, in 2006, I decided to explore Feng Shui, the ancient Chinese art of arrangement. I spent a year studying in New York with a Master who taught the Compass School method, culminating with a three-week trip to China to finalize my credential. It was one of the most pivotal experiences I have had and proved to be a harbinger of the life on which I was about to embark.

Seeing China made me realize that my passion was for people and for the environment. With so much visible poverty and so much visible wealth in China; so much industry and so much devastation and a population so controlled, I thought of my own country and the hidden poverty and excessive wealth: parallels can be drawn anywhere I have been. These discrepancies exist all over the world.

I had traveled enough before that to realize that many people on this planet are hampered by lack, lack of every imaginable resource. My immediate thought was that we *all* need resources of the human kind and the environmental kind. My spiritual heritage had taught me respect for every person and for nature. What better way to serve the planet than to combine my two passions, people and the environment, by creating a business that would provide solutions to business problems while simultaneously offering products I had learned about that could protect the environment and teach respect for nature?

So the idea was hatched on the flight home from China in the Fall of 2006: I would start a "store" to provide services and products to help small business people and their environments become sustainable. I was bursting to share the news with my husband as soon as I got off the plane. Only that didn't happen.

My husband of 20 years announced he was leaving, and then he left. During this period, my father's health declined and he died in August of 2007. Those events were difficult enough to understand and accept, but in addition, the economy had shifted dramatically and my businesses were faltering. I decided once again to put my dreams on hold, close my proprietorships and look for another job.

I was "just above broke," as Mary Morrissey describes. I took a position the following year with a new franchise real estate brokerage in April only to break my foot two months later, a week before corporate training. I could neither walk nor drive, and because the office depended on having a broker in residence, I relinquished my position and sat out the summer in isolation.

My mother was very supportive during all of this. She had been raised by enlightened parents who taught her that men and women should be respected for who they were as individuals; support one another with honesty, openness and without judgment in addition to being capable of taking care of themselves. My mother taught me these values and believed in my ideas. She offered her ideas and questions to vet the concepts I had envisioned. I read voraciously and took some business courses. But then my mother's health declined, she was hospitalized in 2008, and died from minor complications following surgery in 2009. I was stunned and numbed.

For several months, I was consumed with estate matters and completely abandoned my business idea again. I was running on automatic pilot and nerves. I had to put grief aside. But by the end of the year, I had begun to grieve and worry about my future, feeling overwhelmed by an agenda that I had not created. And that made me think about hope and what it means. I read voraciously and reconnected with my spiritual self, and with the business ideas that had stirred within me. The economy was in the weeds, and any applications I had sent out for employment were gently rejected or left unanswered. What could they say to a woman like me, almost retirement age, in an economy like this?

Women are so different from men. Women are the ones who carry on, who bear the burdens and offer hope that everything will turn out all right. As I read a book my mother had given to me *Winter Grace, Spirituality for the Later Years*, by Kathleen Fischer, I was struck by her thought that "It is the women who see things through to the end. Martha perseveres in Gethsemane's dark hour of human failure. Martha provides a strong image of an older woman of faith." From another woman theologian and author that Ms. Fischer quotes, I read that "...the curve of a woman's life span follows the pattern of the seasons. She blossoms in the spring, and there is a long summer of very slow ripening. But the autumn of a woman's life is far richer than the spring if only she becomes aware of it in time, and harvests the ripening fruit before it falls and rots and is trampled underfoot. The winter which follows is not barren if the harvest has been stored, and withdrawal of sap is only a prelude to a new spring elsewhere."

My thoughts in a nutshell! So here I was, no means of support except for my meager savings and a modest inheritance to live out the rest of my days, a lot of property to oversee, with my life expectancy far exceeding the finances and physical stamina to do so. I had met with huge resistance from the established business community because I did not have the liquidity necessary to start a business. I was not experienced enough in "that kind" of business, and by the way, wasn't it a "little too late" to be thinking about starting a career at my age? Really?

I felt a huge weight, and its inertia almost overtook me. When this has happened in my life before, I have taken time away to detach and let go. After college, I entered VISTA (Volunteers In Service To America) and went to Guam for a couple of years. A teacher for the VISTA training said that "when you get yourself in a corner, do what it takes to turn your perspective 180 degrees and see the opportunities open up." I have never forgotten that; perspective and attitude are everything.

So during the winter of 2009-2010, I started the process of "seeking," of looking for ways to go deeper, end my grief after so many losses, and find meaning again. I listened to a tape from Marianne Williamson about transformation. It engaged me and I decided to join her in Los Angeles in early 2010 for a seminar dealing with women's rights and their heritage of taking responsibility. (Does this sound familiar?)

As a result of the "Sister Giant" event in February of 2010, I went to Africa with Marianne and some very interesting and productive women. We attended the Africa Middle East Microfinance Summit in Nairobi, Kenya. Africa was cathartic for me. It was just the place to refocus and let go of the past and all the disappointment I had been carrying around. I met wonderful people, saw gut-wrenching poverty, marvelous animals, but more important, I began to feel connected and focused again. I *felt* hope. I was exposed to new ideas and an attitude of achievement. It didn't hurt to be stranded for an extra week because of an Icelandic volcanic eruption either.

When I returned to Vermont in April, I began my search, again, for a business coach. This time it would be a woman. I felt I was running out of time and didn't want to wait another year to start my business. I had been discouraged by traditional business resources and realized that a woman, who carries hope in her DNA, might be able to understand the pressure, discouragement and circumstances that keep many of us from taking the risk to "Live Our WHY." At the age of 65, I attended the 2010 Smart Women's Institute of Entrepreneurial Learning Expo in Los Angeles. There I met Sheri McConnell, and started on the journey of the rest of my life.

"The jump is so frightening between where I am and where I want to be…because of all I may become I will close my eyes and leap!" —Mary Anne Hershey

Since joining the Mastermind group of entrepreneurial women at the Smart Women's Institute, the ideas, support, assistance and direction I have received has expanded my learning exponentially: it has opened a door to "A New Way of Being., It has invigorated me and finally given me the resources to pursue my purpose and my dream, to leverage my knowledge: to live *My* WHY.

By the time you read this, I will have a website up and be connecting with the world. I will be commenting on events and signs I see in business and the environment that will create opportunities and challenges for us. I will be producing interviews with business leaders from the five key areas in the Sustainable Business Cycle Chart™ that will spark your imagination, get you motivated and assist you with support. There will be people and products to help every step of the way. By connecting and supporting one another, we can all learn how to solve our business problems and save the environment in the process. By creating a community of women with a shared vision of cooperation and co-creation, my dream of empowering other women with ideas to make the world more sustainable by creating profitable businesses and leaving the planet in better condition will have been launched. What more could a person want except to be joined by others in the process?

I invite you to join me at The Global Institute of Sustainable Solutions at www.gissconnect.com where we can discuss and share resources and help each other. As Ghandi said: "You must be the change you want to see in the world."

Evidence seems to be manifesting that there *is* change in the world: physically, financially, emotionally and consciously. The old paradigm of linear thinking is out. The new paradigm of connections and curvilinear thinking is in. One example is:

On June 30th, 2011, 15 women from Vermont, New Hampshire and Massachusetts, three of whom are in their 90s, the rest in their 70s and 80s, were arrested for protesting at Vermont Yankee Nuclear Plant along the Connecticut River in Vernon, Vermont. In their wisdom, they have decided to speak out for a more sustainable and renewable form of energy. They understand that the Tritium and Cesium and other nuclear waste that flows into the Connecticut River and poisons everything around it is bad for our future. They are making a stand to preserve the future. They have witnessed for decades and have taken the action to be heard. They are living their WHY.

As a post script, I have my own doubts and fears, but I have learned to let go of them and ask for help. I realize I may not live to see everything I set in motion be accomplished, but the knowledge of being a part of the productive, and sustainable cycle to create the kind of beautiful world I want to live in and which I believe at my core to be possible and more importantly leave for you, the magnificent creatures of the earth and the children I never had, creates the value that will keep me engaged and excited for the rest of my life.

Constance DeWitt is a New Age Woman who has combined her training in design, Feng Shui and color with many retail and managerial experiences in business and government. Her lifelong love of nature, extensive travel and study of sustainability has led to her belief that we can create profitable businesses while benefiting from each other's brilliance while solving our environmental challenges by following a simple formula.

Constance sees her life's mission as sharing her passion and knowledge of sustainability through five simple steps that produce a dynamic, life-sustaining energy system which has become the foundation for a healthy, industrious and profitable business model. The application of this process to transform business into a creative and sustainable cycle is a dynamic shift in the way we do business: uplifting, motivational and profitable.

Ms. DeWitt is the Founder of The Global Institute of Sustainable Solutions (www.gissconnect.com) providing innovation, human resources and environmentally-conscious products for the entrepreneurial business owner.

CHAPTER 6

The Decision to Lead

by Sue Ludwig

It's a familiar scene.

My husband and I standing in our kitchen talking over the background sounds of our lives: dishwasher whirring, kids talking, dogs trotting across the hardwood floor. I tell him about the business I want to start. I watch as this idea washes over him.

He smiles supportively and says, "All I know is this is going to be bigger than you can even imagine right now."

And he was right.

I could start my story with how my business looks NOW. But that's not the part of the story that you'll find most helpful. What you need to know is the beginning when nothing was shiny or systematized.

When it was just an idea. An intention. A vision.

Because YOU have these things right now. You have ideas and intentions and vision. That's why you're reading this book!

My intention was powerfully simple: to serve an un-served group of therapists who shared the same passion as I do for premature babies. The funny thing is I suggested this idea to my colleagues, hoping that *someone* (one of those charismatic leader types) would jump up and begin the process for the rest of us.

Truly. That's what I was thinking.

An occupational therapist by education and training, I chose many years ago to specialize in neonatal therapy. This means I work in the neonatal intensive care unit (NICU), helping premature and sick babies develop, eat and bond as normally as possible within a high-tech intensive care environment. Physical therapists and speech language pathologists do this as well. We're a vital trifecta in the lives of these babies. I LOVE this work. When I'm supporting a fragile premature baby with my hands, knowledge and intention, I know I am doing my best to affect quality of life; the baby's life, the family's life and my own. It's a continuous loop.

After years of consulting and speaking nationally, I noticed that therapists like me didn't have anywhere to call home. We were isolated and unsupported. Our knowledge and practice varied too widely. We were not a group. Yet here we remained—passionate, educated, driven and hungry for connection.

While I witnessed and experienced these issues, I still sought a leader to save us.

Until I met Christine Kane, who would become my mentor.

She suggested that I could be that SOMEONE. I could just decide to do this. She pointed out that no one was going to anoint me worthy. Only me. All I had to do was step forward into a much bigger version of myself. And lead.

This seemed impossible to me initially. I felt that someone more 'qualified' should do this, like someone with a PhD, an MBA or 30 years of NICU experience. *Anyone* but me.
And yet, no one was doing it.

Lying in bed at night, I considered how I'd feel if someone else did decide to form this group someday. Then I wondered if she'd develop it like a typical association. And that fueled my passion. After all, I had a very clear vision for this group. And it wasn't typical.

After a few restless nights, I made the decision to put my intention into action. It was time. Instead of wondering if I should be the one to create this group, I knew that it was already mine. I loved this group and we didn't even have a name yet.

I began to carve out space for these therapists in the world. And after months of research and work with my mentor, I became President and Founder of The National Association of Neonatal Therapists (NANT). Our home, our group was born!

There are many things missing in healthcare. (Thanks, you say, for stating the obvious.) And I wanted to make sure I did my best to address some of those things through NANT, to help the members as well as the babies.

So we address many of the things I hear families voice concern about across the nation when they have a hospitalized infant: consistency between caregivers and practice, use of the latest evidence and information available, effective and humane treatment, and honest communication. I created member benefits that are both immediately helpful in this regard and completely relevant to neonatal therapists' everyday work. And they USE them, which is great.

AND I wanted something more. Something different. I wanted to bring the art of caring back into healthcare, starting with the NICU. Sadly, there are many real and perceived roadblocks between providing adequate care and exceptional care. Many of these are out of our *immediate* control as caregivers. But we do have control of ourselves. And I believe that the best immediate healthcare reform happens inside of us because of what we bring to the table or the incubator, as the case may be.

So our benefits also address the therapists' life overall. How to be clear, happy and motivated. We want to be a calm, grounded force at the bedside before we touch a little two-pound person. And we want to carry this great energy home to our families, dogs and neighbors.

Whether at work or home, it's all the same life. I've learned a lot about the business of caring. about expectations, delivery, responsibility and excellence. **I'll share 3 of my favorite lessons here:**

Lesson 1: Vision is Primary

I was told several years ago by a colleague of mine that my vision was too big. This puzzled me as I always thought vision to be a rather large concept! What I've learned is how vital it is to stick to my vision. That every decision I make, every new avenue I invest in has to make sense within my vision. If not, I lose the very essence of what I created.

I've turned down tens of thousands of dollars of funding for my company because the funding was attached to conditions that were not in alignment with my vision. They weren't BAD conditions, just ones that I wasn't willing to support. I trusted the money would come in other ways and I let those original offers go. And the money still arrived through avenues that were completely aligned.

When we let go of our true vision, piece-by-piece, it has an erosive effect on our business and our own inner landscape. The opposite is also true. Be true to your vision and watch your business and your world grow in ways you couldn't have predicted.

I continue to serve our awesome members in the best way I know how. And my business brought in more money in the first two months of 2011 than I'd ever made in any previous YEAR of my life.

Vision is primary. Even when it's too big.

Lesson 2: What you Intend, Transcends

My mentor taught me to use intention in everything I do. When I brought *intentional caregiving* to my work in the NICU, it changed my practice. When I brought it home with me, it changed my life. But in business, it's easy to get lost in the everyday lists of things to do—meetings, conferences, email, creating new content or products.

In the midst of that busyness, I step back and notice that whatever I intend transcends. My energy exceeds the boundaries of what I originally intended. If I intend to provide safe, nurturing and skilled therapy to a baby in the NICU, I not only transform how I provide that therapy, but I change the quality of the therapy that baby receives. I enhance the interaction with the nurse who is taking care of him that day and the baby's mother as she learns how to help her baby relax, or eat, or focus on her familiar voice.

That level of intention can't help but leak out into the world.

If I just 'get through' a project, it feels empty and unsatisfying, and is often not my best work. If I intend to create a helpful and functional product for NANT members, I do just that. And in turn, members are inspired. It's that simple and that difficult. It sometimes feels easier to go unconsciously about our business. And maybe no one will notice.

But that's just it. No one will notice. An unconscious business doesn't connect with anyone. I want my business to transcend the boundaries of its focus. Not by scattering my intentions but by living them.

Lesson 3: Form Follows Function

You may have heard this phrase before, quoted first by the American architect Louis Sullivan in 1896. I remember learning it in physiology class my freshman year in college. Basically, it means that whether we're discussing architecture, nature or the human body, form follows function.

The function of our hands is to efficiently manipulate small objects and tools to build, craft, and create. We couldn't do this if we had hooves or paws. Function comes first, form follows, just like the tentacles of an octopus or the design of a beautiful structure. Simply stated, you wouldn't make a Slip 'N Slide out of brick.

I didn't create a business that's all about genuine intelligent connection and then make it inaccessible and cold.

My business should allow its function to dictate its form. I shouldn't create layers of people and red tape between me and my members (or between the members themselves) if the function is education and support. I create, instead, avenues for access, mentoring and real communication. As one NANT member so eloquently stated, this forms "a matrix of support."

NANT continuously receives requests from people who want to be added to our NANT newsletter list. Why? Seriously?

The function of our NANT newsletter is open connection, support, and inspiration. Its form then, takes shape through highlighting members, real stories of clinical and personal trials and success, and useful information written in real language. There's nothing sterile and perfect about relationships. And this one is no exception. We have a relationship and our newsletter is one of the ways in which we converse.

NANT hosted a sold out national conference in 2011! Its functions were collaboration, education and elevation of our field. The FORM this conference took on served all of these functions through every detail, from the flow of the welcome reception to the renowned speakers to the quality of food and surroundings. Anything less would not have produced the same great experience.

Form follows function. Always.

So maybe you're just beginning your business. Or maybe you've been in business for 30 years. We're all continuously learning. Regardless of where you are along your path, remember what my mentor taught me. No one will anoint you worthy. Only you.
We all have a story.

And it's tempting to think that those of us represented in this book have something you don't. Something magical, or lucky. More time, more money, better health, less fear—something.

But we are really no different at all.

The thing we all have in common here is that somewhere along the line, we made a decision. We decided not to stay where we were, doing the same things we've always done. Despite our fear, our doubt, our isolation, we chose to believe there was more to us than our story, more for us than our story might have dictated if we chose to stay in it.

And we started businesses that reflect that highest version of ourselves. My business was and is the expression of my purpose: supporting neonatal therapists and the babies they serve. And maybe, just maybe, changing the internal landscape of healthcare.

Sue Ludwig is the President and Founder of the National Association of Neonatal Therapists, an organization which serves occupational therapists, physical therapists and speech language pathologists who specialize in neonatal therapy. She has been a practicing occupational therapist since 1993 and a neonatal therapist at UC Health University Hospital in Cincinnati since 1996, specializing in assessment and treatment of premature and medically fragile infants in the neonatal intensive care unit (NICU).

Sue is a sought-after national speaker, consultant, writer and educator. She is passionate about changing the culture and practice of oral feeding in the NICU as well as reforming healthcare delivery through the practice of intentional caregiving. She has published articles related to infant-driven feeding, oral feeding and the late preterm infant and quality analysis of developmental care. Sue co-developed the Infant-Driven Feeding Scales©, a widely used assessment and documentation tool for the NICU. She is also a published poet.

Sue has earned the Neonatal Developmental Care Specialist Designation from the National Association of Neonatal Nurses (NANN) and is a member of their Education Provider Committee. She is also a member of the American Occupational Therapy Association. She lives in Ohio with her husband and two children. Visit the NANT website at www.neonataltherapists.com.

CHAPTER 7

Generating Happiness: The Way of the Nurturing Parent

by Michele Eisenberg

Human beings can't help it. At our core, we need three things:

1. We need to feel that we belong.
2. We need to feel valuable and know that we matter.
3. We need to feel loved.

The bottom line of the work I have done over the past 14 years with everyone I have coached, from the CEO and his executive team to the entrepreneur to the stay-at-home mom or dad has revolved around these three needs and how to meet them.

When our core needs feel threatened, we no longer function optimally. Instead, we do whatever we can to get these needs met. The challenge is that most of us seek to meet these needs outside of ourselves without ever being aware that this is what we are doing or that there is another way.

Some people look to their primary relationships to meet these needs. Others look to their success in business or to their wealth, or to the success of their children or to other tangible things in their lives. We all try to meet these core needs in our own unique and creative ways. I have discovered that whenever we look outside of ourselves to meet our core needs, we are setting ourselves up for pain.

I have seen this in the lives of my coaching clients, and I have experienced it firsthand in my own life. The most intense experience I had of trying to meet my core needs through my life's circumstances was in my marriage.

I wanted, more than anything, to feel happy in my relationship with my husband. Actually, I now know that what I wanted even more was to feel loved and valuable and that I belonged and that I mattered, and I was trying to find these things through our relationship.

Of course, it didn't work. My husband could not make me feel valuable or loved any more than he could make me turn purple. Even if my husband had been the most loving man alive and expressed his love to me in every healthy way imaginable, he could not make me feel loved and valued as long as I did not have my own innate sense of being lovable and valuable. We cannot receive things we don't believe we deserve.

I kept trying to get him to meet my needs. The more I tried to earn my sense of my value and belonging from him, the less of these I felt inside. Of course, at the time, I had no idea any of this was going on. All I knew was that I was trying to make my husband happy and improve our relationship.

Then I slowly began to wake up to some truths which helped me find my way free of the painful dynamic we were in. I slowly began to realize that my internal conversation about our relationship was my going back and forth between two parts of me: one who beat me up and told me that if I didn't do better, I'd be alone forever and the other that told me that it would all work out eventually as long as I kept trying. It was like having two internal parents to whom I kept going for advice and emotional support. Their advice and support kept me running in circles and in pain.

Usually, as grown ups, we no longer look to our physical parents for support and guidance. We look to the internal parenting aspects of ourselves, even if we are not conscious of doing this. Unfortunately, most of us have extremely well-developed inner critical and indulgent parents on whom we rely for counsel. This makes hard times much, much harder.

I was no exception. I alternately relied on my internal critical and indulgent parents when I needed guidance. I would swing between them, like a pendulum, which caused me to have the following painful patterns:

1. I resisted growth and change for fear I would lose people I loved.

2. I deferred to others and gave my power away. Because of this, I often felt like a victim.

3. I feared mistakes and failure because I believed they meant I was less valuable.

4. I looked for my value in the details of my life.

5. I devalued my feelings and reasoned my way through everything.

6. I rejected my body and ignored its messages.

7. I ignored my intuition.

8. I blindly trusted others because I did not trust myself.

9. I disconnected from myself, from others and from any sense of spirituality. I often felt lost.

10. I grew mostly through pain.

With the help of my beloved coach, my cherished spiritual teacher, and one of my most healing guides, I learned how to develop and rely on a totally different voice within. This inner nurturing parent offered me empowering support and guidance. The choice to develop this positive inner parent and consistently rely on them for guidance has been not only profoundly healing, but ultimately life-changing, and paved the way for me to change my most painful patterns listed above. As a result, I know the power of love as well as many secrets of happiness.

Here is what I did and continue to do that moves me forward into more love, more happiness and more success:

1. I invite growth and change.

2. I own my power and live as the author of my life.

3. I gave up perfection.

4. I found my value and continually develop my experience of it.

5. I learned how to feel and trust a full range of feelings. I also learned to distinguish feelings from each other, especially the difference between pity, guilt, sadness and remorse as well as the difference between anger and rage: all very necessary and empowering distinctions.

6. I respect and love my body, even when I don't prefer its shape.

7. I developed my intuition and my willingness to rely on it.

8. I learned how to trust myself and, from there, trust others discerningly and appropriately.

9. I connect with myself, with the person I am becoming, with my spirituality and my friends. From here, I can receive support.

10. I grow mostly through love.

None of the above happened overnight. These changes took time. I peeled away layer after layer of who I had become, listening to my inner critical and indulgent parents until I got to more of the core of me. I cried a lot, first out of self-pity, then out of hurt, then out of remorse, then out of gratitude. I learned how to forgive, and how to love. I fell in love. Today, I laugh and love more than I ever have in my life. I am the happiest I have ever been...and I'm excited to know that I'm only scratching the surface of my happiness.

The more I grow, the easier it is to grow. I learned the skill and the power of loving discipline. I consistently return to my nurturing parent for counsel, and therefore, feel less shame, less inadequacy, less pain, and more value, more love, more ownership. It is a never-ending joyous upward spiral.

Living as the author of my life takes courage. There were plenty of times when I felt cowardly and continued to live my life in reaction to the counsel of my inner critical and indulgent voices. By listening to them, I felt disempowered and I grew through pain. My journey was bumpy because I did not initially have a map and I spent so much of my time bouncing back and forth between these destructive voices and therefore in pain.

I am writing this to give you one key awareness in the map that empowered my transformation. It is my hope that this awareness may reduce the pain of your growth and make your journey easier to travel.

If you are like I was, and everybody I have coached, you are confused between your internal indulgent and nurturing parents. The most important distinction between the two is that the indulgent parent lets you off the hook and excuses your behavior. This lack of accountability and ownership is the beginning of the downward spiral. (Kids are often brought up this way so it is no wonder that we lack this skill as grownups.) If you are off the hook, you get to blame. If you blame, it is easy to be a victim. Victims feel powerless and cannot conceive of affecting empowered change. You become stuck. Now what?

In sweeps, the critical parent wants to whip you into shape. Through threats, punishment, and shame, the critical parent keeps you afraid and in pain and fundamentally increases your feelings of anger and rage. Eventually you can't take it any more, so you return to the indulgent parent for a break. There is no way out with only these two on the scene.

Half of the key awareness is that the critical and indulgent parents are two sides of the same coin. Both are specifically designed to give you disempowering guidance, which produces shame and pain.

The other half of the key awareness completes the distinction between the indulgent and nurturing parents: where the indulgent parent lets you off the hook and keeps you trapped in victim, the nurturing parent sees your ownership and knows that with ownership comes freedom.

How does this work? In short, your nurturing parent helps you see, without judgment, the impact of your patterns. If the impact is negative, your nurturing parent helps you find your way to remorse. With remorse comes the choice to forgive. And with forgiveness comes genuine and sustainable change.

For example, after I left my marriage, my nurturing parent helped me look deeply and with compassion at my relationship with my ex-husband. It was painful but also freeing to own the ways that I contributed to the pain and dysfunction of our relationship, and to understand my motivations behind my destructive behavior. With my understanding, my ownership, and the remorse I felt for the pain I caused both of us, I was able to forgive myself and change my patterns. I was also able to see things clearly and not take ownership for what was his. Instead, I learned to set healthy boundaries. If I had not gotten to my ownership, but instead got stuck in blame and victim, I would have eventually recreated the same kind of painful relationship I had in my marriage.

Because I did change my patterns and I grew myself, I felt confident when I found and fell in love with my partner. Because I had become somebody who knows enough of my value, my belonging and how deeply I am loved, this is what I bring to this new relationship and is therefore exactly what I create in it. Of course, my partner, and all that he brings, also has a lot to do with it, but that is a story for another time.

The point is that with the help of my nurturing parent I was able to transform myself, learn how to meet my own core needs and create profound love and intimacy in my most important relationships. Developing my inner nurturing parent is the solution that allows me to be the best parent I can be for my son, the best provider for both of us, the best partner I can be in my relationship, the best coach and teacher to my clients, and the best CEO of my business. And because my most important relationships are healthy and strong, I not only feel free to give my attention to my work, I feel creative and generous in what I give.

It is so much more fun to live freely, in the safety and with the counsel of a trusted nurturing parent, where you feel the security to take risks and learn, the confidence to love and to lead, and the satisfaction of true happiness. I hope you join me here. The choice is yours.

Michele Eisenberg empowers people to generate happiness from the inside out. As a veteran executive and life coach, she has worked with clients all over the world. Michele is known for her ability to help clients create more love, happiness and success in their relationships with themselves, their partners, their children and, of course, as leaders in their lives.

Unfortunately, most of us repeat the painful emotional patterns of our childhood, and these patterns usually get more intense over time. But we don't have to repeat them. We can choose to heal them, if we know how.

Hence, the founding of the Happy Family Network, Michele's passion and WHY. Michele believes that a person's ultimate leadership begins as a parent and partner at home. Over the past decade, Michele studied maps for generating love and intimacy. She has successfully put these maps and principles into practice and taught them to her clients. Her vision is to bring happiness, love and intimacy into families and relationships throughout the world, one person at a time.

The Happy Family Network teaches people how to:

- end shame
- give themselves the love, nurturing and support they seek
- stop dysfunctional and painful patterns of love and replace them with healing and intimacy-producing patterns of love
- use positive parenting skills to reduce negative behaviors in children of all ages and replace them with increased co-operation, respect, ownership, connection, love…
- use children's negative behaviors to teach them vital life skills
- generate and increase love and intimacy in their relationships
- and so much more

Michele knows that when a person is happy in their relationships at home, they can flourish in the rest of their life. She loves nothing more than empowering people and giving them tools to thrive in their families and beyond. The world is brighter when you live in a happy family. It all begins with you. Nothing changes until you do.

Michele earned a Master's Degree from Brandeis University Lemberg International Business School. She received her coaching training and certification from the Coaches Training Institute in 1998, and she is a graduate of CTI's Co-Active Leadership Program. She also received a Master's diploma at the Academy of Intuition Medicine.

Having lived and worked in Luxembourg, France, the UK, Italy, New York and now the San Francisco Bay Area, Michele is tri-lingual, fluent in English, French, and Italian. She has a passion for her work, for children and for parenting. She is an avid student of metaphysics and yoga and loves spending time with friends and in nature.

Michele lives with her partner, Michael, her son, Zachary, their two frogs Toadie and Graby and Ethel the turtle.

Visit www.happyfamilynetwork.com to receive your FREE "Happy Family Blueprint: Building Blocks for a Happy Family."

CHAPTER 8

Are You an Essence-Based Entrepreneur?

by Dr. Jennifer Howard

People often think of entrepreneurs as bold, successful, even glamorous. It seems ideal—an easy lifestyle where your time is your own and you can be your own boss. The promise of autonomy and big bucks sounds enticing, but truthfully, the lives of most entrepreneurs require a deep commitment and large amounts of time. And while many achieve some success, a much greater satisfaction and fulfillment comes from being what I call an "essence-based" entrepreneur.

What is our essence? It's the deepest part of us and in relationship with what many might refer to as God, Spirit or the Universe. Our essence is far more than our quirky personality; it's the source of our purpose and passion. I know these words have been bandied around a lot lately, usually describing a fun pastime or an intense interest. We might say we're passionate about cooking or football, but that's "passion light." When I say passion and purpose, I'm talking about something that comes from our very deepest source, our highest level of existence.

When we come from our life purpose and create a career rooted in our passion, it makes the work required much easier to do. When we're aligned with our essence, we have access to a knowledge and wisdom that allows us to consciously experience our connection with Truth or Being-ness itself. We're actually being who we were always meant to be. It just feels right, and allows us to live an authentic life.

Our "essence connection" is what sustains our interest in our work. It generates the inspiration and commitment we need as we pursue our personal and professional goals. Rooted in this central part of ourselves, we are tapped into our passion and we realize a genuine desire to make a positive difference in the world. In fact, this urge to help others with our work is an indication that we are connected to our essence. Our deepest purpose is to contribute our special gifts to others, and I believe this brings the ultimate fulfillment.

Communication flows so much more easily when we're aligned with our essence. We naturally connect with other people and can experience real intimacy more easily. When we conduct business from this place, we create meaningful and lasting relationships with our clients, customers and colleagues. We're more present in our conversations, and we can hear a deeper level of communication. This benefits us, not only in our work, but also in every relationship we have. From here, we become a conscious entrepreneur.

You also hear the inner conversation that's taking place between your essence and you—your personal sense of self. This conversation often happens without your noticing, because your essence, through your inner voice, is continually broadcasting its reaction to what you're doing. It's responding to what's going on around you all the time. It's a hunch about the next best move for you, and it's the wisdom that tells you who you really are and why you're here. What makes it a conversation is your willingness to slow down and listen, to become more sensitive to the subtle movements of thought, energy and feeling within you and to act upon what you hear, to see where it will lead, and what response it will call forth.

In our culture, we tend to measure success by income, fame and reputation. We are encouraged to compare ourselves with others. Yet we all have our own song to sing, and only we can sing it, so there's no value in comparing our expression with another's. As we step into being an essence-based entrepreneur, we become less interested in the old definition of success, and we begin to broaden our view of success. We observe how clearly we receive our inner wisdom, the alignment of our business with our spiritual values, and how often our actions are guided by the deeper inspiration within us. All these aspects flow from our fundamental connection to essence. Nothing we do and nothing we choose to be is separate from this. Our alignment with our essence determines our quality of life and guides us to take inspired action.

When it comes to taking action, it seems that most of us approach taking action in one of two ways and sometimes we bounce back and forth. The first way can look like getting an idea and running with it. This means taking immediate action. Although this is helpful at times, taking spontaneous action can sometimes lead us down the wrong path. We can end up building a successful business, but remain personally unfulfilled. We may have built a business that isn't connected to who we really are.

The second way of approaching action is becoming trapped in doubt. We have trouble figuring out the best action to take. At first glance this may seem like we're taking time to reflect, but we can get stuck spinning our wheels in the mud of indecision and confusion. We are probably not going deep enough to get traction. This is sometimes caused by our quest for "perfection."

Neither of these approaches produces great results. Instead, we need a third way that's more solidly aligned with our essence. This means being connected inwardly to the wise and discerning part of ourselves that knows what step to take next, the step that leads in the right direction for us at this time. Of course, we'll shift our course from time to time, but this is why it's so important to stay in touch with our internal selves and continue to receive information from our essence. You might remember the personal goals you held dear at age 16, or 21. Most of us have changed quite a bit since then. We've learned a lot and how we see ourselves in the world has been altered significantly, yet our essence—the essential part of us—remains the same.

I recently spoke with two very successful entrepreneurs. They each built their business either when they were young and didn't know themselves well, or chose what seemed like the easier path at the time. One person said her coach urged her in a certain direction. The other said that she fell into it and it seemed right at the time. Both careers worked fine for a while, but then they reached a point where they had achieved success, yet didn't feel happy or fulfilled. They had made choices not aligned with their essence, and so their work eventually felt like drudgery. It's important to ask ourselves, "Will this choice move me forward on my essence path? Is this decision in alignment with my highest/deepest connection?"

The Internet is flooded with people who've created the perfect system, formula or methodology to guide the budding entrepreneur to success. There's nothing wrong with that, of course, as we need to develop tools for our businesses. A problem arises when we believe that a formula alone will guide us in the right direction. Using the cookie-cutter approach without altering it often doesn't work for the essence-based entrepreneur. This type of coaching often focuses on financial reward, and it's easy to buy into this singular type of success. There are people who've made millions of dollars following this path themselves and many by coaching others to do the same. But our internal guidance is ultimately the source of our fulfillment and satisfaction.

If we do the work to identify our mission, and we feel a strong sense of purpose in what we do, we may find it looks startlingly different from someone else's business plan. Imagine three accomplished painters side by side at easels, gazing at the landscape before them. Each will see the view differently, because we don't perceive in identical ways. One artist may focus on the foreground, while the next is fascinated by the waves splashing against the rocks. The third is intrigued by the clouds over the horizon. All of these paintings are beautiful in their own right. No two works of art are alike, and so your essence-based business will have that specific stamp of you, your own unique perspective.

Another important aspect of being an essence-based entrepreneur involves furthering our education. We continually study our craft and build our knowledge base. We also acquire new tools needed to build our businesses, and our commitment to learning works perfectly in tandem with our intuition. We continually use our growing knowledge, skills and experience but lead with our internal guidance.

When we make an effort to consciously connect with and live from our essence, we're not only aligning with our highest energy, we're lining up with the highest and deepest energy that exists, existence itself. When we make this connection, we experience a clarity, confidence, and empowerment that isn't ordinarily available to us. How do we do this? There are several ways to get started.

To develop, deepen and clarify our connection to essence, we need to turn inward, be contemplative. This can be greatly served by meditation, because when we turn down the mental chatter that distracts us and we begin to quiet our mind, we become open to the deep communication. There are many types of meditation, from one-point focus with a mantra, centering prayer, silent, to chanting and guided meditations. Whatever you choose, I encourage you to practice every day if you can. Meditation can also help us release emotional blocks holding us back and it does wonders for the stress we carry with us.

Along with a contemplative practice, the essence-based entrepreneur will engage in personal work. Whether its psychotherapy, coaching, energy psychology, energy healing, a specific spiritual discipline or an entirely different modality, we continually seek to know ourselves and let go of the thoughts and beliefs that no longer serve us. We may have anxiety and fear that lowers our energy, makes us unsure of what to do next and stop us from seeing the possibilities available to us. With our ongoing personal work, we can release our stuck energy and connect with our essence more easily.

Sometimes we may ask for guidance, and at first, it might seem difficult to be clear about the answer. It may not show up immediately or in a way that we can understand at the moment. We might come across an answer through a random conversation, a book, or a snippet of a song. Pay attention to the six languages of our inner wisdom: thoughts, feelings, body sensations, mental images, intuition, and inspiration. Did a thought occur to you that seemed to make sense? Did it feel like you heard something out of the blue that then made sense to you? When making a decision and considering your options, does a specific option make you feel good or uneasy? Check in with your body—do you have any physical pangs or sensations that confirm something you're considering doing? Watch your mind's eye. You may find clarity in an image that flashes across your mind. Sometimes the answer to your question comes as a hunch or a feeling of absolute certainty. This can be your intuition. And sometimes you may feel suddenly inspired to act in a situation. When we cultivate our connection to essence, we can consistently access one or more of these languages. The more we use these tools, the easier and more frequent the guidance will flow through us. In this way, we take inspired action.

As essence-based entrepreneurs, we love what we do because we've identified our passion, clarified our mission and we've finally come to awaken and live our life's purpose. Our essence informs who we are and all of our choices and ultimately all that we bring to this world. As a conscious entrepreneur, your business will grow and thrive as you do. Your life and relationships will be energized and enlivened. Imagine the possibilities of living from your essence! What song will you sing?

Dr. Jennifer Howard teaches the art of Conscious Living. She is equally at home sharing ancient spiritual wisdom, the latest scientific understanding, and proven and practical life-changing techniques culled from over 20 years as an internationally acclaimed coach, licensed psychotherapist, teacher, and energy healer. As a professional speaker and author, Dr. Jennifer's energetic style, along with her sense of humor, helps her audiences—beginner and advanced alike—assimilate what is being taught, even when the material appears to be complex.

She has offices in New York, leads a variety of teleseminars and is a leading thought leader on spirituality and psychology. Having frequently appeared as an expert on numerous national network television shows, including The Maury Povich Show, Turning Point, America's Talking, Rolanda, Charles Perez, Les Brown, News Channel 12, she is also the host of the popular radio show, "A Conscious Life." Dr. Jennifer Howard, a Huffington Post blogger, along with one of 15 experts participating in the Walk With Walgreen's national wellness campaign, was named one of the TOP 25 Celebrity Doctors on Twitter, one of the Top 100 Health websites and has been dubbed "The Funniest Shrink on Twitter."

Dr. Jennifer, as she is known in social media, is offering a free downloadable MP3 of her meditation and a handout that accompanies and deepens this article. Go to www.drjenniferhoward.tv/essence and visit website: www.drjenniferhoward.com.

CHAPTER 9

From Depression to Divine Purpose

by Anita Pizycki

My mother called on a crisp cold day in February. Looking back, her call began a very difficult journey of illness and death. But also one of deep connection to purpose, though it would take many months for me to realize it.

After a bit of chitchat, my mother gently informed me she had lung cancer. The malignancy in her top right lung was inoperable. As she explained her treatment, I understood all too well. I had been driving my spiritual Kabbalah teacher, Anne, to her doctor's appointments for breast cancer. Anne had become like a second mother and best friend to me. I now had two mothers with cancer.

During these events, I attempted to find balance between work, family, aging parents, and for myself, as this is what I taught my coaching clients. Little did I know that any balance in my life would be totally blown apart by the events of the next eight months.

At that time, I owned and ran two businesses. I operated a coaching practice, guiding accountants and lawyers around their businesses and their life. Then, as a chartered accountant, I ran the office and all the financial aspects of a small construction company I co-owned with my significant other. Getting away to visit my mom or take Anne to appointments while balancing all this wasn't easy—and that was only the start.

In May, I received a call that would change the rest of my life. My partner called to say that an accident occurred on the construction site involving a three-year-old child. Later that day, we learned this precious child had died. At first I felt shock, then horror, and then extreme sorrow. I actually felt my heart break.

The next few days were almost unbearable having to go over the event with police, ministry authorities, insurance adjustors and victims' counselors. After each meeting, the counselors told us to go home, take care of ourselves, take care of our staffs, as we, too, were victims of this tragic accident. Nevertheless, I felt overwhelmed by grief and loss for the young family. I would just lie down and cry.

As if these events were not enough, in June we learned my partner's sister-in-law, Karen, had a relapse—her cancer had returned. Only 39, Karen had two small boys and a loving husband. She passed in early August.

The Fall became filled with increased cancer care for Anne and flying to help my dad with my mom, whose condition continued to worsen. One of my dear friends, Paul from my Kabbalah class, learned he had cancer also. Anne passed in November, Paul in December, followed by my mom in January. In eight short months, I had dealt with five deaths. With their passing, I also lost my spiritual community at a time when I needed it most.

I spiraled into a deep depression. My broken heart completely shattered into pieces I didn't think could ever be repaired. Even with years of spiritual training, I couldn't make any sense of it all. I had days where I would lose my will to live. I couldn't see the point. Then I would remember I had a 16-year-old daughter who needed a mother. Remembering that kept me here, but each day became harder and harder to get through. By May, a year after the tragic accident, I returned to bed most days by noon. To keep grief at bay, I read books on depression, grief, and spirituality.

One day while reading, I couldn't stop crying. I became scared. I called my partner, Dixon, asking him to come over, saying I really wasn't well and I needed him here. He was by my side within a few minutes. He held me and asked what would become a very important question. He asked, "*What do you need?*" I thought for a minute and from somewhere deep inside I replied, "I need to go to Lily Dale."

Lily Dale is the oldest spiritualist community in America, nestled in a tiny western New York town, less then two hours from my home. Anne had sent us there once to learn mediumship from Rev. Elaine Thomas who, in Anne's opinion, was the best.

"Why don't you go next weekend?" Dixon suggested.

"No," I protested, almost subconsciously, not even sure where the words were coming from. "I don't need to wander the town; I need to be in a spiritual class." I intuitively understood I needed a *structured learning environment*. I needed people who could bring me answers to what I didn't understand about all these deaths, provide emotional support, and offer healing for my broken heart. Today I am sure the guidance I received came from spirit because going to Lily Dale had not been a thought before that moment.

I soon learned that Elaine Thomas' school, Fellowships of the Spirit (www.fellowshipsspirit.org) had a Spiritual Insight Training II weekend coming up in just 10 days. I'd taken SIT I years prior and never had found time to complete the two-part course. Since they are only offered several times a year, I had further confirmation I'd received divine guidance.

After the first evening of classes, I knew I'd made the right choice. I felt more like myself then I had in over a year. I truly believe that depression is caused when we become disconnected from our spirit. That weekend helped me reconnect to my spirit again.

By Sunday, the staff began encouraging us to attend the two-year ministry school. I deeply wanted to, but knew I could never afford the $8,000 to $10,000 it would cost, never mind the time away from my floundering businesses. Yet, each time someone asked if I planned to attend, I burst into tears. I knew Spirit wanted me to take this path. I would need to trust Spirit to provide the funding.

Every year, all of the family visits my dad in Florida. Since most of us still live in Canada, it's one of the few times we all gather together. I hadn't mentioned going to ministry school to my dad as I knew he felt I should focus on getting a job. So he surprised me when, as we prepared to leave for home, he wrote both my sister and I a $5,000 check. I almost fell out of my chair. My father is a generous man, but he had never done anything like this before.

The two years at Fellowships of the Spirit were critical to my self-healing and full recovery from the depression. At school, I found answers to my deepest questions about life and death. I received hundreds of healings to put my humpty dumpty heart back together. I gave readings and healings from Spirit to my classmates. And most importantly, I truly learned how Spirit and I work together. I learned how Spirit provides me with guidance.I need only listen to my intuition.

During the second year of school, I wanted to return to accounting work to become more financially stable. I asked Spirit to help me find a job I could do easily in my current state of mind, which still required gentle self-care, life balance, and healing. I applied for jobs but had an eerie amount of non-response. I felt Spirit's urging to attend a local accounting association dinner. I casually let everyone know I wanted accounting work.

Within a week, I learned of a client who was in and out of the hospital due to liver disease. It was a gift from God. Not only would the work be easy and familiar, I felt like I would be really helping a family in need. The part-time job also allowed me to continue coaching my current clients.

Attending ministry school and having experienced all I had, made me realize just how very much I wanted to make a difference in the world. I began asking Spirit for the inspired direction my coaching practice should take.

I have learned that when I ask, Spirit provides, though I might not always recognize the answer at first, or it might take an evolution of events before that answer becomes clear. One day while reading my email, a newsletter from Mary Allen (America's Peace Coach) popped into my inbox—an odd occurrence, because I filter this type of mail to a secondary folder to read in my spare time. Since Spirit oftentimes utilizes odd happenings to gain attention, I opened it. Mary mentioned a free teleclass with Adam Urbanski, The Marketing Mentor. I signed up.

Adam's material impressed me because he taught how to create and market products and programs for information-based businesses—just what I needed at that time. When Adam invited us to join his weekly program, I wondered if I should sign up. As I thought about how the information had come to me, I accepted it as from Spirit. I trusted this class would somehow be good for my business. Even when I had trouble signing up online, I didn't take it as a sign to stop (as we spiritual people do sometimes). Instead, I called the office and got it done. The call to a real person only supported my feeling more that this was a good move for me. The program also included a ticket to Adam's event in California. At the time I thought, *"Well that's nice but the travel costs will make the trip impossible. I'll just enjoy the weekly class and that will be enough."*

Once again I found a *structured learning environment* proving itself as a valuable asset. Adam's weekly calls kept me going forward. Then, as the emails for the upcoming California event started to arrive, I felt torn. How could I justify spending over a thousand dollars to attend? That's when I started noticing people, newsletters, books and articles all mentioning how we have a huge reservoir available to us. This triggered my memory of thousands of travel points I'd saved for years for a someday, round-the-world trip. I booked a flight, hotel and car—all for less than $100. It felt so freeing to follow my heart's intuition after so many difficult years.

The conference provided invaluable content and business connections, but Spirit had something even better planned. On the last day of the conference, Sheri McConnell spoke on the use of for-profit networks that not only provide training and skills to their members but also create a place of connection and belonging. She talked about how she did this while still having time to raise four kids and have balance in her life.

During her talk, all that I desired to create as a heart-based coach came together for me: I truly believe that we go through challenging experiences for a reason. Hearing Sheri speak, I knew I had experienced such a profound sadness so I would seek out community and structured learning for myself. In doing so, I'd soon come to realize this is what I needed to create for others.

I've observed wonderful teachers and classmates who were totally connected to their purpose and their bliss while performing their healing services for others. I've also noticed how many of them struggle to create successful businesses doing what they love and feel called by Spirit to do. Unfortunately, many have no choice but to keep stifling day jobs to provide for themselves and their families. As a healer, I can work directly with a handful of people. As a business coach to countless spiritual entrepreneurs, I can facilitate healing to a huge global community desperately in need.

So IASE was born: the International Association of Spiritual Entrepreneurs (www.iaseconnect.com). IASE forms a perfect vehicle for me to teach, coach and create a community where spiritual business owners can come to connect, learn and grow their businesses. Just as I first realized I needed *structured learning* when my life became stuck, IASE offers structured learning that takes into account the uniqueness of the spiritual business owner.

As these realizations came to me, my heart soared as I caught a glimpse of the fulfilling purpose I came here to serve—my WHY. My goal is to be a guiding light of success for spiritual entrepreneurs who are called by Spirit to step up, feel the fear, and do it anyway. I now know that *consistent action guided by spirit equals limitless possibilities*.

Anita Pizycki is a chartered accountant, business coach and spiritualist minister. She has been coaching business owners to make more money in less time for over eight years and is now focusing solely on assisting Spiritual Entrepreneurs. She is also Founder and CEO of the International Association of Spiritual Entrepreneurs (IASE) where like-minded business owners come to connect, learn and grow their businesses. She has seen many spiritual business owners struggle to make a living doing what they love and feel guided to do. Her mission is to help 10,000 Spiritual Entrepreneurs create wildly successful businesses by taking consistent action inspired by Spirit all while maintaining balance in their lives.

She has grown as a person and as a business owner through structured learning environments that were dedicated to a specific outcome. Her goal is to provide that structured learning environment for Spiritual Entrepreneurs. Membership in the IASE has many benefits including monthly teaching calls by experts. Subjects covered change year to year but include topics such as visioning, successful money mindsets, turning intuition into action, planning, goal setting, time and energy management, money mastery, marketing, social media, heart-based selling, creating a support team, and life balance, etc.

She has also created products and programs that are specifically designed to support the spiritual business owner. All programs are easy to follow and lead business owners to taking action while providing support. Virtual and live events allow fellow spiritual entrepreneurs to meet, share their struggles along with their wins, and most importantly, support each other in achieving their goals.

Anita lives in St. Catharines, Ontario, Canada with her partner Dixon, and her teenage daughter who comes home during summer breaks from university. Visit Anita at www.iaseconnect.com.

CHAPTER 10

Beauty from the Inside Out, in Business and in Life

by Becky Reese

Most women struggle with taking care of themselves. If you can relate, you might be in the same place I was years ago, not knowing where to begin or how to take care of myself. Taking care of yourself might even seem like a selfish thing to do. Or time-consuming. Or a waste of your precious time. Trust me, it's none of those things. Whether you're a stay-at-home mom, mompreneur, or a new or seasoned woman in business, you've most likely got "people-pleaser" syndrome. It's one of the most widespread "diseases" us modern girls have, and it's largely responsible for all the exhaustion, stress, and burnout we feel.

Or is it? Hey, who's really running the show here, anyway? You see, when we aren't taking care of ourselves and setting clear boundaries around what we will or won't do, we give in to stress. We surrender. We give up. We let circumstances and other people have power over us, and we feel helpless because of it. It's natural. After all, this is what we're taught as young girls, right? Be nice. Be quiet. Be subservient. Fold your napkin on your lap. And whatever you do, don't rock the boat or there'll be hell to pay.

But when we realize there are other ways to approach life, everything changes in profound and meaningful ways, and our life becomes our own again. I hope the following story of my experiences will help you see how.

I am the wife of a millionaire. My husband and I have worked hard, made wise investments, and climbed the ladder of success that has led us to a place of financial stability and a little beyond. So I should be happy, right? However, I've learned that money doesn't solve everything. Money doesn't make you beautiful. Money doesn't create a solid marriage. Money doesn't give you self-worth. Money doesn't hug you, love you, inspire you, bring you peace, or comfort you in the long run.

Before I got hit over the head with a major wakeup call, I was living a good life as far as my financial statements, but on the inside I was crumbling like a sugar cube. I was living on the edge of stress. For the last 18 years, my world consisted of caring for my husband and our five children and helping out with our multiple businesses. It was a routine I had mastered well. Take care of everyone else and forget about me.

For so many years, I spent my time, energy, and efforts trying to make everyone else happy but I couldn't find even an ounce of happiness in myself. I should have won awards for people-pleasing, I was so good. I thought if everyone else was happy, life would be a-okay. If my kids were happy, there'd be peace at home. If Mike was happy, our finances would be steady and stable. If my parents were happy, I could be the good daughter.

I took care of everyone around me and neglected myself along the way. It got worse when Mike started his own business after years of working for others. He always had the "play big to win" attitude and he was definitely living his philosophy. But before our finances leveled off to a comfortable position, our debt was piling up.

As the numbers went up, so did my anxiety. No matter what we did, it seemed we were just borrowing from Peter to pay Paul. Bills freaked me out. Living expenses freaked me out. I'd lay awake at night wondering what I could do to ease the financial burden, worrying about how it would affect our children and wondering if money would one day completely disappear.

I worried about everything. My weight. My health. My children. My marriage. The finances. When I wasn't worrying, I was fixing everyone else's problems and making them happy. It was the only thing that afforded me temporary peace. The anxiety plus my penchant to people-please was a coupling that ultimately sabotaged me on the inside and on the outside. By the time I realized I had no happy place to call my own for these reasons, I had already spent years unknowingly being pummeled by self-doubt. It's one of the main reasons I landed in therapy three years ago and goes hand-in-hand with the anxiety. While on one hand, I was able to laugh at myself for doing something silly or stupid like trip or mispronounce a word; on the other hand, deep down I felt overweight, fashion-illiterate, and purposeless.

My weight issue was a big deal. Five babies will wreak havoc on your body. No doubt about that. I wouldn't trade any amount of pounds for my beautiful children, but seeing my body change in ways I couldn't keep up with chipped away at my self-esteem. But here's the funny thing. Even when I lost weight between babies three and four, I still wasn't happy.

So I started experimenting. I started doing things to mask my insecurities and the truth of what was going on inside of me. I tried hair extensions. I tried makeup. I tried jewelry. I turned into a fashion wannabe. I loved browsing through fashion and beauty magazines and admiring the beautiful women photographed on the pages. I wanted to look like them. Maybe that would supercharge my spirit and make me feel good. Or worthy. Or enough. Isn't that what we all just want to feel?

News flash. Even when I adorned myself with pretty jewels and couture dresses, I may have looked fabulous on the outside, but I still felt nothing on the inside. I spent so much time on diets it was like a full-time job. When my nutritionist told me, "See a therapist, Becky. I bet your anxiety is what's keeping you from losing weight," she was right. It was ironic; anxiety was the main culprit in my battle of the bulge.

It was the people-pleaser in me who was carrying around all this anxiety, manifesting as extra weight. It was the little girl who, along with her brother, had tried desperately to keep the peace and keep quiet, as my mother would go into another one of her screaming spells, a horrible side-effect of her manic depressive illness. I lived in constant fear. Fear that I would be the bad girl that would make my mom upset and ruin everyone's day. I was burdened by thinking it was my responsibility to create a home atmosphere of peace, of happiness, of calm. It was too much weight for any little girl to carry, and as I became an adult, those same feelings trailed behind me. Can you relate?

So many of us base our level of happiness and contentment on what we look like or—here's a big one—how much money we have. I can tell you that I have experience in both areas. In an article entitled, "Love the One You're With" Geenen Roth wrote, "All we ever have is now. If you can't look around now and see the abundance in your life, you won't be able to notice it in five years either, no matter how thin you are. Happiness is not about changing your circumstances but changing the eyes through which you view your circumstances." See? Perspective.

In 2007, I lost my best friend and sister Carol. It was through her death, I came face-to-face with the troubling fact that I was lost. With her gone, I noticed how much I had depended on and needed her. Life is fleeting. We all know it deep down in our hearts, but it usually takes us being sucker-punched by a tragedy to truly appreciate that truth. Not only did my sister's death make me grateful for the close relationship we shared, it also created in me a deep hole I was unable to fill.

I had immersed myself in motherhood and supporting my husband as he bettered himself in his personal and professional development. Like most women, I fell into the trap of putting everybody and everything before me...all the time. Carol's death left me to question who I was. It put me on the track to seeking more out of myself, more out of life, more out of the mere existence I had been living for so long. I knew I had to get myself out of the rut I was in. I had to confront my fears and brush them aside. I had to step out of the comfort zone I was in. I had to stop paying attention to what others thought or said about me.

I was finally ready to do what it took to take care of me. If you're on your journey of self-care, do your best to ignore the naysayers or those around you who are negative or who don't notice. Remember that you are the best. You are beautiful. Don't you ever forget it. That goes for all you working moms as well. After all, caring for a family is a business, too, when you really look at it. You have multiple hats to wear and endless things to juggle. You work 24/7, and you always have to watch your pennies. Sound familiar?

And here's something else I realized about self-care. We don't take care of ourselves so others can take notice. We don't take care of ourselves so we can show the world how extraordinary we are. We take care of ourselves because it's the right thing to do for our well-being and it makes us better people.

The thing is, you can't really understand what it is to love yourself until you get there. And that process, if/when it happens for you is completely individual. The experience of the "a ha" moments or mental clicks going off that connect the dots for you is very personal and based on your own life experiences, past and present. When it's time, God will help you see what you need to know.

For me, it was the moment I realized, despite having what others/society told me looked like a supremely successful life, I finally understood that "outside" success couldn't possibly fit the bill. I had to find a way to get comfortable in my own skin. And when I did, everything I thought I was searching for faded into the background and I took up my life again, where each day, I live from the inside out with grace, humility, and unwavering faith. Yes, that spiritual knock upside the head opened my eyes to who I am deep down, but you can be sure, I'm still a work in progress!

My relationship with myself is the key to all the good and positive relationships I have with everyone in my life, including those I work with. I know your business is your baby. I know you want to see it succeed, but at what price? Let me ask you this. If you knew today was your last day on earth, what would you do with those last 24 hours? Really think about it. What is THE MOST important thing you would do? Whatever that is, I bet you'll find a big part of YOU ripples through that final analysis. Now let that filter through everything you do, each and every day.

Once you make that special journey to really understanding yourself from the inside out, you'll see how much easier it is to take care of yourself. Then your life—and your business—will naturally take care of themselves. Learn to be kind to yourself. Do not compare yourself with anyone. It's a waste of your precious energy. We are all exquisite, unique beings. Celebrate your uniqueness and everything else that makes you who you are. You are strength. You are love. You are beauty. Now go out there and get 'em. I'm rooting for you!

Remember, life is how you live it, not how you spend it!

Becky Reese is dedicated to the belief that all women should feel beautiful. Her first book, available September, 2011 details her struggles and triumphs of finding inner peace and beauty. Her clothing line will debut in Spring of 2012 and will feature running clothes for sizes 8 and up. Becky is passionate about offering functional and fashionable sports clothes to women of all sizes and shapes. She started Sexy Moms Running Club in August and loves the idea of getting more women together through running!

As the youngest of eight children and the mother of five, Becky values the importance of family more than anything. She is an author, entrepreneur and philanthropist who is dedicated to helping families, especially children, in need throughout her church and community. Becky lives in Northern Michigan with Mike, her husband of 19 years, and their five children.

Visit Becky at www.marriedtoamillionairebook.com and www.sexymomsrunningclub.com.

CHAPTER 11

Emotional Resilience—How to Bounce Back

by Jennie Sutton

You may be wondering why I want you to take control when all around you, it feels that your world is falling apart.

Well, let me start from the beginning. You see, I commenced my professional career as a registered nurse. My vocation was in palliative and terminal care, providing comfort for those coming to the end of their lives. It was at this time, that I learnt early on that *"life is what you make of it."* Yes, we may well be dealt a bad set of cards, but even then there is something to be grateful for.

Consequently, I became aware of how, when faced with death and the bereaved, it's really important to be able to bounce back and keep your own 'tank' full. By not taking all the emotional baggage with me, I was able to continue to care from one patient to the next.

Whilst nursing I learnt many lessons that have changed my perception of life. It was about developing the ability to bounce back through emotional resilience. This can mean different things, to different people in different situations. For me, as a cancer nurse, it was about supporting people to get the very best out of the time they had left. I spent much time talking and listening and learnt that the power of conversation can never be underestimated.

The First Lessons of CHAT

Choice

Choice brings with it an opportunity which you don't know is available until you think about it.

Humor
Humor connects people and laughter is a great healer.

Aspirations
Aspirations only happen if you take action, so don't leave yours in the trash.

Thanks
Being thankful for the small things will make you value the big things.

So what's the moral of these lessons?
Life is not a rehearsal. If you stay in a rut, all you'll see is the ground beneath you, as you calculate each and every step. You'll miss the sky, the clouds and rainbows of life. So don't wait—take action. In essence, this chapter will build upon the lessons of CHAT and take you through four key principles to enable you to bounce back.

Before then, I'll share with you my own definition of emotional resilience:

"Emotional resilience is the ability not to dwell on something that's gone wrong, but an opportunity to learn and move forward, accepting that things that don't go right are just part of life's tapestry."

So now it's your turn...

I want you to think about what emotional resilience means to you. Perhaps think of an occasion when you felt emotionally resilient and what it was that enabled you to feel that way. Or think about someone who you admire because of their emotional resilience. What is it about them that demonstrates this? The person could be a friend, family member, a colleague or a celebrity.

Having identified these qualities and characteristics, how about using some of them and making them work for you, too? Here I've put together some simple tools that will enable you to bounce back at any time.

Let's take a look...

The Principle of Flexibility

A ball, when it hits the ground, has the flexibility to move in one direction or another, depending on the surface of the ground, the speed of the ball and what the ball is made of. In other words, the way the ball bounces is made up of a number of flexible factors.

Being emotionally resilient enables you to have that same flexible approach to decision making, too. People who have this quality make decisions, take action, stand by their judgements, and yet are equally prepared to change their minds if need be.

Decision Making and Choice

The tool below will help you to balance your judgment and decision making. It enables you to manage risk through a simple framework of...

___ Identifying what your core obligations are, what you must fulfill and take responsibility for in any of your roles (as: mom, partner, daughter, boss, colleague, etc.)

___ Leading you to acknowledge your own responsibility, flexibility of choice and decision making

___ Clarifying what is NOT your obligation, liability or responsibility.

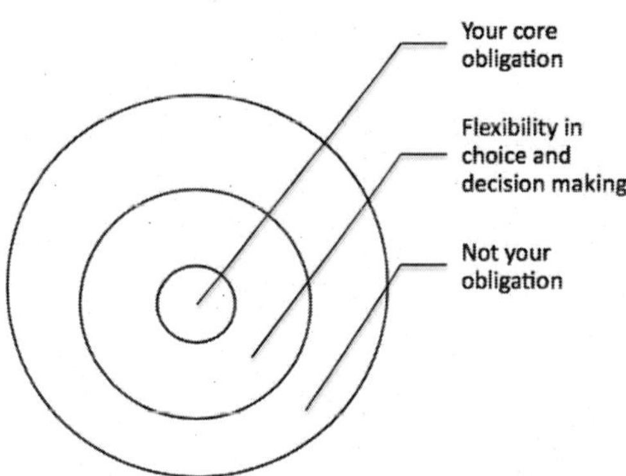

You see, you are someone who can make decisions.

The Principle of Fun

Regardless of what age and ability you have, playing with a ball has a sense of fun, bringing a smile to your face whilst playing or evoking fond memories from your childhood. For me, the memory of loud laughter and family banter between father and teenagers while playing ball in our garden brings a huge sense of enjoyment to me.

Having emotional resilience is about making life fun. I don't mean when someone is feeling really low or going through bereavement, you crack a joke. I mean making people smile over the simplest of things. This could be sharing a funny memory or a story. Sometimes it's just about finding the 'funny' in the situation because everyone's path to happiness is so different. You see, laughter connects people on the emotional level. Perhaps that's what makes us human!

Having a positive attitude is contagious and you feel great, too. For me, choosing your attitude is like choosing what clothes to wear in the morning. It's a conscious choice. I can either wear something drab or colorful. I know which one I'd prefer to wear!

Tool to Attitude and Laughter

Below I've put together a simple list that you can practice and implement easily into your everyday life. Remember, having fun is good for you, so give yourself permission to use it and enjoy the experience.

Fun with the Outside World	Fun with our own Life
1. Enthusiasm and optimism is contagious 2. Connect and build rapport 3. Exercise and enjoy the fresh air 4. Spread good news 5. Every day learn something new	6. Plan for something exciting in the future, once done - replace it 7. Keep things in perspective and seek for the 'funny' 8. Take a positive approach and remain upbeat 9. Use a journal to record funny occasions and jokes 10. Plan and program your mind for a positive day

Now look back over the above 10 points and think about these questions...

___ What makes you laugh in your work?

___ What makes you laugh away from work?

___ Is there an opportunity that this laughter can be a fusion of the two?

___ If so, how can you make this happen?

The Principle of Focus

Now we take a look at throwing, hitting and kicking the ball. Whatever the game, be it baseball, basketball or soccer, the principle is constantly the same. It's about focusing on hitting the target, getting the ball in the goal or making that all-important home run. To have emotional resilience, you, too, need to have focus. Focusing on achieving the goal or outcome you want in life will build your armory in emotional resilience.

So let's take a look and explore this principle further...

Have you ever noticed when you get focused on a goal, suddenly barriers appear? You see, at that very moment we create our own obstacles. Think about it. Before a goal is set, there were no barriers to its accomplishment because we never thought of it.

For example, you may want to attend some self-development program that you think will equip you on the path to your success. Once you've set the goal, you may find that the blocks suddenly arise. Maybe something like the following...

"I can't do that, as I don't have the money." "I have other commitments that day," or "it's too expensive." None of these considerations were relevant until you created your goal and focused on attending the workshop.

So what can you do?

Well the easiest way is to avoid barriers and have no focus or goals at all. This is why so many people don't bother setting goals in the first place. They don't want to deal with the obstacles in achieving their aspirations. The moment we set a goal and the moment we choose the direction, the barriers become real.

But I'm guessing you do have some focus, and that's why you're reading this chapter.

Tool to Achieving Your Aspirations

The following checklist will enable you to keep your focus. Remember, barriers are just life's tests to see how badly you want your goal in the first place!

Follow this checklist...

___ If you've got an obstacle in front of you, celebrate as you are on your path to achievement

___ Think about the obstacle differently—ask someone you trust for their opinion

___ Look at the obstacle from a different perspective

___ Use your energy to keep focus on what you want, rather than on what you don't want

___ Look up from the detail and plan ahead whilst keeping your eye on the target. Remember, a turtle only knows where it's going if it takes its head out of its shell.

___ If faced with a challenging conversation or situation rehearse, rehearse, and rehearse. Then you can take comfort that you've explored all eventualities and boosted your confidence at the same time.

___ Focus on one thing rather than spreading your time around too many things.

___ Keep the end result in mind. Your journey ahead requires more than an overnight bag. Don't dwell on things that don't work. Just take the lessons from them instead.

The Principle of Flourish

Like any ball game, the more you practice, the better you become, and you enjoy greater control of the game. This is the same in the game of life. The more you control your emotions, the more resilient you become. This, too, takes practice with a heightened amount of self-awareness.

In other words, don't let past experiences influence you from moving forward. I like to call this *"looking at yourself through the rear view mirror."* You see, when you drive a car, you use your rear view mirror to assess what's gone before you. To me, if past events dictate our future, we would spend our lifetime always looking in the rear view mirror and never achieving our dream. So, the more you hang onto self-doubt or self-limiting beliefs, the more you'll focus on what you don't have.

Tool to Change an Awful Day into an Excellent Day

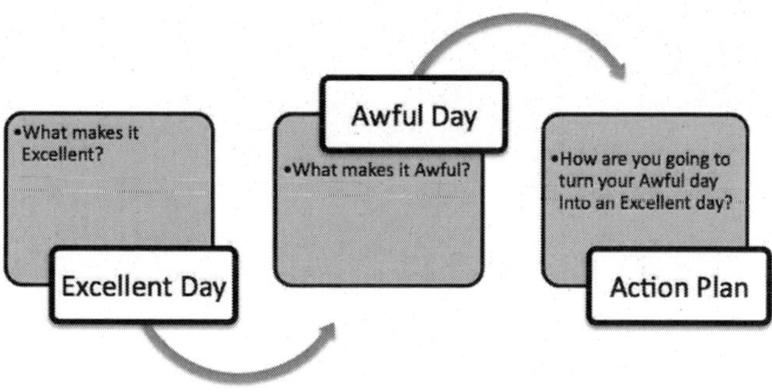

Here is a checklist to turn your day around...

___ Take a leap to push yourself as it really expands your horizons

___ Take a walk, allowing yourself space to ponder, create and imagine

___ Imagine yourself being emotionally resilient as your unconscious will not know the difference between what's real and what's imagined

___ Open your mind and relax and take some deep breaths

___ Give thanks for the little things and changes you've made each and every day

___ Focus on one thing and make it happen, and be aware of the *"should've, could've and would've"* syndrome

Now Hit the Curved Ball

I started off telling you about the lessons of CHAT and my experience with those at their most vulnerable. And yet, they still had the ability to bounce back.

Emotional resilience is something that we all can master. It's a strategy that just needs nurturing and practice. Although we also need to accept that at times we can still be emotional, it's the recognition of those times that will give us strength by reflecting and planning to do something for the next time.

Now, I invite you to be flexible in your approach to life, have fun and keep focused on your goals. Finally, remember to flourish every day, look for the good things and turn the not so good things around.

Finally, go on—grab yourself a bat and hit that curved ball high into the stands!

Jennie Sutton started her career in nursing, then went into leadership within healthcare as a result of her passion to make things better. Better for those who received care and better for those who delivered care. Jennie enjoys getting people to realize their potential and believes that the way to facilitate that is through stepping out of your comfort zone whilst being supported in the process.

Jennie currently combines her training, coaching and speaking business www.enablingsuccess.com with that of being a GP Practice Manager in Cumbria, in the UK. Jennie is also a mother of four children and Founder of a number of social enterprises, ranging from Eden Women's Theatre Group to a Community Involvement Group in Health.

Jennie is someone who makes things happen. 'No' is not an option. and provided the outcomes or actions make her MAD (Make a Difference), Jennie's talents to make things come to fruition are her resourcefulness and creativity.

Section Two

Transformational Transitions

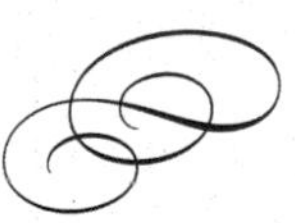

CHAPTER 12

The Missing Piece

by Daria Boissonnas

Once upon a time in a remote village, there lived two wise ones. Each lived alone in a small hut on opposite sides of the village. The wise one who lived on that side was very strong but could not see, having been born blind. The wise one who lived on this side could not walk, and had a voice that was barely above a whisper.

People from miles around visited the wise ones for their valuable advice, taking care of them in return. Although the two were always in demand, they considered themselves rivals, each jealous of how well people regarded the other.

One day, a great fire began to descend the wooded mountainside towards the village. Everyone in the village grabbed their loved ones and escaped down the road to the sea, a walk of two days. In their rush, nobody remembered the two wise ones.

As smoke filled the village, the blind one searched desperately for the other one, finally hearing that soft voice calling for help. Humbly, the blind one offered to carry them both to safety if the quiet one would be their eyes and guide their way. It was quickly agreed.

As they traveled, one on the back of the other, the two rivals discovered how much they had in common, as well as their individual strengths. Along the way, they became great friends. By the time they reached the sea, they knew that by working together, they could be far wiser and more effective than before.

The blind one was called Mindbody. Mindbody was strong and knew what actions to take to make things happen, but could not see which direction was best.

The quiet one was named Heart. Heart always knew why, and what was best, but had no legs to do anything about it.

Today, when Heart guides Mindbody and Mindbody takes actions with Heart, all is well in the world.

Dreams

When I was a little girl, I knew exactly what I wanted to do. When I was 19, however, with a career choice and independence looming ahead of me, I concluded it was not possible to make a living pursuing my dream. I set it aside and moved on.

Oddly, after that, no job or business seemed to satisfy or turn out spectacularly well.

Without the heart, the mind/body is blind. For two decades, I walked around blindly trying this and that, but nothing seemed to work. I held great jobs and felt empty. I implemented fabulous business plans and brilliant product ideas, and each one did…okay.

Nothing seemed to work out in real life quite as well as I felt it could inside. Today as a mentor, I find that I was not alone: many entrepreneurs with enthusiastic big dreams for changing the world are frustrated by stunted revenues and dead-end ventures. They are left scratching their heads, wondering what went wrong with their business, or worse, doubting themselves.

Here is what I have discovered through my journey and my clients': when things keep failing to work out brilliantly, you are missing a key piece of the puzzle. You are missing a piece of *you:* your healing gift, and your ability to share it.

You have a gift for the world, a unique focus that comes through your heart. When shared with others, your gift transforms the world. In my terminology, as a healer to other healers for 14 years, it creates healing. Healing is not about waving your arms over someone who leaps out of a wheelchair. It is not about hospitals or surgery or anything gross.

Healing is the most powerful type of permanent positive change there is. Healing is that "a ha" moment where you make a shift and can no longer return to the old, smaller way of doing things. Healing sheds limitations and creates an upward spiral of transformation.

The good news for entrepreneurs is that healing is so valuable, so different from other forms of change, that you can easily build the lucrative business of your dreams upon it. Healing is priceless, permanently increasing many qualities of life that we seek, especially in business: efficiency and effectiveness, connection and communication, harmony and beauty, wisdom and growth, meaning and fulfillment, and so much more.

The funny thing about your healing gift is that it comes from exactly who you are at your core. You are preprogrammed to succeed at it, though many of us get bogged down in doubt and fear (and the more gifted you are, the more bogged you can get!) The more you align with the core of who you are, your Inner Healer, the more your greatest gift will flow. And along with it comes untold new levels of joy, love, achievement, service, wisdom, wealth, wellness, and a deep inner peace.

It seems obvious now that what I was missing in my two decades of frustration was me: my healing gift and my dream of sharing it. When I began realize this, however, it did not help. I knew I had to add more of "me" into my business, but had no idea what that "me" was! Often when we bury our dreams, we push them so far down that we forget them ourselves. I see this over and over in my clients, other creatives who heal, as I help them rediscover their gifts on a new level and do what they were born to do in a magically joyful life and business.

However successful you are today, the more you express your healing gift through all you do, the more joy, money, and success on all levels will pour into your life and then through you out into the world. Your life and business will reach new heights unimaginable to you in this moment.

As for me, I have just finished my first book, *Gift of the Healer*. Though

I saw it in my childhood, today I *am* a writer. In the end stretch of completing the book, I finally let go of the last few tatters of resistance and "why nots" that had distorted my world for decades. It was a humbling experience I cannot fully describe. As if to cheer me on, the Universe has supplied a series of astonishing and downright miraculous transformations in my relationships, business, income, state of mind, health, and personal outlook. As I look at myself and out at the world as a *writer*, everything else clicks into perfect place and perspective. All is as it should be…all is as it always has been.

7 Steps to Awakening Your Healing Gift

How do you find something if you have buried or forgotten it, or are not sure what it looks like? To find and share your healing gift with the world, you must open the spigots to your gifts. You have every resource you need within you and at your fingertips to reach your goals. In a sense, you don't have to *do* anything to achieve this success and bliss as much as you must train yourself to get out of its way.

Here the 7 steps for fully awakening your healing gift and sharing it with the world. For even more details, download our free *Trail Guide to Awakening Your Inner Healer* kit at www.giawaken.com/freekit.

1 — Know who you are. This is the oldest and best spiritual advice on the planet, for a good reason. When you find your full healing gift, you will discover that all your quirks, personality traits, experiences, body features, preferences—*everything* about you contributes constructively to your healing gift. Know yourself and you know your healing gift. Know yourself and you find your gateway to wealth, health, and happiness.

2 — Build your base. As you explore your gifts, create support structures around you. Nourish and exercise your body, mind and soul. Build a meaningful network you can tap—and then practice asking for help. Create an environment that soothes and supports your mission. In this way, you will be fully nourished enough to more powerfully help others.

3 — Explore Possibility. My clients are unique and highly talented, and to implement their healing gift in the world they often end up innovating new businesses or jobs. The lesson for all of us here is this: do not expect to find a cookie-cutter healing gift within you that fits in someone else's box. Explore what else is out there. Explore within. Dream. And then blaze your own trail.

4 — Be the Change (Practice). Your gift is powerful enough to change the world and valuable enough to found a business. Now build the routine of a master healer who expresses his or her gifts in a big, successful way. Train your body and mind to express your potential. Master the art of self-motivation. With these positive habits, the rest is easy.

5 — Move Beyond Doubt. Doubt is the killer of dreams. It is far more lethal than fear, a mere byproduct of doubt. Doubt arrives when we disconnect from our inner knowing, that sure place within that knows who we are and what to do next. Practice faith in yourself and your gift. Test out your inner guidance and observe your results, until you can discern and trust it. Every answer you need is already within you.

6 — Let Go of Resistance. It is much easier to follow your calling than to resist it. Like a migrating bird, your healing gift knows how to find its home, no matter how far off-course life blows you. It can be difficult to see your own resistance, however. Working with a mentor or coach can help, as can regular healing sessions, practices, and seminars. Your healing gift is a powerful source of joy and income, and when you let go of your resistance, it will bring you home.

7 — Step It UP. Like a vine reaching for the sun, your healing gift can grow and expand forever, especially if you give it something to reach for a little higher than it is right now. Bring many things into your life that allow you to stretch and expand: follow people who do what you want to do, hire mentors, and join groups that support and stretch you.

Rinse and repeat. Let these seven activities be ongoing. Establish routines with them, and then adjust as needed. Do this, and you will create an upward healing spiral that lifts you ever further into living the life of your dreams with grace and ease—one that allows you to help others more effectively.

Daria Boissonnas is a writer, healer, and spiritual mentor. She helps highly creative leaders to unlock their greatest healing gifts and transform the world. Daria is the author of *Gift of the Healer* (www.giftofthehealer.com) and the Founder of the Global Institute for Awakening (www.giawaken.com). She is available for private and group consulting, as well as interviews and limited speaking engagements.

Daria lives near Madison, Wisconsin, with her husband and the four most amazing kids on the planet. She has a BA in Economics from Cornell University which she uses more often than you would think.

For more information, download your free *Trail Guide to Awakening Your Inner Healer Kit* at www.giawaken.com/freekit. Register for a free *Companion Action Guide to Gift of the Healer* at www.giftofthehealer.com.

CHAPTER 13

Living Real and Raw

by Rachelle Anslyn

The chase left me feeling empty. I didn't even realize I was in it.

I started with a purpose, my WHY, and in the process of getting my message out there...I got lost in the matrix only to go through the birth canal and discover a profoundly transformed WHY.

I teach bio-individuality, meaning what works for one person may not work for another, so I wanted to be clear—this goes for the food you eat, the way you move your body, how to live your life, grow a business, express your purpose, love in relationship and on and on. What I want to share with you is my path of discovery...how I found my true WHY and true way, and yours may be radically different than mine.

Probably the first business principle I was taught when I was still in school to become a holistic health coach was this mantra "I'm not a health coach, I'm a marketer." I heard this time and time again in learning about creating a business...and I lived it. I learned business and marketing, invested in all of the right info products and coaching programs and learned a lot. However, what it also did for me was left me disconnected from who I truly am and how I really want to serve (and along the way had amassed a huge amount of debt)... I finally realized the truth is I don't want to be a marketer.

I want to be a connecter. I want to create sustainability in my life through healthy choices, community and collaboration. I would rather grow my business organically than massively. Again, bio-individuality; I finally came to the truth of what works for me, and it comes in a very different package than long sales letters and following blueprints from the most successful coaches.

So many people who are going for million dollar businesses give everything back to growing that business; their time, money, energy and then the business is what needs to be sustained verses their life. Striving for abundance and success in the material world created a disconnect from the truth for me.

Abundance, as beautiful as it is, when it is made to be about getting more and more and more...it becomes an addiction not a Universal Law.

The truth is. I am abundant now. I have everything I need in every moment of my life. Feeling connected abundantly to source leaves no room for lack in our lives. I check in with myself, "Am I okay?" Yes, I am in this moment and every moment I have checked in, regardless of my bank account or credit.

External wins and losses can shape your entire existence if you are driven by them.

I awakened to something deeper that would drive my life. My WHY has become about living real and raw. Living the path of evolution, being willing to be vulnerable enough to share the light and the dark shadows of the path to inspire connection on the deepest level with others. Living connected to truth, living in truth.

So let me get even more transparent here, building a business based on ego wants and needs is the shadow. Mine looked like this…

Shadow
Part of me was building my business to create worth for myself, to challenge how I show up in the world, gain confidence, to be seen and heard, to be successful, to be somebody, to be important, to make money, to create safety and security, to have nice things, to feel good, to be who I thought I wanted to be, to project an image.

Then there is the light, the other side of the shadow that comes from our true nature.

Light

I have always been a natural coach and had a lot to offer, am deeply caring, compassionate, a good listener, problem solver, intelligent, insightful and I thrive in supporting people.

When I was trying to create self-worth out of success, what I had done and accomplished actually diminished my self-worth. My true worth comes from me just being me, being present, meeting the eyes in front of me; this is the source of our inherent worth, our true abundance, our true connection and creative force.

Shining (or playing a bigger game), abundance, manipulation masked as authenticity are a few shadows I've seen played out in marketing. I already spoke to how abundance can be made a shadow when it becomes an addiction to more. For insight into the manipulation that is being used in marketing check out "Start With Why" by Simon Sinek. The last shadow I wanted to call out is around shining.

Shining bright doesn't come from stepping into the spotlight and getting a high from your accomplishment. There is a difference of shining your true essence and shining because you need to prove something to yourself or the world. Shining creates competition, ill feeling, and is about outdoing each other. Shining that comes from an open heart, a willingness to see the one in front of you, as a divine being... that is where the beauty of humanity can truly emerge. Your essence comes from shining in your everyday moments, being a light that is connected to something deeper within you which is the true source of power and wisdom.

I'll give you a little context for where this is all coming from (to read the full story go to www.concentricbalance.com/2011/07/awakenings). I had an awakening in my body during the time that I was teaching my Body, Food and Love program that you can find at www.bodyfoodandlove.com. It was an experience that has left me more connected to my body and my intuition than ever before. After that, I went to Eden Unplugged (a retreat for evolutionary entrepreneurs at www.edenunplugged.com), which awakened me to community. Within a month after the retreat, I had given up the life I had so lovingly created and was grateful for. I gave it all up, my land, my partner, the house we built, my business as I knew it, my comfort, my security, my safety, everything I loved most in my life. I gave it up because I was being called to something more. Something deeper.

In my 20s, I had immersed myself in personal growth to alleviate emotional pain. I found a place of relative comfort in my life, which in retrospect, I can see what I actually did was learn how to out-think my emotions. I learned how to be very practical and rational and move through things with the will of my mind.

Through this awakening, I also tapped deeply back into my emotions. I realized that when I am not afraid of my own emotions I can be with others in a clear, loving presence that embraces all of who we are and the human condition that we live in. That's when I began to really look at the shadows.

The both/and—living the paradox. We don't get rid of the shadows, we acknowledge and bring them to the light. We make friends with them, love them and accept them. Only when we can love the shadows within ourselves, can actually truly love each other.

Facing the shadows is uncomfortable. I've been getting really, really uncomfortable in life, and on the other side of that, I can know that I am actually always okay. I see what we do as a culture…chase the comfort, the ease, the happy life, great body, perfect partner. It is all for the illusion of safety.

What if we all got wickedly uncomfortable? Gave birth. Connect in with source. Went deep, deep, deep.

I've gone through massive deconstructing of my whole life to reconstruct in truth and alignment. This isn't something we do once, get it down and remain that way in our lives. It's important to have the breakdowns to allow for the reevaluation, reassessment, realignment, and reconstruction. What we see as truth for us one time becomes only a fragment of truth or completely not truth at another time.

Now I am establishing a life based on my connection to source, myself and community. Why is community so important? We get to practice giving and receiving on a moment-to-moment basis in community. We get to have our light as well as our shadows reflected back at us in community. We get to face things that we don't want to face. We can consciously choose to see what we don't want to in order to bring that to light as well. Drop into deep, deep love. Self-love, then loving others.

My hope is that my vulnerability, authenticity and transparency helps heal others.

What was I chasing; self-worth, recognition, admiration, financial freedom, attention, and love are all with in me already.

I still love appreciation, acceptance, recognition, attention, and love from the external world...and I know if I tap into my own source, I don't need it from others. I don't have to seek it and prove it...I have to be it. My job is to see it in others, and love others deeply. I look at any judgment that comes up, anything that keeps me from fully seeing and loving you for the essence and beauty that you are...anything that keeps me separate, and I take a look. I see what I do not love in myself. I find love and compassion...then I can fully love you. Then I can fully see you.

There is the 'being' and the 'doing' in life—living the spiritual and the physical. I am still working with these edges, balancing and being the bridge of the physical realm to the spiritual realm.

My WHY. My own evolution, which leads me to being more whole and fully able to love you. To live and breathe my own self-worth so that I can see yours. To shine authentically so that you are seen through my light.

When I look deeply into the eyes of another who is willing to be fully seen, I see nothing but beauty.

Relax into enough. You are enough, you have enough.

Rachelle Anslyn is known for thinking big and living an extraordinary life. Her passion for being authentic, creative, and vibrant has taken her to explore the depths of what is possible. She has traveled over 30 countries to work with clients, for volunteer aide, to study with yoga masters, and for the delight of cultural wisdom. Rachelle has studied over 100 different dietary theories and learned straight from leading health experts and doctors such as Deepak Chopra, Andrew Weil, Sally Fallon, Mark Hyman, David Wolfe and many, many more.

Rachelle graduated in 2009 from The Institute of Integrative Nutrition in New York City. Her mindset mastery came from attending The School for The Work of Byron Katie in New York City in 2001. The following year, Rachelle staffed The School working directly with Byron Katie in Los Angeles. Rachelle has also studied with yoga masters around the globe in several traditions including Kundalini, Iyengar, Jivamukti, Ashtanga, Vibrant Living Yoga and Yoga Synergy. Through her experience with self-inquiry, yoga, nutrition and the healing arts, Rachelle has cultivated a full spectrum mastery of living a vibrant, purposeful life.

Rachelle has had over 12 years experience in the health and wellness field. She believes through awareness we evolve into who we already are, which is Radiance. Rachelle shares her gifts through insightful coaching, practical raw food workshops, inspirational yoga, and life-changing retreats. Concentric Balance is an inquiry and implementation method developed by Rachelle, utilizing her clients' natural strengths to create a shift in the core of their being, which then begins the ripple effect into their self-transformation. Her mission is to facilitate that shift and create an effect that goes beyond us as individuals; into a Happy, Healthy, Radiant WORLD.

CHAPTER 14

Broke That Glass Ceiling… Now, Breaking Barriers to Help Others

by Gayle Joplin Hall, PhD

A radio talk show was on daily, so I toyed with the idea of calling in to ask what I should do with my life. At the age of 28, I was working at a mundane job and felt like I was wasting away. I envisioned owning my own company in advertising sales. I drummed up the courage, made the call to the radio show, and began speaking live with the psychologist. His final comment was something equivalent to "whatever you decide, don't ever be in sales, nor should you ever own your own company." Those words sparked my fire!

Immediately following, I called a national advertising specialties company. I was hired over the phone. Wait a minute…what was I doing? The president explained this was straight commission. The outcome was to achieve accounts by knocking on business doors, otherwise known as cold-calling. Panic set in. My emotions shifted between sheer excitement to feeling totally mortified.

Calendars were best to sell because of high profit. I was advised by the company president to enter small shops and avoid corporate offices and hospitals, because those were difficult for a seasoned professional. Very quickly, I became discouraged with the greasy "quick-lube guys" gazing at me and jeers from women at beauty shops. Since I am a nonconformist, I decided to implement my own sales techniques. Resiliency kicked in.

Knowing myself, I boldly thought, "Why can't I go and sell to hospitals if I want to?" I had never taken baby steps before and I was not about to give up on my dreams now! Not only did I decide that I was going to sell to hospitals, I also resolved that I was going to call on the largest hospital in Kansas City. It took me six hours the first day to pinpoint the proper building for public relations. This was not located at the hospital. My freshly pressed suit had become wrinkled, my make-up and hair were dripping in the 90-degree heat, and my nylons stuck to me like bubble gum on the bottom of a shoe. I already decided I was not going to sell calendars, just because I was 'supposed' to. I parked four blocks away so nobody would recognize me getting out of my dilapidated car. Nervously, I toted that heavy briefcase in the door. I was quickly greeted with, "We're not interested." Gingerly, I proceeded toward the desk near the gatekeeper who had rudely spoken. As she repeated herself, I picked up one of her cards, gave her some of my promotional items and asked who the head buyer was. As she threw my specialties in the trash, she explained the same man had been calling on them for the past 12 years and they were not interested in anything I had to say or sell. I left, after telling her that I would be back again.

Although I was quite familiar with rejection, I must say that my ability to drag myself to the car after facing the gatekeeper's harsh tone and humiliation toward me was difficult. The prize for that hot summer day was the business card I had snatched off the desk before leaving. That one little card listed every buyer's name. I felt like I had hit the jackpot. Once inside my car, I slithered out of my sticky pantyhose before I began the 23-mile drive back home. I was not discouraged because God had spoken to me. My heart was floating in the clouds!

Every Monday morning at 9am for the next five months, I showed up at the PR department with food. The first time following my initial visit, the identical rude gatekeeper had the supreme look of shock on her face as I walked in with fresh bagels. She explained they were not allowed to accept gifts. I told her these were not gifts, just breakfast. I left a stack of cards and pens on another desk as I exited the building within 30 seconds. My mission was accomplished. By the end of the first month, I had met all of the eight buyers, except for the main one. The ladies looked forward to me stopping by those Monday mornings, month after month. I kept asking for business and left promotionals behind; however, I still only knew the head buyer's name. I had never met her. The parking space four blocks away seemed reserved for me. By the end of the fifth month, I realized it was my moment to make a big change.

As I walked through the familiar doors at 12pm, the building was quiet. I had decided to switch it up and arrive at a different time of day. Instead of going in at my usual 9am, I showed up at noon. I was carrying a tray full of fresh limeade drinks (try doing that while walking four blocks in high heels). The woman, named Diane, appeared from around the corner. Finally, this was my moment. Diane asked me if I was Gayle, the one who had been coming by every Monday for half a year. The head buyer asked me if I had some time, took one of the limeades, and we sat down. Diane told me that she had a huge television campaign approaching and needed some fresh ideas for breast cancer awareness. She asked me if I had ideas she had not seen before. I explained to her that she was putting me on the spot, but that I worked well under pressure. Her hard-hitting response was akin to, "Good, you have one day to put together something that will make me want to do business with you. I have only worked with men and I work well with men. Women don't last too long in your industry." Scared out of my wits, but knowing I would bust my butt to deliver what this head buyer wanted, we agreed to meet the next day at noon. I worked up a mock vinyl shower hanger with the hospital's logo for self-breast exam.

During our meeting, Diane became my buyer. Custom graphics were produced for the largest hospital in Kansas City. The product was flashed over various networks during National Breast Cancer Awareness Month. The buyer was so pleased with my innovative idea, I was invited to sit in and contribute during brainstorming sessions at most of the public relations and marketing meetings. You see, I became a valuable part of their team, not just another salesperson off the street. I learned what they wanted and needed. I was valued and respected by them. The best part of my selling career with the hospital was waiting for my phone to ring and making the sale. Not only did I sell to the largest hospital in Kansas City, I gained the business of four other hospitals, as well. I never sold the same products to any competitors in the same industry.

Oh, yes…I should mention that I lost my parking space four blocks away. You see, I bought a brand new Cadillac within two months of making that big, first sale at the hospital. Then, I started taking some of the buyers out for lunch in my beautiful car. The shame of being poor was wiped off my face and removed from my spirit.

I broke the glass ceiling and busted through the doors in the advertising market, calling on hospitals when I was clearly told by the president of the company I worked for, to "Never even try to sell to a hospital." I guess they had no clue who they were talking to. I took a chance in believing in myself when others doubted me. It paid off. Some may have heard what the talk show host said as rejection. I saw this as a possibility to better myself and earn a good living.

After 10 years, I burned out on selling and knew I wanted more out of my life than making money. At the age of 38, I entered college as an older-than-average student. I completed my undergraduate degree in less than four years and my Master's degree in less than 18 months. My doctorate was a living hell, due to experiences with my department chair. Nonetheless, I not only survived, I graduated with my PhD in Psychology and maintained a 4.0 GPA. Yes, I own those bragging rights.

Since the age of 19, I had always volunteered with numerous organizations. It seemed natural for me to become a college professor. I love teaching and learning. My students admired me and held me in high esteem. God kept pushing me to do more, even though I was working hard with my students teaching them service learning. As I prayed and meditated, God was telling me to reach a global audience so I could teach on a worldwide platform. In December of last year, I announced to my students that I was taking a sabbatical from being a professor so I could teach and reach others as being directed by God. Oh how I miss my students and if not for email, I would be lost without them now!

My business ventures include trademarking and forming my own company, Dr. Hall on Call™. I am known as The Happiness Life Coach™. I apply positive psychology in business and all areas of life. I use an eclectic approach when guiding people toward finding their true calling and bliss. As a keynote speaker and author, my passion is domestic violence. I work online and in person with women, victims of abuse, executives, soldiers, and special populations. We conquer behavioral problems such as anxiety, panic attacks, depression, PTSD, OCD, and work to resolve relationships, self-esteem, marriage and dating, love, and more. I am writing my first two books (just signed the contract), have co-authored three books, edited textbooks, am a mentor, and a professor. In my spare time, I love to travel, make others happy, and live the fullest life we are all supposed to live.

So now you may be saying, "You make this seem so easy. I cannot do what you did!" I am going to tell you some dirty, little secrets about me. Here is what you may not know:

- I was emotionally and psychologically abused throughout my entire undergraduate career. Yes, I was a victim of domestic violence.

- I lived in my car for four days with my baby son because I was so ashamed and could not go to family members, nor to a hotel, for fear of being found by my abusive husband.

- One time I was so miserable and desperate, I thought of suicide. It was the easy way out. Did not want to leave that legacy for my children.

- On 9/11/2009, I suffered from a nervous breakdown. Not proud of this, just the facts.

- I have had my heart broken too many times to count by the ones I have loved the most- especially men.

What can you do to make changes in your life and create the life you deserve? Here are five important bullet points to remember and implement NOW:

- Realize that when someone tells you "No," (like when I heard a constant "no" for months on end at the hospital), this does not mean no, forever, it merely means, "no, not right now."

- Create a dream board or vision board. See yourself living the life you want to live.

- Surround yourself with only positive people who will support you in your endeavors.

- Find a mentor. This is paramount.

- As you look into the mirror every morning, repeat this and make it your mantra: "I am beautiful! I am gorgeous! I am worthy of this best life now!"

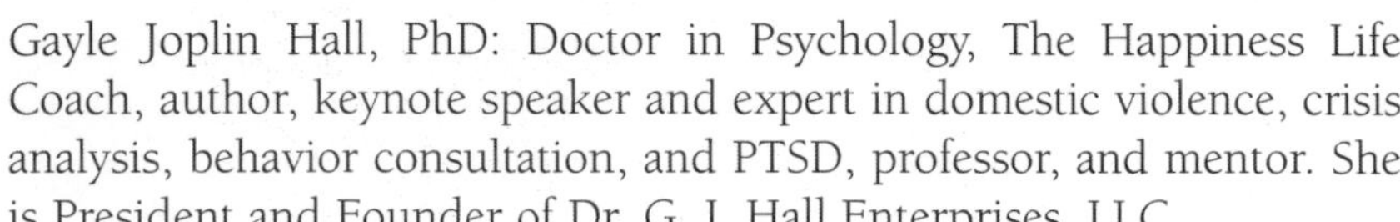

Gayle Joplin Hall, PhD: Doctor in Psychology, The Happiness Life Coach, author, keynote speaker and expert in domestic violence, crisis analysis, behavior consultation, and PTSD, professor, and mentor. She is President and Founder of Dr. G. J. Hall Enterprises, LLC.

As a people lover, it was only natural for Gayle to leave corporate America after 15 years and cross over to academia. She became a professor in college. Her students adored her. Nonetheless, God was constantly tapping on her shoulder to reach out to bigger audiences and teach more people. In December of 2010, Gayle took a sabbatical from teaching, to brand her life coaching business. Hence, the formation and trademarking of Dr. Hall on Call™. Her company is based on the philosophy of positive psychology and the law of attraction.

Gayle has studied people and human behavior for over two decades. What she noticed was a common factor among people everywhere—we have choices to be happy with our lives or to make changes. Many people remain stuck in their situations because of fear. As a victor of domestic violence, Gayle realized this about herself. Fear of failure had kept her from pursuing her dreams of fulfilling her mission to reach global audiences with multiple platforms. This included starting her coaching business, speaking engagements, co-authoring books, and writing her own first two books about domestic violence. She is now transparent and shares her stories, life, and wisdom with the world.

"It makes me a better person to be a part of something bigger." As one of the touchstone quotes in Gayle's repertoire, this has grounded her for over 20 years. Gayle has donated over 5,000 hours of service to domestic violence and served 32 families with hospice during their times of need. Her service work encompasses the homeless population, the isolated elderly, Veterans and the USO, homeless children and the YWCA, and BACA.

Caring, compassion, dedication, happiness, integrity, laughing, loving, and serving…these words embrace Gayle Joplin Hall's core belief system. Gayle will guide you in decisions about love, relationships, careers, goal-setting, anxiety, dating, divorce, meditation, fear, PTSD, conflict resolution, children, happiness, LGBT, stress, spirituality, and more. The value she brings to each person's life resonates long after she is gone.

Contact Dr. Gayle Hall so she can help you discover your bliss and passion. To schedule your "Hall-Call" or to book a speaking engagement, visit www.drhalloncall.com.

CHAPTER 15

The 5 Unintended Mistakes Spirit-Rich™ Entrepreneurs Make in Business (*...and how to avoid them!*)

by Baeth Davis

Do You Want to Make Money Doing "Work You Love" Without Sacrificing Your Spiritual Development?

Being spiritual and being successful, even wealthy, in business ("spirit-rich™") are not mutually exclusive. You probably know this—but do you hesitate to say the word "spiritual" in the same sentence as "business?" Are you afraid that it won't be accepted in your business world? Well, good news. You don't have to tattoo "I'm spiritual" on your forehead or start a mantra-chanting group at lunchtime (though that may have stress-reducing benefits!) to have a spiritual experience in your business.

Let's put 'spirituality' and 'business' together...

As a spirit-rich™ entrepreneur in business, you offer your clients **meaning, value, transcendence, connection and authenticity** through **your products, programs and services in exchange for profit.**

It doesn't matter if you are a life coach, an online marketer or an artist; if you bring value to your work, you are bringing spirituality into your business, even if you never directly state it as such.

Currently, you may fall into one of two categories:

1. You're a **spiritual seeker** who wants to know why it's important to learn business principles.

2. You're a **business person** who wants to know why it's important to incorporate spiritual principles and practices into your business.

If you're in the first camp, it's essential to get over the mindset of "I'm spiritual, so don't talk money to me" because money is good. Everything in the Universe is made up of energy. Money is a form of energy. In of itself, money is neutral. It's how you use money that matters.

Your relationship to money is also an accurate barometer of your own self-worth. Denying yourself material abundance only limits your ability to fulfill your spiritual purpose. If you're worried about how you're going to pay the bills, where will you find the energy to pursue your dreams? Having financial security allows you to live your vision with more enthusiasm and ease.

If you're a business person wondering what spirituality has to do with business, I offer you this perspective: the true bottom line of business is to give value and to receive value in return. The main return in business is profit. If you give great value, you will receive value over and over again. This is also the main goal of a spiritual life—to give to others the absolute best you want to receive for yourself. (In the Landmark Forum organization, they call this the "Platinum Rule.")

Businesses that stand the test of time offer their customers transcendent value and service. Your successful business is an opportunity for developing your spiritual self. You either give value to others or you don't. Your business may succeed on the financial bottom line without giving true value—but eventually, it will falter and be found out.

Spirit-rich™ businesses operate on the fundamental spiritual law that states, "What you give is what you receive." As a spirit-rich™ entrepreneur, you have the magnificent opportunity to make a powerful difference in the world when you translate your spiritual wisdom and insight into a business offering that helps others feel better about who they are, and makes their lives easier, more productive and more fulfilling.

Ultimately, the best businesses, no matter what they're selling, strive to make the lives of their customers and clients better.

How I Came To Do What I Do…

I currently have a successful business **helping you identify YOUR Life Purpose and get paid for your passions**. I identify your Life Purpose using a system called hand analysis. "Hand analysis" is scientific, non-predictive palmistry. The amazing thing about hand analysis is that it allows me to determine your **specific** Life Purpose. Your Life Purpose is in your hands—literally!

I am not a fortune teller. I help you **identify your Life Purpose** and then we **use a business coaching model** to make that purpose a reality in your day-to-day life.

Before I became a mentor to spirit-rich™ entrepreneurs, I used to work in marketing. When my boss told me it would be another five years before I'd clear $40,000 a year, I knew it was time to move on.

As a last ditch effort, I even offered to work on commission without benefits for new projects I delivered to the company, but still he refused. I got the message: my success lay elsewhere. As I packed up my office, a co-worker wished me well and said, "Baeth, this is perfect for you. Whatever you put your mind to, you'll succeed at. I wish I had the guts to leave."

Once on my own, without a paycheck or a plan, I managed to acquire a business loan from a family member. I used this money to live on as I cobbled together a not very successful venture as a manager for artists with an emphasis on promotion and marketing.

I was getting closer to my true path, but hadn't quite hit the mark. I was working long hours, but not making much money. And I hadn't yet figured out how to attract the ideal clients, so I had to deal with a lot of neediness, drama and irritation from my current clients. I was burnt out and running low on cash. I was desperate and depressed. Would I ever find my Life Purpose, my right life?

Right about this time, a friend urged me to get a hand analysis session.

I'd never heard of hand analysis and was very skeptical, but after her umpteenth urging, I broke down and consented. Ever the networker, I invited over eight friends to meet the "hand analyst."

Well, was I ever in for the surprise of my life! This woman, a complete stranger, took her hands in mine and said, "You're not living the life you are meant to live."

This wise observation sent me over the edge into a one-hour crying jag. I barely heard the rest of what she said between blowing my nose and wiping my eyes. But what I did hear stays with me to this day: "You are very sensitive. It's a gift, not a weakness. You have an ability to help others on their path. You have a special message for a large audience. You're a writer, a speaker, a teacher."

I was hooked! I set out to learn everything I could about hand analysis so I could provide similar "wake up" experiences to others. Within a year, I began reading hands professionally.

To supplement my hand analysis income, I took a job as a personal assistant. Within a year, I decided it was time to make my living full-time reading hands. Once the decision was made to read hands full-time, it became clear that I needed to leave Los Angeles and travel around the U.S. to find out where I really wanted to live.

I decided to fund my trip by reading hands in all 50 states. I would stay with friends to reconnect with them as well as reduce my travel expenses. I anointed this adventure "The Hands of America Tour." I even had magnets made for my car to announce my arrival into each new town. (Shyness is not my challenge.) I gave notice at my apartment, gave away most of my furniture, put my excess stuff in storage, bought a car online and headed East.

My first stop was Colorado. While in Colorado, I met my former husband and current business partner, Mark, and moved fully into my new work identity as a spiritual guide with a message. I was officially a spirit-rich™ entrepreneur!

While dating, and then engaged to Mark, I continued to travel—and made it to about 10 states analyzing hands before settling down in our new home of Tucson, Arizona.

But the challenges of my journey didn't end with this new level of enjoyment in my life. Oh, no. In fact, the massive mistakes were still around the corner!

Mis-Takes = Opportunities for Re-Takes

I now see mistakes as opportunities to learn, to find a better way, to improve upon a previous choice, experience or method. As my success grows on a life-scale, so do the importance of my mistakes.

Unintended Mistake #1
You Can't Have a Balanced Life AND a Profitable, Successful Business

Many spirit-rich™ entrepreneurs are born nurturers. Being a nurturer is a personality trait.

As a nurturing entrepreneur, you may develop the unconstructive habit of putting everyone else's needs before your own. The challenge, of course, is to learn to nurture yourself so that you can help others effectively. Being a martyr has gotten a lot of press over the millennia for being the trademark of a "spiritual" person, but it won't grow your business and it probably won't help you walk on water. It almost surely will make you tired and very possibly, ill.

I had to learn this the hard way. As the word-of-mouth spread about my abilities to determine someone's Life Purpose via their hands, I received more and more business. During one trip to New England, I was seeing eight people a day for one-hour sessions. By the end of one month, I had lost my voice, come down with bronchitis and ended up in bed for six weeks!

I had made more money than I ever made before in such a brief span of time but it cost me my health. I started feeling sorry for myself. I started thinking on the downward spiral: "But what I'm doing helps people! Why would it make me sick? It makes no sense. Maybe I should drop this whole thing and go get a "real" job and just read hands on the side."

But being the plucky gal I am—this line of thinking lasted about two seconds. I told myself, "Baeth, snap out of it! Take your own advice. The same advice you tell every client that walks in here: 'in order to serve others, you must first learn to serve yourself.'"

I realized that I was trying to make up for lost time by saying 'yes' to everyone. I didn't want to let anyone down. I didn't want to be perceived as selfish or un-nurturing. I wanted to serve everyone who walked through the door at the expense of my own life's balance.

But I finally knew that if I was to truly serve, I had to be healthy, and to be healthy meant taking care of me. So nowadays, I work with clients three days a week. Monday and Friday are my marketing days. Weekends are for playing. I raise my rates as my skill and experience continue to grow. I eat well, get regular massages, go to the gym five to six days a week and get eight to nine hours of sleep per night. I pamper myself with manicures, pedicures and a wardrobe that flatters my appearance.

I know the hours I spend in self-care will more than make up for themselves in enthusiasm, joy, and happy clients. I now make more money working less hours helping MORE people. I've been on the other side, bedridden, unable to serve anyone. Cramming in one more thing today will not help you tomorrow. In fact, it may just cost you your ability to enjoy tomorrow. Indeed, the more you serve yourself, the more you will be able to serve others. And what could be more spiritual than that?!

Unintended Mistake #2
You Can't Be Spiritual AND Be Wealthy

If you're over this one, or it never applied, bravo! For the rest of you, please keep reading!

Here's a clue: this issue about the seeming incompatibility of spirituality and wealth isn't really about spirituality or money—it's about self-worth.

I've discovered that receiving income for doing something I love to do is a total blessing, the ultimate in working satisfaction. Each time I'm paid feels as good as the first time I was paid for reading someone's hands. In giving value, value is returned.

However, I've consistently encountered reluctance among my clients when it comes to receiving full value for the services they offer. They have all sorts of reasons: "the economy where I live can't support my higher rates," "people will judge me," "it's not right to be paid for something that's fun to do," "I'm afraid to ask," "it's not spiritual to be paid," and on and on.

The most common excuse I hear is, "Why would someone pay me that much for my services? Who am I? I don't know if I'm good enough to do this." Bull's eye! Low self-worth in action!

So my question to you, dear reader, is this: What is your excuse for not receiving full value for your magnificent services? Once you've identified your core excuse, I invite you to dig a little deeper. What is the fear beneath this excuse? I bet you'll find that the core issue comes down to one thing again and again—low self-worth.

To be truly spiritual is to know yourself—to know your worth, your limits, your talents, your challenges. To be spiritual is to be willing to accept that you have something to offer to others. I dare say, to be spiritual is to accept your spiritual assignment here on planet Earth with gusto, joy and commitment and spread your wisdom far and wide.

If you choose to take on this assignment, to live your Life Purpose full-out, no excuses, people will gladly pay your full fee and enthusiastically send you more clients.

If you don't value what you have to offer, why would other people? When you receive a fee that reflects the true value of what you have to offer, your clients perceive that value. In perceiving that value, they get more OUT of their work with you because they've put more IN. One healer I know explains it this way, "I find my clients actually facilitate and speed up their own healing when they invest in themselves."

Unintended Mistake #3
As a Spiritual Person, I Don't Need a Plan—Spirit Will Do It For Me

This is one of the trickiest of all the challenges facing you as a spirit-rich™ entrepreneur in business.

Meditation, prayer, and yoga are just a few ways you can connect more deeply with yourself. However, even the most dedicated student of spiritual understanding won't go far in the business world without a vision, a plan for that vision and measurable goals and results to determine if the vision has succeeded.

Spiritual practice is a brilliant way to connect with and focus on your vision. In fact, Napoleon Hill, author of "Think and Grow Rich" says it all with his book title. When you "think" on your vision, your entire brain chemistry reconfigures so you start noticing opportunities in your world that will help you achieve your vision and "grow rich."

Here's a simple example: Some years ago, I wanted a teal-green Ford Explorer. As soon as I made that decision, I started noticing teal-green Ford Explorers everywhere I went. Not long after that, circumstances aligned that allowed me to purchase the exact model I desired. I've since sold that vehicle. I have no doubt that when the time is right, all circumstances will conspire to help me manifest whatever my next desired acquisition might be.

But manifesting a car is small potatoes! How about manifesting the life of your dreams? Right down to the high-thread count sheets on your bed and your dream lover laying beside you?! Not to mention that fabulous career that you wake up to in the morning filled with joy and enthusiasm because you've been granted another day to serve your clients and help them achieve their dreams. Yes, I believe that's what it all boils down to. **When you fulfill your wildest dreams, you become the inspiration for others to do the same**.

But getting clear on your vision is not enough. **You have to believe in your vision like you believe in gravity.** You have to know it's a sure thing—**just a matter of time and determination.**

First **you find your vision**, then **you focus on your vision regularly**. After those two steps have been undertaken, it is imperative to **listen for guidance**. This report is a perfect example of listening for guidance. After following the suggestions of one of my marketing mentors, this report was the result.

What kind of help do you need? Are you willing to do whatever it takes to educate yourself and find the help you need so you can go to the next level? If you're lousy at making a plan of action, that's okay—there are plenty of experts to help you do it.

To review:

Step 1: find your vision
Step 2: focus on your vision daily
Step 3: listen for guidance
Step 4: take action on that guidance

We all plan and organize information in different ways. That's perfectly fine. If you're listening for your inner guidance, you will make the choices that are right for you. But this is the key—**one must decide and take action**. Meditating might lead you in the right direction, but it probably won't be enough. You need to move ahead with the wisdom your spiritual practice has provided for you.

Unintended Mistake #4
Handing Over Your Inner Knowing to the Guru

Okay, here's the deal. Whether you are a predominantly intuitive person or a predominantly logical person, you are intuitive. Your intuition serves many purposes: to protect you, to inspire you, to guide you, to heal you, to support you. Listening to our intuition takes practice—a lot of practice for some, not much practice for others. Nonetheless, it's an art that is worth fostering—primarily because it will make your life a heck of a lot easier and help you develop your business on your own terms, in your own authentic way.

There are many ways we as women devalue and ignore our intuition. We discount it, we rationalize it, we laugh at it. The most common mistake we make in not trusting our intuition is to hand over our inner knowing to someone else. This "someone else" fulfills a particular role for the spiritually-oriented woman in business. This "someone else" is typically a boss, partner, guru or "expert" who tells us what we have to do to succeed and more to the point, who we have to become to be accepted by them.

Because most of us seek approval, whether it's conscious or unconscious, people we perceive to be in positions of power can sometimes become parental figures for us. This puts you in the dangerous position of taking actions that will please and appease the "parent" (read: boss, associate, teacher, guru, leader, etc.) Each time we do this, we lose a little bit of power and put the opinions of another higher than our own inner knowing.

Nobody knows what's best for you—no matter how convincing their argument, no matter how compelling their threats of loss. The profoundly gifted spiritual teacher, Osho, said the real meaning of "guru" is "Gee, You Are You." In becoming your own guru, you will find whatever you need to fulfill your business objectives. There is nothing wrong with seeking the help of other leaders, experts and teachers—as long as you are on a level playing field.

If you find yourself hesitating to speak your mind or voice your objections, then you've probably just given away your power to the outer guru and ignored the inner one—YOU. Of course, there is a price to be paid by heeding your own inner knowing: not everyone is going to like it and not everyone is going to approve. As women, we sometimes sacrifice our own integrity to avoid conflict and not rock the boat. However, the price you pay over the long term is not worth the damage it causes to your self-esteem, not to mention your ability to have a successful career.

As a spiritual mentor, my main focus is to help you discover and live your specific Life Purpose—not just from a career standpoint—but on a life-scale. Recently, I had an insight that stopped me cold. I thought to myself, "Now I get it! Now I understand why so much of humanity avoids living their Life Purpose. No, let me revise that. They don't avoid living their Life Purposes. They actively seek to create drama and pain to avoid even knowing what their Life Purpose is!" Why? Because **your Life Purpose can only be experienced if you are willing to endure the hardship of exposure, the vulnerability of showing the world who you really are**.

And this is some kind of challenge—especially if you encounter disapproval from your boss, parents, spouse, children, etc. If your own tribe won't support you—well, you have two choices: back down and live in constant dissatisfaction, or trust your intuition and take the wild ride of authentic living. I've had to suffer the rejection of several bosses and teachers in order to have a successful business. Each one told me some variation on the same theme, "Baeth, it's my way or the highway." Well, I'll take the highway, thanks. The journey is so much more fun when I get to do the driving!

Unintended Mistake #5
It's All About the Money

Once your business is prospering, it can be very tempting to look at how you can make more money and yet more money. Certainly, the dictionary would argue that the primary purpose of business is to make money.

But as a spiritually-oriented business woman myself, I only want to attract money in way that reflects my most deeply held values and beliefs. I believe I am here, ultimately, to serve. It's easy to become overwhelmed with all the options and choices out there for making your business grow. In fact, it is possible to become so immersed in the "how" that you forget the "why."

Why are you growing your business?

Is there a reason larger than the bottom line?

I've watched some women lose sight of why they went into the business in the first place once the business started booming. A form of greed took over and quality got sacrificed for quantity. We all know the stories of successful businesses that expanded too rapidly in the quest for profits and soon had to close all their shops to stave off bankruptcy. This issue brings me back to the previous mistakes we've explored together.

If you keep your life balanced, give full value and receive full value, make a plan for your vision and trust your intuition, you'll know how much to do and when to do it. I know you've heard this a million times—but it's really, really true—everyone really IS different. So what works for you might not work for someone else and vice versa. Keeping **a balance between meaningfulness and profitability** is the mark of the truly enlightened entrepreneur, the evolved spiritual woman in business. It's not either or. It's both.

Now that you know what to avoid, here's what you **can do**:

- Write a list of goals, affirm the goals in the present tense, and follow the affirmation with the reward you'll give yourself for achieving the goal.

Recently, I set the goal of getting a massage once a week. Once I achieved that goal, I rewarded myself with a new fall coat. I really enjoy rewarding self-care with more self care!

Here's another example:

Goal: To receive $5000/week Affirmation:
Intention Statement: "It is December 31st and I am receiving $12,000/week, every week."

Reward: "My reward for this is to take a nice vacation with my beloved and donate to my daughter's high school sports program."

Plan: Now make a plan to hit this target and measure your progress.

- Make list of 10 creative habits that you can do daily or weekly to nurture yourself and do some of them. Examples: get a massage, go dancing, take a 20 minute nap each day, listen to an entire record album and read the liner notes.

- Ask yourself: What is the spiritual mission of my business?

- What is that action worth to me and to others financially?

- Set a schedule to meditate 30 minutes a day and study business principles 30 minutes a day.

- Ask yourself before every action, "What's my desired outcome?"

- Check in with yourself throughout the day and ask, "What is my intuition telling me about this?"

- Set financial goals for the week, month, and year with the reward for each new level

Baeth Davis is "The Palm Pilot for the Soul of Your Business™" and the owner of The Hand Analyst, Inc. She has been helping spiritrich™ entrepreneurs build six- and seven-figure businesses that are both purpose-full and profitable for 10 years. Her motto is, "You, too, can get PAID for Your Passions!" This year, she celebrates the 11th anniversary of being in business.

Baeth won the coveted 2007-2008 Glazer-Kennedy Information Marketer of the Year Award. She competed with three other finalists before an audience of 600 people at the annual Glazer-Kennedy InfoSummit in St. Louis, MO. The winner was chosen by audience vote. Audience feedback attributed Baeth's win to her inspirational and compelling presentation style as well as her generosity with her business success strategies. She shared over 160 pages of her marketing copy, sales strategies and results with the audience members.

When asked why she thought she won the contest, Baeth replied, "When the contest application came in, I had this very strong feeling that I had to enter it. It wouldn't leave me alone. When I found out I was among the finalists, I was stunned as I was up against some very stiff competition. My intention at the live competition was to basically inspire the audience with this message: 'If a hand analyst can have a successful, profitable business, ANYONE can, including you!' When people came up to me after my presentation to congratulate me, the main thing they said was, 'Baeth, I know now I can do this. Thank you for inspiring me.' Hearing that they were inspired, I thought, 'mission accomplished!' If I can help even one business owner to think bigger, dream bolder, and go for what they want, I know I'm doing what I came there to the planet to do. My goal is to be of service to others through love and inspiration."

Baeth has been featured in Cosmopolitan, Women's World and the LA Times and heard on NPR, Radio Europe and BBC-5. She has been seen on network TV and presents her work nationwide at conferences and healing centers. Baeth is committed to helping entrepreneurs discover, live and share their Life Purposes so their lives are purpose-full, prosperous and of service to others.

CHAPTER 16

5 Keys for Embracing the Process of Change

by Lisa Dewar

"It wasn't supposed to turn out that way!" I exclaimed. Life was sweet and all was going well when suddenly a medical diagnosis flipped everything around. After 17 years of marriage and working as a team in Christian ministry, my 43-year-old husband, Darwin was diagnosed with an inoperable brain tumor. Within three months he died, and life as I once enjoyed changed forever.

Perhaps you have faced similar situations in your life where unexpected events left you having to re-define what "normal" was and redesign life from that moment on. For some people, such a crisis would completely destroy them and may even need years or decades to recover from it. Sadly, some never recover. A year before the diagnosis, I had been experiencing tremendous growth and shifts in my understanding and mindsets around creating wealth and owning a business. I had enjoyed the learning tracks I was on and was moving forward in my plans to launch a transformational life coaching business when the loss occurred. "What now?" I asked.

Starting a business can be a daunting task, requiring a lot of time, energy and focus, even in the best of circumstances. The demand on all these resources had just increased as I looked to provide an environment for me and my three young children to grieve, heal and rebuild. Being a spiritual person, I took time to pray, seek counsel, and listen to the inner voice of my heart to determine how best to overcome the seemingly huge obstacles before me. I decided to take that first year, live off our savings and a limited stream of income to focus on healing and re-establishing a safe, stable home for my children. Although it was the most difficult season of my life, it became a defining year. To many people's surprise, I did not despair, lose hope nor lose a sense of who I was. This became key to my moving forward with fresh focus and joy. Years before, I had started a journey of growth and transformation that had built into me the solid foundation I needed to walk through this crisis and to re-invent my life. I had come to know and embrace who I really was at the core, how I was wired and the rewards of not settling for life in the comfort zone. Even though my circumstances had changed and now my future would look different, my identity was still intact.

Over the years, I had discovered that a primary key to living on purpose is knowing who you really are. Many people search for their purpose as if it was something to be found or attained. Many end up wasting a lot of money, time and energy in this pursuit. In my experience, as you seek to connect with your heart, identify your core values, strengths, unique passions and personality, your purpose becomes revealed and you begin to naturally step into it as you align your actions to live true to all that is you.

As I processed the unexpected turn of events, I was tempted to allow the pain to determine my decisions. I considered giving up on my entrepreneurial dream and delve into a 9 to 5 job to create a more stable income. This would not have been wrong and sometimes it is actually the right course of action to take. In my situation, it would have been more detrimental and stressful if I had chosen that route at the time. My kids needed me to be available and have flexibility in my schedule as each of us walked through a season of grief. Circumstances change, dreams evolve, but who I was as a person had not changed and what I had to offer the world had actually just increased. It was that understanding that motivated my decision to continue on my entrepreneurial journey, and to leverage my resources to create the purpose-based business I had dreamed of. With the help of a few coaches, some friends, and spiritual guidance, I moved forward with fresh focus and deliberateness. I surrounded myself with people who were doing what I wanted to do and who supported my decisions. Life is a series of choices. You either let circumstances define your future or you make choices to create the life you want.

As I stepped forward there were 5 key principles that helped me gain clarity and guide my decisions as I embraced the process of change.

Your Responses determine your future.
It is not what happens to you that matters but how you respond to what happens to you. Trials and change are normal aspects of life that no one is exempt from. Whether it be momentary setbacks in business, customer dissatisfaction, or family crisis, how you choose to respond to life is key to living on purpose and in passion. The late Jim Rohn, author and motivational speaker, once gave the analogy that your life is like a sailboat. The same winds blow on us all, good and bad. What determines where we end up is not the wind but the setting of the sail. Are you passively letting life's circumstances carry you along, hoping it will end up where you want it to? Or are you deliberately responding with choices and actions that keep you moving in the direction of your dreams?

Relationships are your business.
When difficulty hits, you may be tempted to become bitter, pull back into your own resources, abandon your faith and trust no one. However, that only moves you further away from living true to who you really are and fulfilling your purpose. In addition to taking care of myself, nurturing my relationship to God, my relationship with my family was paramount. As I reflected on my options now faced with being the sole provider and creating a secure future for my kids, I saw how the entrepreneurial lifestyle was the ideal setup for me, especially now. Freedom of time and quality of life for my family were some of my initial *whys* for even considering owning a business. These same *whys* motivated me to continue on that course even though my circumstances had changed.

Drawing upon my experience with non-profits as a leader and visionary, both working independently and as part of a team, I realized that successful people don't attain success on their own. I was not meant to do it alone. Businesses are built on relationships. Building and nurturing meaningful relationships, personally and professionally, is essential to your success. I accessed the resources I had in existing relationships with people who were my raving fans, mentors, neighbors, friends, family, and other supporters. As well, I reached out to build new relationships with other entrepreneurs who provided the inspiration, mentoring, joint-venturing and practical helps necessary to stay the course. Which relationships do you need to nurture for support and inspiration? Who do you need to add to your success team?

Real you.

Understanding who I was and what my greatest strengths are provided me the essential components I needed to be more intentional in my decision-making. Over the previous 15 or so years, I had been actively engaged in not only coaching others in areas of personal and professional development but also experienced tremendous freedom to live more authentically. The foundation of knowing who I was and loving how I am wired to function provided the platform to re-invent my life drawing upon existing internal and external resources. Using personality profiles, feedback from trusted friends, hiring a coach, listening to my heart, and seeking spiritual guidance all served to confirm who the real me was, and helped form the basis of my identity. Through identifying your values, passions, strengths and personality styles, you too can develop the strategies to align your actions to live on purpose.

Marcus Buckingham in his book *What Successful Women do Differently* reveals that the most successful women do not live balanced lives but rather strive for imbalance. His findings highlighted the fact that to live a life on purpose and within the bounds of your passion you need to do what he calls "lean into your strength zone." As you operate from the areas of your greatest strengths, you experience a richer, more fulfilling life. Instead of trying to do it all, and dwelling on what you can't do, gather a team to do the things you are not good at, so you are free to do what you do best and love. Surrounding yourself with others as part of your team helps fill in the gaps and do what you are not meant to do. These may include a bookkeeper, an accountant, a housekeeper, and others. This establishes the systems needed to make your life and business more impactful and meaningful, and frees you to do what you love.

Re-invention of Life.

Modern society promotes the recycling and re-using of materials in a new way than originally used. This is a smart move and kinder on our environment. Similarly, I realized that I had core personal assets that could be drawn upon to use in a new way. Based on my education and experience of almost 20 years speaking, and coaching others in areas of personal transformation, spiritual direction, leadership development, and effective communication, there were a lot of options to leverage. Although I functioned in these areas in a non-profit context, tapping into some areas of expertise in a new way was exciting and life-giving. I learned how to re-invent how I offered them to the world and create a purpose-based business based on my strengths, experiences, passions and unique personality. Living authentically from the heart is becoming recognized as essential to business and corporate productivity.

In his book, *The Heart of Coaching*, author Thomas Crane, discusses the importance of connecting with your "centre" in improving business relationships. He acknowledged that "some of the most profound movement I have made on this journey has come from consciously attempting to bring more of my heart into my relationships and coaching practice." As you live and work from a place of truth and integrity, aligning your actions to your authentic self, you find fulfillment in functioning in the arenas that are your strongest points. In what ways do you need to re-invent what you already have to create a purpose-based business?

Resilience.

The most successful people don't give up, but rather learn from their mistakes and demonstrate a resilient spirit. Resilience is defined as the power or ability to return to the original form, position, or state after being bent, compressed, or stretched. It's like having elasticity. One of my mentor coaches Valorie Burton, in her most recent book, *Where Will You Go From Here* discusses the quality of resilience thoroughly. She says that "the essence of resilience is your ability to effectively navigate adversity and courageously face whatever life throws your way. Though you may be bruised and battered by challenges, your spirit still soars."

Undergirding resilience is the belief that you can overcome any experience and that you can actually become a better person because of it. It is seeing obstacles as opportunities to grow rather than give up. Burton relates resilience to "tempered glass" which is glass that is made stronger due to repeated exposure to heat and cold. She cites one definition of *temper* as "to make stronger and more resilient through hardship." This reflects another belief that resilient people hold on to which is that the process is just as important, or even more important than the result. In the heat of battle, your character gets tested and can become stronger, allowing you to emerge victoriously and with even more to offer the world. Your response and resilience go hand-in-hand to empower you to break through those emotional roadblocks to be better equipped to carry out your dream.

In times of crisis and unfortunate circumstances, many people come face-to-face with where the cracks are in their foundation of identity, security and worth. Many experience an identity crisis as a result and experience confusion and disorientation.

When adversity or unexpected events threaten to sabotage your goals, remember that it is not just about achieving a dream but it's about who you need to become in order to achieve and successfully live that dream. As you choose to move forward, realize that what seems to be an obstacle is actually an opportunity for you to develop the character and skills you need to attain your goals and create the life you dream of. Stay true to who you are. Focus on your strengths and not your weaknesses. Let your responses and not your circumstances determine your future. Businesses are built on relationships. Surround yourself with key relationships that will help support and empower you as you embrace the process change and emerge with increased compassion, courage, and the needed character to passionately pursue the life you were meant to live.

Lisa Dewar is a speaker, transformational life coach, and communication expert. She is the author of *Let the Real You Step Forward* and the Founder of the Global Institute for Spiritpreneurs. Visit her at www.lisadewar.com and download your free "Creating Your REAL U Blueprint" or to receive her weekly coaching tips.

CHAPTER 17

The Bliss Is In the Breakthrough

by Karen Dodd

"Your work is to discover your work and then with all your heart, give yourself to it." —Buddha

Have you ever had that nagging feeling that you were meant to serve at a higher level or make a bigger contribution (after all, isn't that why we're here?) but you can't quite put your finger on what that is?

As an only child who moved from school to school due to my father's career, I was shy and never felt part of the "in crowd." One of my most painful memories in my last year of high school (when we had moved yet again) was eating my lunch in a cubicle of the girls' washroom because I didn't have anyone to eat with.

My Story

I now know that my mother did the best she could with what she knew, but I was literally criticized every day of my life and wasn't encouraged to make my own decisions. I grew up extremely insecure, with low self-worth and really, no real sense of who I was. Add to that the need to gain praise and recognition from others, and I really didn't have the tools to build a healthy self-image.

Going from junior high to high school, I had been told by my mother than I wasn't good enough to go to university, so I chose the business and commerce program which basically meant I was destined to become a secretary. So, that was the first job I fell into.

From there, I was very fortunate to get promoted rapidly within a large corporation, but after seven years, I knew in my heart that I didn't have the personality to tolerate the corporate gamesmanship that permeated that organization. I didn't realize that I had an entrepreneurial mind back then, so after I left that company I was either pushed ("You would be so good at this!") or fell into a number of careers, none of which were fueled by passion.

Oh, along the way I started several entrepreneurial ventures of my own and I was considered to be successful. But deep in my heart, I knew this wasn't "it." But what was "it?" Even as a young child, I somehow knew I was destined to do something special that would influence a lot of people. But how would I ever get in touch with what that was?

Fast forward to 1992, when I married my second husband, a successful businessman who loved me unconditionally and had the exact opposite upbringing to me. Although one of six children with only just enough money to make ends meet, he and his siblings were told by both parents that they could do or be anything they set their mind to. Wow, there must have been a reason this man had been put in my path!

Our wedding was like something out of a fairy tale, but the first 12 years of life together resembled something out of a nightmare. Before you jump to the conclusion that my husband was abusive or anything like that, I assure you he was not. He was, and still is, a kind and loving man who supports me unconditionally. But as second marriages often go, our finances were being drained by an ex-wife and two confused children.

Somehow we stayed together, and almost 12 years to the day, I remember him calling me out of a meeting and telling me that at last, our financial obligations were over. It was time that we could actually start building a life for ourselves. It was like the weight of the world had been lifted from our shoulders.

And then, one fateful day in October, 2005, I got a call at one of the four jobs that I was working simultaneously, that my husband had suffered a serious ladder accident in our home. I remember coming back to our house and seeing a three-foot pool of blood on the kitchen floor, where he had fallen 15 feet onto ceramic tiles. He sustained injuries to three of the four quadrants of his brain, shattered his left arm and had multiple injuries to his back. The ambulance had to pull over on the way to the hospital as they'd lost his pulse.

Over the next year, he valiantly fought his way back to being able to work again. As we were both self-employed, there were no benefits and as we had just started to get our financial heads above water, we had no reserves to get us through. I remember the banks started calling within days of his accident and had it not been for both our parents, we would have lost our home.

Brain injuries, as you might have heard, change your life forever. Not just of the person who was injured but also that of their spouse, family and even friends. The person injured is often angry, defiant, compulsive, and on a rollercoaster of emotions. Miraculously, he didn't remember anything about his accident. I remembered every gory detail, and it kept coming back to me in nightmares. I was inexplicably angry at him for somehow having caused this near tragedy.

Two years after "The Accident" (it became like a third entity in our marriage), we separated—not once, but twice. I remember someone saying to me, after learning my story, "And of course you got counseling when you were going through all this, right?" It had never occurred to me, as I was so busy working four jobs and taking care of my husband and all the devastation left in his wake.

I'm happy to tell you that after a year of on and off separation, our missing cat got us back together (that's another whole story in itself) and we recently celebrated our 19th anniversary. No, it hasn't been easy, but getting back together was the best thing I ever did. For our 17th anniversary, he surprised me with an eternity band; 17 diamonds for 17 years. Within a month, one of the diamonds fell out. Go figure, the Universe knew that although we had technically been married for 17 years, we had actually only been together for 16 because of the separation. You can't fool Mother Nature!

When the Second Shoe Dropped

Shortly before we got back together, I had started having some health problems of my own. My weight had plummeted almost 30 pounds and I had extreme pain everywhere below my waist. I often could barely walk and the crashing fatigue was something I had never known. It took another three years to be diagnosed with an auto-immune and inflammatory disease called polymyalgia rheumatica.

It's still something I struggle with every day.

Sometimes, when nature slaps you up the side of the head, it takes us awhile to pay attention. This was the Universe's way of making me focus on my priorities, as I entered my 50+ years. Someone once said, "Sometimes we have to lose our self to find our self." It took me awhile but eventually I got it. I knew I had to start living my passion and I didn't have the ten years it often takes to build one's ideal business.

Senior-preneurs, Boomer-preneurs, or…?

I'm fond of saying that either you choose your particular niche or your niche chooses you. In either case, the market that you serve or the problem that you are best known for solving, usually comes from your personal experience. I say *usually* because it does occasionally happen that someone is simply in the right place at the right time to take advantage of an opportunity and they just kind of fall into their business. But more likely, what you do best and with the most passion, comes from your compelling story.

So, why wasn't I using my own compelling story to connect with and solve problems for my obvious niche?

Hmm, an interesting dichotomy, don't you think?

Here I was, frustrated at being a "me-too" in my niche. I was tired of being told by younger entrepreneurs to "shake my booty" (my booty shakes all by itself, thank you very much!). Although I have huge respect for young mom-entrepreneurs, I don't have much in common with them. I've never had children and I've not had to deal with their particular types of challenges.

When considering my own compelling story, I realized that the majority of my clients and those with whom I resonate, are—guess what?

They're just like me! Have you noticed that as well?

When I started to do more research, I discovered that the fastest growing segment of the small business market is entrepreneurs over the age of 50.

As a woman in the 50+ category, I hesitate to refer to myself as a "senior-preneur." I could live with "boomer-preneur," but when my partner in success and virtual assistant, Tracey Ehman, came up with 'Fifty Plus and Fabulous,' I thought, *that's it!*

Who Is That 50+ and Fabulous Woman?

She could be an empty-nester, transitioning in her personal relationship, or considers herself a late-bloomer. She's someone who, in the second chapter of her life, isn't willing to live one more day with her music still in her. She wants to fulfill her lifelong desire to share her passion with purpose and profit. This now forms part of our mission statement with the Global Institute of Small Business Marketing, where as CEO, I have finally found my passion.

Depending on where the 50+ woman falls in the roughly three-decade age spread, she could have been a freedom fighter (okay, not literally but she still had a ways to go in dealing with Neanderthal male bosses) or a "wisdom rider," simply in a place of knowing and of grace. She often has sacrificed what she'd really like to do in order to raise a family, stayed in a job just to pay the bills, or has taken until now to uncover her passion.

Supporting, Inspiring and Educating the 50+ Woman

In researching this segment of women, I found that she is being quite well served in the areas of health, wealth, diet and lifestyle. But, not so much in the area of entrepreneurship.

Would your product or service contribute to this particular woman's goals and aspirations? Professions that come to mind that could be of support in her entrepreneurial quest could be: professional organizers, image consultants, bookkeeping and accounting, career counseling, web and graphic designers, social media and SEO consultants, and of course, coaches. I'm sure you could add to this list.

I believe that our strengths and our weaknesses are very close together. For example, one of the 50+ woman's strengths is definitely her experience and wisdom. Her corresponding weakness can come from the fact that she learned to communicate in a very different way than is necessary today, with the emergence of the Internet. So, all of the professions I listed (and more) can be critical to the success of the 50+ entrepreneur.

She Has Affluence and Commitment

I didn't actually go to college until I was in my 30s, where I had to take time away from my business and finance myself as a "mature student." I noticed very quickly that the few of us older folks who were spending our own precious time and money, tended to take our education very seriously. We didn't skip classes, not do assignments or laze around just taking up a seat.

Similarly, it's been my experience when working with the more mature entrepreneur that she is more likely to have the funds to invest in herself and she is very committed to getting the support she needs to launch or grow her business. She also has what I call a greater "sense of urgency," because she doesn't want to take the 10 years that her younger counterparts took to build their businesses. If you provide any of the peripheral services needed to run a business, you can help the 50+ woman to greatly shorten her learning curve.

What I Have Learned

First and foremost, I have learned that you *can* teach a Fifty Plus and Fabulous woman new tricks! A lot has changed in the last five plus decades but I know that staying interested in other people and being willing to think outside the box is critical to being successful. I have learned that I have more tenacity that I ever gave myself credit for, both in my personal and my business life.

For me, hiring a mentor to work with each year for the past three years has contributed enormously to my growth. I don't think I could live long enough to learn it all myself.

On the personal side, learning to forgive—both myself and others—literally is what has set me free from guilt, resentment, and anger.

Wow, this piece took a *long* time for me!

Doing this work was like looking at a picture within a picture. Initially, I dwelled on all the people who had done me wrong. But upon further examination, I discovered that it was only *me* that I had to forgive because I was the only one that I had steadfastly refused to acknowledge and love unconditionally.

It's Never Too Late

With 65 to 95 percent of jobs in the world being provided by small and medium businesses, and one in five being owned by the 50+ entrepreneur, this segment of "wise women" definitely deserves more than a cursory glance.

If you are a Fifty Plus and Fabulous women still looking for her passion, I urge you to not to wait another day before finding your purpose and stepping into your brilliance. As George Eliot said, "It is never too late to be what you might have been."

I wish you more love, joy and happiness than your heart can hold!

Karen Dodd has become known as the Entrepreneur's Marketing Expert and is fast becoming the leader of authentic marketing for solo-entrepreneurs in every stage of building their businesses. In her current company, the Global Institute of Small Business Marketing, Karen brings her 30 years of experience in marketing, client attraction and coaching. She specializes in teaching entrepreneurs how to take the task of marketing and apply it to making authentic connections and solving problems. Her company also teaches its followers and members how to market online, identify and refine key brand differentiators, and most importantly, how to create the space for their businesses to grow energetically, but gracefully.

Teaching sales and marketing for two of the largest vocational institutes in the country, and consulting with numerous companies in the private sector, today Karen specializes in working with small business owners, mentoring them to combine their entrepreneurial passion with growing a profitable, equitable business. Under the Global Institute of Small Business Marketing umbrella, members can enroll in annual programs ranging from $197 a year to $25,000.

Karen's goal is to create a breed of entrepreneurs who reflect the change she'd like to see in the world. "Marketing is energy," she explains. "It's all about real people making real connections, solving your ideal clients' problems better than anyone else in your niche, and paying it forward to create the space for everyone to grow."

You can visit Karen, access her free CD, and find out more about her and her company at www.smallbizinsitute.com Karen lives in beautiful Lions Bay, British Columbia with her husband, a laid-back Mexican beach dog, and two assertive cats.

CHAPTER 18

Positive Thoughts and a Vision Board

by Dympna Fay-Hart

I was born into a large Irish family in Chicago in the 1960s. My parents, both Irish immigrants, came to this country separately in search of better lives, leaving behind all they knew. They were work-horses who bred eight thoroughbreds—four brothers, three sisters, and me.

My mother's working life began as a cleaning lady for the Heinz ketchup family in the late 1950s, but she got fired when she was caught throwing a party while they vacationed. I love telling that story. From Tralee, a small town in Ireland she moved to Chicago where she met my father, an Irish homebuilder. My mother, her name was Mary Fay, taught me how to have purpose at a very young age. She was high-powered and ahead of her time to say the least. My siblings and I fondly call her "Mother Mary" and I believe somehow the Beatles met her and their song "Let It Be" is about my mom. Hey, if Mia Farrow's sister Prudence is Sexy Sadie, I am announcing, my mother is the "Mother Mary" in "Let It Be." *In my times of darkness, she is standing right in front of me, speaking words of wisdom…let it be.*

My mom died suddenly at 63, in 1998. We worked together as partners in real estate. I was hesitant to join her, as I had spent a lifetime as coffee girl, bank deposit runner, cleaning lady, and the multi-tasking office gopher. Our family-owned business was a real estate firm in Chicago. My mother was enormously successful in sales and, on several occasions, I witnessed her talk the shoes off people's feet. She never took "no" for answer. One of her successful tactics was disarming people with her charm and wit. On occasion in her cold-calling days, people hung up on her, a lot. She simply called them back and asked, "Did I catch you at a bad time?" Many words she spoke just once have stayed with me for a lifetime: "Clothes make a person, but you can't buy class," is one of my favorites.

With eight children, it was at times challenging for her to be in the office for long hours. Although it was just down the street from where we lived, she still came home to be sure we hadn't burned down the house. She arranged with the telephone company to have a "business line" ring in the house, and she would answer the phone in her sing-songy Irish brogue: "Fay Real Estate, how can I help you?" We were military-trained to immediately stop screaming, talking, and laughing when the "business line" rang. My mother had her own "hand signals" and trust me; those hands were registered with the FBI. Let's just say with eight children, she was a strong woman.

My mother and I began working together in late 1993. Our ads featured our pictures with a catchy slogan, "Together we're #1!" Her success evolved accidentally from her philanthropic endeavors. She heavily supported our church and many other causes, ranging from hunger to families that fell on hard times in our community. We had four successful years working together as realtors, before she died very unexpectedly. The torch was now passed. I must pick up the pieces of something very broken and make it work—all on my own. I saw first-hand my mother's love for helping others and elected, as a tribute to her, to first take some time to heal and then to take a closer look around me at areas that could benefit from my volunteering.

I took all that she showed me and submerged myself as a silent good-will ambassador to my community. It was very therapeutic, and before I really knew and understood what was happening, my business began to flourish. I was busy—I mean really busy. My church asked me to be the president of my women's council, a women's shelter contacted me to assist in finding needed items for battered women, local government bodies were asking for time toward improving various causes in my industry, and my real estate business was going through the roof. It was happening—I was finding my purpose in life. I was earning a living, a very good living, and fueling my business with a plethora of quality clientele: the return of my philanthropy was developing a sphere of influence in contacts for my business.

In 1996, I had the good fortune to have my third child. I was elated. Around this time, my career and long hours outside the home were taking a toll on my marriage. I continued to work, and my husband was supportive at the time my career was peaking, but as a couple we were not growing together, and we divorced in 2003 after 15 years of marriage.

I began buying real state to ensure peace of mind for my single life in retirement. Over the course of seven years, I was carrying and personally managing seven properties, translating to roughly between $2 million and $2.5 million in mortgages.

I realized the need to get organized and to create goals for myself. I knew I had a recipe for success—but I was like a downed, sparking electrical wire that needed to be reconnected, rewired, and reattached. So I began creating a mental list of my accolades and eventually put pen in hand. The list started out slowly but seemed to grow rather quickly, and I began to enter thoughts of accomplishments I had already achieved, and also a few that were on my bucket list. I was always competitive in nature, but now I had a desire to braid my sales career and philanthropy into something more. By my 39th birthday, I was encouraged by my younger sister to enter a half triathlon; while I was in okay shape, I never imagined I could complete any triathlon. I didn't break any records doing it, but I finished with a sense of great accomplishment. As my big 40th approached, there was an award that had always intrigued me and was on my mental vision board: to be one of the top "40 under 40" realtors in Illinois. It seemed the moment I thought of it, my phone rang, and I was to be one of that year's recipients. I was climbing a career in great strides and dominating my market place. I felt like I was on top of the world.

My company, Century 21, had a lifetime achievement award based on years of service, high sales volume and philanthropic contributions to communities. There were only 47 inductees in the world, and the average age for this pinnacle award was between 50 and 60. The year I turned 40, I was inducted into Century 21's International Hall of Fame—and the youngest to do so. Congratulated by our Guest Speaker, General Colin Powell in Las Vegas at our international convention, I was, as my friend Cathy would say, "The cat's ass"...until that is, the recession knocked my "triple-decker ice cream cone" right on the sidewalk!

My hard work and years of planning for retirement were fast evaporating before my eyes—the now 18 years I had invested, the financial planners, the real estate purchases, and the stocks were all dissolving, actually plummeting. I began to wonder how I could survive this. I had three children who I was predominately supporting on my own. It felt like the perfect time for a big fat pity party for 'lil 'ol me. "This sucks," rang through my head daily, but I had to go on and know in my heart that things will not always be this way. I told myself: "I have to reinvent, recreate, draw on my resources from all that I have experienced and somehow, some way, find gratitude for all the good in my life that I seem to have misplaced. I have to pray."

As women, we are always prepared for a disaster. The good news is that we were all born with the "coping with disaster chip." I simply needed to be reminded of this. My inner voice that was normally so present and aware of my surroundings was stolen from me in the trauma of what was taking place in my financial world. But, words my mother told me were coming back to me: "Smile, even if you don't feel like it—someone out there is having a worse day than you, and when you smile at them, it will force them to smile back…"

I needed to remind myself of a word I love: "Determination." Defined—a willingness to try, to fail, and to try again.

I remember one day last year watching the news about the trapped miners in Chile. When one of the 33 miners reached the surface after being in darkness 2,300 feet below ground for 69 days, his first words were, "God must have wanted us to change." I thought of those words for days, no, for weeks. In my plain language, I was drinking the wine all these years, but this new life now has me squashing the grapes.

Change. It shows up like uninvited guest. Two things can happen when an uninvited guest shows up at your home. It can be startling, uncomfortable, silencing, and intrusive; or, change can be warm, new, sporadic, and an opportunity to break out the fine china and serve up some goods times to your uninvited guests. The choice is yours.

I have a rotating vision board in my home office with words and photos of things I want—some material items, some words and phrases I love to read over and over again. Some of my favorite sayings through trying times: "The light comes in through our broken places," by Ernest Hemingway. We do not truly appreciate the goods times, until we have experienced bad ones. Celebrate. Be kind to yourself in the process. We deserve to celebrate and honor our lives. Express gratitude, no matter how great or how small, for all the relationships we have. Speak up; realize your ambition. It is never too late to dream—if you can think it, you can have it. Playright Marsha Norman said, "Dreams are illustrations from the book your soul is writing about you." Inspire others, keep your sense of humor, and listen to yourself.

Dympna's professional career in real estate started in 1993, at Century 21 McMullen, what is now considered the hallmark of franchise offices. Developing her skill as a new agent within the organization, she quickly honed her knowledge of the industry, as well as her expertise in the Chicago area real estate market. She received her broker's license in 1996 and is now considered one of the top agents in real estate market.

Dympna became increasingly involved in philanthropic and community efforts which play a significant role in both her professional and personal life. Today, she is a highly-accomplished and respected real estate businesswoman with a large client referral base and a wide network of contacts, both national and international.

Her articles on real estate have been featured in the *Chicago Tribune*, *Chicago Agent Magazine* and *At Home* magazine. Dympna has been a panelist at international conventions revealing her successful entrepreneurial business strategies combined and balanced with her philanthropic endeavors.

Dympna's impressive sales results have earned her numerous accolades and recognition as one of the industry's top producers. In addition to being a leader in her industry, she has received the highest pinnacle awards in both sales and philanthropy. Her overall attitude and enthusiasm has been an inspiration to her peers and the foundation for her success. You can learn more about Dympna at www.fayhart.com.

CHAPTER 19

Become the CEO of Your Life!

by Linda Spevacek

Have you ever faced a difficult challenge, the kind of challenge that will inevitably result in decisions sure to be unpopular with some of the people closest to you and misunderstood by just about everyone else? Decisions that you know via your intuition are essential, but you just can't get your head around how everything will possibly come out ok in the end?

"How did I get myself into this situation?" I found myself wondering. I was at the peak of my career, or so it would look to someone from the outside. I was running my own successful investment consulting company, partnered with some of the best in the business, working on big, complicated, interesting deals, making plenty of money, happily married with two young boys, and able to manage my schedule so I could be home in time for the school bus. I had methodically and strategically built my life to arrive at this pinnacle!

Yet I felt stagnant. Been there, done that. I knew I needed to make some career-changing decisions. My gut told me that there was more important, more impactful, more satisfying work that I wanted to be doing, but I had no idea what that would be. Furthermore, I felt trapped. How could I just throw away all of my training and experience? Not to mention the fear of financial ruin. The challenge felt enormous.

Take the "B-School" Approach

Today, as a coach, I work with smart, experienced, and accomplished business people across the globe. And most of them, when faced with a personal or professional challenge, feel exactly the same way I did when I was trying to figure out why I was not completely fulfilled in my career. They wonder, "How did I get to this point? I thought I was on the right track."

These feelings of confusion, sometimes combined with a little dose of guilt or shame ("How can I possibly complain—things really aren't *that* bad!"), often push us backwards, right into the waiting arms of our existing, unsatisfying situation.

By necessity while dealing with my own challenge, I discovered that there is an alternative. As smart, analytical, business-oriented thinkers, we can tackle life's challenges in the same way we approach business challenges, as a CEO would. We simply need a process—think of it as a personal strategic plan—to analyze the situation, set a new direction, identify the steps to move from where we are to where we want to go, remove or overcome obstacles in the way, get into action and stay on the path to successful achievement of rewarding and fulfilling goals. In other words, we need to become the CEO of our lives!

However, as I began to apply business school techniques to the design of a personal strategic plan, one fundamental and monumental difference between planning for organizational change and planning for individual change became clear. For most business challenges, there are generally only one or two correct solutions. Across a population of individuals though, there are an infinite number of right answers. The key is to find the right answer *for you*. And the only way to find the right answer *for you* is to ask the right questions.

Questions are the "secret sauce" to the simple but powerful 3-step process for personal change called: Become the CEO of Your Life.

C is for Clarity

The first step is to find *Clarity*. Complete and total clarity provides direction and also, surprisingly, unprecedented freedom. Imagine your life without second-guessing yourself, without hesitation, and without regret. Clarity provides freedom from these thoughts for true peace of mind.

Finding clarity can be elusive. When people are asked the direct question, "What do you want?" answers tend to be vague and unfocused.

More exploratory questions take a different approach and lead to deeper, richer answers. Questions like these:

"What do I want to feel every day?"
This question is a terrific alternative to thinking about what you want to *do*. When you think about what you want to *feel* instead, you will achieve much greater clarity about not only the activities you are drawn to, but also the kind of atmosphere and environment you want, who you might want nearby, and what kind of impact you'd like to have.

"What really matters?"
This question focuses your attention on issues that are important, and will also help you identify things you may be able to eliminate or let go of.

"What's missing?"
The answers to this simple question tell you exactly what you should seek to add to your life.

"What do I feel compelled to do before I let more time slip by?"
Not everyone feels like there is something of vital importance that they want to accomplish, but if you do, I highly recommend that you respond! Nagging feels of regret over unpursued dreams are one of the largest sources of pain that people carry. If you are passionate about a cause, an activity, or a group of people, then get involved!

And finally, this question:

"What is my purpose?"
Knowing your purpose is the simplest and most satisfying direction-setting tool there is. When you build a life based on your purpose, your course is clear, choices become easy, and self-doubt simply fades away. Imagine waking up every day knowing in your heart that you are on the right path!

E is for the Ability to Execute Your Plan
Once you have achieved Clarity about your direction, the next step is to create and execute an action plan. Although this step seems simple and obvious, it is unfortunately where most people get hung up.

What stops people from reaching for their goals and dreams? Although lack of resources is most often cited ("I don't have the time" or "I don't have the money"), the real reason is usually a mindset problem caused by fear, doubt, and lack of self-trust.

We must find a way to overcome these personal obstacles. Once again, applying business concepts, thinking analytically, and asking the right questions will lead to solutions.

"What is stopping me?"
Have you ever sat down and considered what boundaries you place on yourself? For most of us, these fall into four categories: Resources (time, money, labor); Beliefs ("I'm too old to start something new"); Fears (fear of failure, fear of injury, even fear of too much success!); and Influences (concerns about how other people will react).

Resources
Resource constraints are factual and can be handled as you would any business limitation. Time management, delegation, partnering, asking for help: find ways to leverage the resources you do have rather than let resource limitations actually stop you cold. The only question you really need here is:

"Where can I find the resources that I need?"
When you begin to list all of your potential resources, I guarantee you'll have more than you could possibly use.

Beliefs
Beliefs are thoughts that limit your ability to take action. Fortunately, there is a simple and familiar business tool that you can use to assess whether you need to continue to let the belief hold you back: the Cost/Benefit analysis. Only this time, do it in reverse. Ask yourself:

"What is the benefit of this belief?"
A female executive client lacked confidence in her ability to "be a player" within the inner circles of a male-dominated industry. She listed the benefits of this belief as: "I'm off the hook—I don't have to even try to compete at their level. That saves me from ever failing or being embarrassed."

"What is the cost of that same belief?"
The instant that same executive identified the cost as: "I'm losing out on multi-million dollar deals because of my fear of stepping up!" she immediately took action. She contacted the largest professional association in the industry, got onto their schedule to make an educational presentation to a very senior level audience, joined a committee, and within six months was elected president of the association. She's definitely "a player" now!

One final question:

"Am I willing to continue to let beliefs limit me in any way?" Yes or No? It is your choice.

Fears
Fear stems from two sources: the known and the unknown. The fear you know is grounded in past events and, contrary to popular wisdom, the past does not have to be repeated! Instead, why not use your past to guide you toward a better outcome next time?

To address fears that you know, ask yourself this question:

"What lessons from my past can I use to help me move forward?"
Remember when you first burned your hand on a hot stove? Life lessons are often similarly painful! But you didn't stop cooking, did you? Consider how your mistakes have shaped you, taught you, and honed your skills. When you think about it that way, you can almost welcome failure for the valuable lessons you will learn! Seriously, despite your fear, any outcome, even a failure, is better than not trying at all, isn't it?

Fear of the unknown is often worse than the fear we know. This fear often looms like a huge, scary cloud, thick with dreadful possibilities. Fear of the unknown requires a different strategy than dealing with the fear we know. This fear requires courage, and a terrific question to help you gain courage is:

"What would change if I could absolutely trust in and believe in myself?"
Answering this question presumes courage, and the answers could astonish you. Imagine all that you would try, taste, participate in, and

accomplish if you had complete self-trust! Isn't it worth choosing to believe in your courage over choosing to believe in your fear?

And finally, try this question, even in the face of fear:

"If I can't change it, can I just live with it?"
Sometimes an apparent obstacle isn't really an impediment at all, but an excuse. Consider whether you could simply work around it. Over time, you may find that the problem, even fear, simply disappears.

Influences
Keeping up appearances and worrying about what others think probably stops more people from realizing their dreams more than any other obstacle. Simply ask yourself this:

"In which areas of my life do I heed the wishes of others over my own desires?" and then this: *"Why do their opinions matter more than mine?"*

Again, it is your choice whether to let the influence of others stop you. Consider too, that the people we let influence us are often the people who love us the most. Wouldn't they be horrified to know that they were an unwitting impediment to your happiness? And won't they be so proud of you when they see you taking decisive action to achieve your dreams?

O is for Organization
The final step to becoming the CEO of your life is to build a supportive organization around you, but in this case not your physical organization, not your staff or desk or filing system or time management system. The organization to cultivate, nurture and learn from is a powerful and experienced team that any CEO would envy: your Internal Advisory Board. Whether you recognize this team as the voices in your head, your intuition, or just your gut feeling, learn to tap into your personal wisdom.

There is only one question you need to ask this team when dealing with any challenge imaginable:

"How would a CEO handle this?"
When you view challenges from the perspective of a CEO, everything

changes. You are in charge. You are experienced. You are capable. You are respected. You are admired. Trust your personal wisdom, your Internal Advisory Board, and you will find that you already know how to handle whatever surprises life presents.

I mastered this process to remake my career and now I rely on my CEO perspective every day. So can you. Let Clarity, grounded in a sense of purpose, guide your direction. Choose to Execute your plans and ideas without the boundaries of limits, fear, or outside influences. Tap into the wisdom of your supportive Organization as you would a trusted advisory board. Follow these easy-to-remember, three simple steps, and you, too, will become the CEO of your life!

Linda Spevacek is an executive coach, speaker, blogger and author who helps people achieve professional success while still feeling fulfilled in their personal lives. Linda comes from the fast-paced world of deal-making and investments, so she understands the drive to succeed, as well as the pressures success can bring. She specializes in asking clients the challenging, thought-provoking questions that lead people to find their own answers for powerful results that actually last!

Exploration of "purpose"—that personal self-discovery of who you are and how to leverage your unique talents into building a life and career that feels authentic and satisfying—is built into every coaching program offered. Linda is trained and certified in helping people define their purpose. Clients say this discovery is not only one the most meaningful experiences of their lives, but also surprisingly fun and enlightening.

A group of Linda's clients awarded her the nickname "America's Launch Coach" prompting her to name her coaching company The Launch Companies LLC. Linda offers individual and group coaching nationwide over the phone and web. Each coaching program provides a step-by-step system for success, from developing a rock-solid foundation to finding breakthrough solutions to problems and achieving profound personal discoveries. Titles include Your Life/Your Dreams, Create Your Vision, and Discover You, Inc. All programs are deliverable as workshops for corporate clients. In addition, Linda is Co-Founder of Corporate Umami Enterprises LLC, which helps organizations *Create Wow! in the Workplace* through the power of an engaged workforce and more effective leadership. The Corporate Umami sessions are sensory, interactive, and uniquely different from conventional corporate training programs.

Linda is a graduate of Colorado College and has an MBA in Finance from the Anderson School at UCLA. She serves on several not-for-profit boards and is an elected town planning and zoning commissioner. Linda loves nature and the outdoors. She can often be found playing tennis, skiing, riding her lovely Arabian mare or hanging out anywhere near water. She lives in Connecticut with her husband. They have two grown sons.

Linda is proud to be featured in the book *Roadmap to Success* alongside industry giants Steven Covey and Ken Blanchard, available on her website www.launchcoach.com. A live, 10-minute presentation of "Become the CEO of Your Life" is on video at www.youtube.com/lindaspevacek. The vital questions from the program are available for download as a free e-book entitled *50 Questions That Will Change Your Life* at www.launchcoach.com/blog.

CHAPTER 20

The Transitional Road

by Kathy Stover

When I look back over the years, I can see that my entrepreneurial spirit was a big part of me even as a child. I grew up in a neighborhood with mostly boys, and at 11 years of age I knew that if I was going to make money, I would have to compete with them. I understood that in order to thrive, I was going to have to be smarter and think one step ahead. I intuitively knew that how I presented myself and my lawn-mower would determine if I got the job.

All the boys in the neighborhood were charging 50 cents to cut lawns. For my first job, I showed up with my lawnmower adorned with a beautiful pink satin ribbon and a plan. The plan was to only charge 25 cents and cut the lawn in a pattern that was both beautiful and impressive to the eye. I just knew that when all the neighbors saw how beautiful that lawn looked that I would be able to raise my price to 75 cents and corner the market because the patterned lawn would be the talk of the neighborhood. I was right, they loved it! But my competition was sure unhappy that I was taking away their business and making more money. This created my first joint venture. I taught the boys how I cut the patterns in the lawn and set up deals where we split the money we made cutting lawns. It was a win/win situation for everyone and everyone was happy. I had achieved a newfound respect.

Although I didn't know what to call it then, I saw that what I desired or wanted to achieve, I could picture in my mind and visualize the outcome. I also knew that I had to establish relationships with competitors in order to work cohesively and that helping others had to always be a part of the plan. This entrepreneurship, thinking outside the box, was going to set a pattern to be repeated over the course of my life.

When I was in the fifth grade I met the love of my life. I didn't know it then but we were destined to spend our lives together. I just didn't expect it to start so early. When I was 16 I found I was pregnant. I was shocked. How could that be? I was just too young. But I knew in my heart I wanted to keep this child. To try and keep us from continuing this relationship, my husband's father signed him up in the Marine Corp. He was 17 at the time. But we were married before our daughter was born. We set up house, two young kids with a baby. What a sight we were! We were so broke. We ate a lots of mac and cheese and were always scrambling for the next buck. Life was a struggle.

When we were stationed in Twenty-nine Palms, I found myself working in a gas station pumping gas and checking oil. While stationed in Hawaii, I taught other Marine wives how to change their oil and do a tune-up. They would buy the parts and I would charge them $10 to learn. Things were just never easy although I always had an underlying belief in a God who would solve my problems and take care of us.

One of the defining moments of my life involved my daughter. I very badly wanted her to attend a private Catholic high school. I had determined that a private education would be best for her but the cost was entirely out of the question. I went to visit the school and talk with the nuns. After hearing my story and my struggles, one tiny little nun said she could tell I was having trouble humbling myself to ask for help. Her response has stayed with me my entire life. She said if I never humbled myself when in need, it would not allow those that have the ability to give to experience the joy of giving. The spirit of giving is one of the guiding forces of my life today. My daughter not only attended and graduated from that school but went on to attend college.

I was so happy when I had the opportunity to enter the corporate world of sales at 25. This world allowed me the stability to contribute to my family and allowed financial security. I made a lot of money and spent a lot of money! I loved everything about the world of sales and management. The challenges and rewards were a perfect fit. This job was to sustain me for the next 25 years.

After I left the corporate world, my husband sold his business and we moved from the city to a small mountain community. This was an exciting time for us. With money in the bank to take away our fear of financial insecurity, I had no doubt in my mind that I was going to be successful with my Internet endeavors and life was good.

Then the bomb hit. It was the call that still rivets me today. My biggest cheerleader, the man who always told me no matter what, I could do anything I set my mind to do, was diagnosed with terminal cancer. My dad. My dad taught me to believe that whatever it is that you do if it is done with passion and purpose, it will catapult you to success. I've always believed that to be true. My world was rocked.

I continue to hear my dad's voice; yes he still cheers me on. I understood the importance of multiple streams of income so I went through the motions and became a notary so that I could do mobile loan signings. Times were good in the mortgage industry. I was also very successful in an up and coming network marketing company. My love of everything Internet and my desire to always help others guided my path. Because of my sales background, some dabbling in multi-level marketing, Internet marketing was very appealing to me.

The easiest sale was to put up an auction listing on eBay. This took care of my desire to sell and brought in money at the same time. I found that I was able to go to garage sales and resell just about anything or sell items found in my own home. More importantly to me, I was able to teach others how to do the same thing I was doing and make money themselves. Even then I had the mindset of abundance although I sure could not have put those words to it at the time.

As I continued to sell different types of items on eBay and started promoting products of others as an affiliate marketer, my multiple streams of income continued to grow. This process was one of plenty of trials and errors. It was not as simple as it may sound now, but I knew not to leave before the miracle.

We are all familiar with the collapse of the economy. It hit us hard, too. We lost hundreds of thousands in the stock market and more in mutual funds. My notary business dried up overnight with the downturn in home sales. The MLM closed. We had to sell various items and try and eek out an income. It was a scary time but somehow I knew things would be okay. Past failures do not dictate future success and sometimes the baggage of our past can limit us from achieving the things we so desire. What I desired was not going to be thwarted!

Then I discovered the little blue bird…Twitter. At first glance, I thought it was a passing phase, much like Myspace, but the lightbulb flashed in my mind. Big time! I could see how I could market business and the creativity started to flow. I was on again!

The most important thing is to believe in yourself. Believe in your dreams and your goals and the ideas that come. Surround yourself with the support of people who not only also believe in you but will help you along your journey. Honest evaluation is so important to keep us on the path. Often times the advice of others has been instrumental to me. Not only have they seen something I might have missed, but their objectivity might be the key that turns the lock. Like-minded individuals not only inspire, but they remind us to not set limits on what we can achieve. They help us to dream bigger.

I, from time to time, will chase the shiny object. This is probably a result of my extreme creativity and my passion. How do you like how I covered that one? I'm thankful that I can use my God-given talents to share these gifts and make money while doing so. Throughout my life I have had a mentor or what some would call a coach. They have helped me to see the big picture—the whole picture—and to stay focused and forge ahead. They have each had different ideas of what has worked for them, but the common ground has always been to believe in myself and know that I am capable of big things, of great things. They were each put in my life at a particular moment for a particular reason.

This past year, I have been working on expanding my spiritual growth and moving ahead through the shift and tide of change occurring in this new phase of transition in business. At the urging of a mentor, I began with a simple gratitude list, listing all of the things that I'm grateful for. When I got to about 42 things on my list, I was stuck. Then it came to me. The object of this exercise is to fully realize that I'm grateful for everything. From the simple things like having food on my table to the great big things. When I remind myself of this, I see the big picture of a spiritual principle that guides my life.

Written affirmations are a very integral part of my spiritual growth. Affirmations have been around for a long time and are very powerful. They are simply thoughts of mine that I know to be true that when written and visualized, come to fruition. For example, one of my affirmations is that I am a strong, creative, vital woman who has the ability to lead others. What the mind believes the mind can achieve. Simply repeating this verbally is just not enough. I must write it down. A written affirmation is a proof of a willingness to go forward. In my daily life, I have five affirmations. From time to time during the day, I will write other affirmations when the thought comes.

Practicing these principles on a daily basis has changed my mindset and has moved my business beyond my wildest expectations. The gifts I receive are monumental, and I continue to learn so much and remain teachable.

Always remember…

Move beyond your comfort place, success awaits you in the space, the spot you never dared to go, so you can share all that you know.

Kathy's corporate career spanning over 25 years ended six years ago as she retired out early by choice. She decided to pursue her vision and passion to help others by enlisting her 20-plus years experience as an Internet and network marketing entrepreneur to work from home.

Kathy Stover is a "Social Media Evolutionary." A social media marketing strategist and consultant who manages and teaches thought leaders, transformational leaders and business owners how to successfully market and brand themselves via social media through the shift and tide of change occurring in this new phase of transition in business worldwide.

Kathy's intuition and marketing savvy provides her the ability to move within her client's niche, understand and connect with their clients on a level that provides them the edge to move through the ever-changing realm of social media successfully.

She is the Co-Creator/Co-Host of the "Celebrity Creators" Show, a weekly live show featuring special expert guests, covering interesting and helpful topics to assist online marketing and business entrepreneurs to build, grow and expand their online and offline presence in today's ever-changing economy.

Kathy is a wife, mother and grammie as she is fondly called by her three grand-children, and lives in the Sierra Nevada Foothills in Grass Valley, CA. Visit Kathy at www.kathystover.com

CHAPTER 21

Quitting Is Not an Option

by Michele Modellas

I woke at 5am, excited and ready for the day. It was The Day I had been training for the past few months—My first Triathlon! I eagerly gathered my gear I had packed the night before, ate my oatmeal, and took a few sips of my spicy hot chai tea. I loaded my bike in my Celica and off I drove to the race course at the lake. As I approached the lake, I could see the buoys that mapped the swim course. I stopped and took a deep breath to take it all in! Was I really about to swim, bike and run miles and miles, something I hadn't even thought of doing a few months prior? I found a parking spot and went to find the rest of the women I had been training with. I remember, vividly, that morning and the feelings of calmness and preparedness for what I was about to tackle. At the same time, I had no idea what to expect from each segment of the race. Would I be exhausted after the first part? The second part? How long would it all take me? What I did know was I had physically prepared for the day, I held tight to the encouraging words from my trainer and I was confident in my mindset to finish. I was determined that quitting was not an option! For me, it didn't matter how long it took, but that I finished and finished well!

Personally, I can parallel participating in a triathlon and "succeeding" as an entrepreneur. I had decided to become self-employed quite a few years ago, and I was thrilled that I could determine my schedule, the client base I wanted to work with, and income potential. I've had an entrepreneurial spirit since I was a young girl and liked to be involved in multiple projects at one time. When I began my venture with my meeting and event planning company, I wasn't really sure exactly how to run my own company, but I knew I had skills and experience from my many years of working for employers in this line of work. I had supportive people in my life who believed I could do whatever I set out to do, and I had faith in myself and my decision to risk what it took to be self-employed.

During the past years of being self-employed, there have been ups and downs in client contracts and personal life challenges. But, I have never had a single regret of working for myself. When you know deep within that you are meant for more than what "society" says should be the "normal," it's that driving force that has kept me going and pursuing to overcome any obstacle that comes in my path.

In 2005, shortly after leaving a traditional J. O. B., my mom was told she didn't have long to live. During the next 10 months of her life, I was grateful I was self-employed and could have the flexibility to take her to doctor appointments, be with her the many days she spent in the hospital, and spend some quality time I would not have had if I had to report to an office for work each day. She passed away, and then it seemed a spiral of events occurred, which included my main client contract abruptly ending and me filing for divorce from a 23-year marriage. I began to second-guess everything about my life.

I was confident God would allow me to continue in my line of work, and provide for me, but it was during that time I discovered my quest for real purpose. I also discovered I had been living in such complacency over the years. With a false sense of security and self-satisfaction, I merely thought I was satisfied and was pleased with all the things I could do and be for everyone. I truly was unaware of the degree of troubles and deficiencies in my life. With so many balls to juggle, I did a pretty good job keeping them in the air.

While I loved what I had done in the past with event planning, I discovered what I was passionate about was to encourage women to "live a life by design, by pursuing their purpose and passion" and am in the process of launching the Global Association for Women in Transformation.

"You are so much more capable than you even realize. When your body wants to quit, you have to overcome that with your mind and push yourself harder." My triathlon trainer, Rachelle, inspired me on a whole different level with these words when I was comparing myself to others who seemed to be "passing me up" with their timing. I held onto these words when I would get tired and wanted to slow my pace. "You are not being fair to yourself if you only compare yourself to the ones passing you and you don't see your own success when you are passing up others. Everyone is at a different phase of training," said Rachelle as we were biking that warm August morning. That particular morning ride seemed much more challenging for me despite the prior months of practice. Even though it seemed harder that day, I pressed through and kept up the pace and went the distance. I laughed when we were done with the ride and someone checked my bike. The brakes had been slightly on the wheel the entire time. "See, you were keeping up even with the brakes on," said Rachelle.

It goes without saying that struggles, challenges and just plain life can come up against you when you are on course with your business. It's those times when you have to keep moving at your pace and not compare yourself to anyone else. Maintain your integrity, keep your passion and purpose. I hold close this mantra I made up years ago, "I won't let nothing or no one take me out! This journey is not in vain…I'm Staying Strong and Focused in ALL circumstances. I have one life and I'm Loving it!"

It has been the words of so many supportive people in my life that remind me to believe in myself and lift me up when times get rough. It's loving words like Dee said to me, "Walking through tough times show a person's true character…you look good walking Shelly." And it's also bold questions like Lisa G asked me, "Michele, how long will you keep going the way you are? When are you going to make a change?" Those people in your life that know you best are the ones who will be "in your face" because it's for your good and also to gently listen when that is what's needed.

As a new business owner just starting out, I knew I could call on my friends to help me in crunch times and when workloads were heavier and I didn't have permanent staff. I think those growing pains of starting a business are part of what establishes your business character, and we all need to experience those tougher times. It makes the "easy" times that much sweeter!

The biking segment of the triathlon was my favorite. It was the time where I now know I could have pushed myself harder, but I thoroughly enjoyed all those miles on my bike, being outside in the open air, either passing up other cyclists or being passed up myself. It was all well with my soul. My training had allowed me to be able to do that. I actually sang out loud while out on the course. Similarly, my many years of meeting planning experience have allowed me to arrive at a meeting and know it will flow smoothly because of the preparation I had put into all of the preplanning. And, when something unexpected happens, I can remain calm and handle the situation, knowing all other aspects are in order.

"One thing about you, Michele, is that even with so many challenges, you have and are going through, you look for the positive and aren't afraid to try new things to make yourself a better person," said Gerald one day after a swim, bike and run training day. Determination to press through to make your dreams come alive, whether personal or professional, is vital to be a Smart Woman who lives her WHY!

Sheri McConnell is an inspiration in so many ways and imparts what she knows to help other "Smart Women." Since meeting and interacting with Sheri, clarity to launching the Global Association for Women in Transformation has come about and I'm thrilled at what's coming next. Finding people who have paved the way and achieved the type of success you are looking for is key to moving forward. Just as it is with hiring a trainer to help me prepare for a triathlon, knowing there are others who have gone before you makes all the difference. No matter where you are on your journey of business, enjoy every part of it—the hard times when you start to second-guess your purpose, as well as the more simple times when all is flowing well. The determination you maintain, the mindset that you won't quit because you know without a doubt that's not an option, and knowing you are aligned just where you should be, will keep you pressing forward despite any obstacle or life intrusion that will come your way.

When you realize you are no longer satisfied with being complacent doing and living as others think you should, and you know deep within your soul you are pursuing your God-given purpose and passion, that's when your life will be opened to experience fulfillment. I was a business owner doing what I have done so many years, in a profession I still enjoy. But it is what God is moving me into that is lighting up my heart and countenance! As I make preparations for speaking engagements and writing books and materials, my hunger to see women move out of complacency and into a rich and full life, living it by design and pursuing their purpose and passion, is what energizes me.

As I was starting the run segment of the triathlon, I knew in the back of my mind that was the part I least enjoyed. I decided to focus on mini-distances during that part. As I was running on the hot, dusty course, I set a goal that the water stand was going to be my first accomplishment. Tasting the cold grape Gatorade was refreshing. The sweet liquid on my lips was the prize I needed to continue on. Rounding the corner at the halfway mark, seeing the calm empty lake, and knowing I had swam that course, was a visual of how far I had come. My body physically got a little taller at that point and my confidence was boosted as I recalled all I had already done. When I saw the grass area of the course, I knew the final goal was within reach. Being completely focused on getting to the finish line, there was nothing that could distract me! Yes, I was tired, my legs were telling me they were exhausted…that would be enough to want to quit. As I approached the pavement, I knew it was almost over. All of a sudden, I heard a familiar voice yelling "Go Shelly," I looked up and spotted my beautiful red-headed friend, Dee, the final encouragement I needed to keep my legs moving across that finish line! DONE! What? I did that? Wow!

My training prepared me to the place of nearing the finish line, encouraging words from others are what sustained me during the course, and my God-given determination is what kept me from giving up before crossing the line and my time being recorded as evidence I earned the title of being a triathlete. What a surreal feeling and a confirmation that if we dig deep enough within, we really have what we need to pursue our passion!

Staying focused in whatever business or personal venture you are working is a first step. Not letting outside distractions and negative influences consume you and keeping life in balance with your body, mind and soul is essential. For me, God being the one I pursue first is what keeps me going. He lines up everything else. I may make a plan of action, but He directs my steps. His provision is more than enough for me to live a successful life. And the most beautiful part is that I get the pleasure of knowing that when I am aligned with His will, moving and accomplishing what He sets up, my hearts desires are fulfilled, completely!

Michele Modellas is the owner of Meeting & Management Solutions. She works with associations and corporations to expand their organizations and marketing in the area of meetings and special events. She is also the Founder and CEO of the Global Association for Women in Transformation—Helping Women Create a Life by Design by Pursuing Their Purpose and Passion. It is her desire to be a woman of influence and inspiration in the U.S. and abroad and see people hunger to live a rich and full life, beyond what they can imagine! Michele also speaks to groups on various topics, including the area of moving out of complacency and into a life by design.

Section Three

Living in Daily Discovery

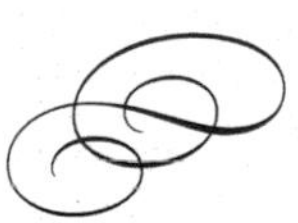

CHAPTER 22

My Safari to Success

by Meredith Hill

The word "Safari" means journey in Swahili. For 10 years, I planned incredible safaris and was blessed to explore southern Africa, both physically and through my clients. Sounds romantic, right?

Rewind 10 years earlier. I left an amazing job on Wall Street where I had everything—recognition, multiple six figures in pay, invitations to high profile parties, and a promising future. Yes, I had it all, except one thing—a passion for my work. I might have kept a smile on my face all 50 to 60 hours a week (sometimes 80 hours), but inside, my soul was dying.

So, I did a courageous thing. I left it all and traded it in for a life of entrepreneurship. I followed my passion. Definitely a good move, believing that's all I needed to be a success. Very stupid (well, if you want to be nice, call it naïve.)

If I only knew then the bumpy ride I would have for the next 10 years, I probably would have stayed. Over the next 10 years, as I planned safaris (journeys) for many, many travelers, I would experience one hell of a journey myself. I may not have encountered meat-eating predators—lions, leopards and cheetahs like my clients, but I certainly felt like that many times.

Even though it was a tumultuous journey with more peaks and valleys than the state of Colorado, I wouldn't trade it in for the world. I learned incredible lessons and have come out on top, with the world in my hand and more fulfilled than I could ever imagine.

If you are reading this and are thinking about leaving a J.O.B., or if you have left the J.O.B. but continue to struggle to get by, please know this: you can follow your passion, have your own business and be a success. They are not mutually exclusive, which is how it felt for many of my years in between.

I want you to know that you can have a successful, thriving, sustainable business doing the work you know in your heart you are here to do. As you help others, you can make lots of money…there is nothing shameful or wrong with this. You can attract wonderful clients to your business—people who make you light up with joy and feel so grateful you get to touch their lives. You can have this hugely successful business AND find balance, too. You can have a happy, healthy marriage, live in that dream home, drive a fun, sexy car, give birth to amazing children, be a great, well-rounded mother, and most importantly, make a positive difference in the world.

How do I know this? Because I made it happen (well, maybe not the sexy car, I am still in mini-van mode). When I left my Wall Street career, I jumped into entrepreneurship with excitement and too much confidence. I soon realized, I had a lot to learn. But it took a while for this stubborn Taurus to embrace the lessons, release my cockiness and be humble.

It took hitting rock bottom. Six years into my entrepreneurship journey, my life was unraveling. I woke up one day and decided to be honest about my situation: my marriage was falling apart; my children were trying to get my attention with acting out, unusual behavior and strange medical issues; my business' financial state was non-existent. The only thing that did have my attention was my business. But it wasn't giving me anything back.

The stress and lack of boundaries leaked into my personal life. There was no "off" button because I worked from home. I wanted to prove to my clients that I was good, so I would spend countless hours on trying to be an instant expert on all parts of the world. In between cooking dinner and baths, I would run up to my computer and try to "squeeze in" more work. My children would look at me with big sad eyes and ask "Mommy, why do you have to work? It's bedtime." My relationship with my husband also suffered. We were two ships passing in the night. We hardly knew each other any more.

One day, I decided to take notice of the train wreck about to happen—my family was falling apart. I thought long and hard about giving up, and I almost did. But I didn't. I wanted to prove to my children that you can follow your passion and make a profitable business out of it.

Instead of giving up, I went on a mission to learn everything I could about marketing and success for the entrepreneur. I read books, took online courses, went to workshops, purchased home study systems. You name it. Eventually, I got my business partner on board and together we learned even more. And slowly, but surely, it worked.

One of the most important lessons we learned is that marketing alone will not fix the problem. We discovered that we had to take a holistic approach to our business—incorporating marketing for sure, but also, mindset and support. And as we worked on all three, our business took off. We went from $96,000 in revenue to just over $500,000 in revenue in three short years.

It's what the business numbers have done for my life that I am most grateful. I pay myself a salary. I treat myself when I feel like it. My children are thriving. My relationship with my husband is a million times better. We were able to take my family on several dream vacations. I have help in the home. And the list goes on.

But, just when it was time for me to sit back, relax, and take in our success, the entrepreneurial bug bit yet again. Truth is, in my last 12 to 18 months in my travel business, I was questioning whether or not I was truly following my passion—because I think it can change. What I learned about myself was that I was a teacher at heart and didn't feel I was using this gift to its greatest potential.

So I decided to take Maya Angelou's beautiful advice: "When you learn, teach." I turned to the travel industry and started teaching what I had learned about building a successful travel business. And I had never felt more fulfilled in my life. I realized there were thousands and thousands of people I could help with the knowledge and experience I had accrued. But this also created a source of tension and fear. I realized that I had to choose one path. Choosing the path of teaching and mentoring in the travel industry meant that I had to give up my travel business. It meant giving up my identity.

It took a lot of courage, but I made the decision to start over and have recently started the Global Institute for Travel Entrepreneurs (GIFTE). I found it so amazing to realize that the acronym of my new venture was GIFTE. My 10-year journey of owning my business had been about discovering and claiming the power of your own gifts and then using them to drive your business.

As I look back upon my success and embark upon a new entrepreneurial venture, I see a direct correlation between my success and my ability to practice and hone 7 habits. I call these the 7 habits of highly successful, soul-inspired entrepreneurs. When you follow these habits, you will find a direct path to success.

The 7 Habits of Highly Successful, Soul-Inspired Entrepreneurs

1) Stretch—Don't ever get comfortable. Don't ever stop learning. Realize you can always do more. Stretch yourself by having a voracious appetite for books, doing things before you feel ready, and always listening to the quiet voice of desire (not the loud obnoxious one). The most effective way to stretch yourself is to hire a mentor. Think about yourself as a slinky. If you hold each end of a slinky in your hands, you can stretch the slinky as far as your arms length. But, if you give one end of the slinky to someone else, you can stretch the slinky far more…maybe two or three times more. That's what a good mentor does for you.

2) Set Clear Intentions—I used to go through life by default. It's so empowering to sit down a few times a year, and map out what you want in life. It's exciting when it starts to happen. For example, my business partner and I talked about attracting billionaires for clients. We talked about this for at least 18 months. And then one day, a billionaire showed up. Then another one. Then another one. Talk about empowering! You can control your destiny…but you need to give clear direction. Make a habit of setting clear intentions on a daily basis.

3) Seize Opportunities—one of the greatest lessons I learned is that once you set an intention, the path to your goal will NEVER be illuminated at once. Instead, what happens is opportunities show up. You have got to be willing to seize the opportunities, even if it feels uncomfortable.

In fact, the path of entrepreneurship is mostly uncomfortable, because if you are feeling comfortable, it's time to move forward.

4) Surround Yourself with a Supportive Tribe—I did NOT grow up in an entrepreneurial family. In fact, my father had two jobs during my entire childhood—for which I eternally grateful. But that means that I was navigating this entrepreneurial world solo. You can't do it alone. You need support. You need to surround yourself with people who "see" you more than you see yourself. People who will cheer you on when you are seizing opportunities that scare you to death. People who will lend an ear when you feel you can't do it anymore. People who will celebrate with you…because they GET how meaningful those successes are. People who simply understand without you having to explain.

5) Stay Focused—As creative types, we entrepreneurs get very distracted by bright, shiny objects. But that is only going to hurt you in the end. Be disciplined with your focus. You can't chase two bees at once. Pick one thing and focus on it until completion. Then move on.

6) Skin in the Game—A recent college study found that people are FAR more likely to expend effort to avoid losing a dollar than they are to gain a dollar. In other words, people will move mountains so they don't lose money, but are much less motivated to make money. As a business owner, the purpose of your business is to make money. But because of this natural human behavior to get comfortable and not have as much incentive to make money, putting skin in the game changes this dramatically. Now, all of a sudden, you have a new, bigger motivator than simply making more money to move your business forward—the fear of losing money. I have seen this with myself and many clients—the moment they put skin in the game, they do things they never dreamed possible. It's amazing and very exciting.

7) Surrender—Surrender is NOT giving up. Surrender is taking your focus off your fears, or as Lynn Grabhorn (author of *Excuse Me, Your Life is Waiting*) calls them, your "don't wants." Realizing that you've been rowing your boat upstream, surrender is the moment you let go of the oars. The moment you take your focus off your don't wants and let go of the oars, you release the resistant energy that's been preventing all your wants from flowing to you. Surrender is taking focus off your fears and putting focus on your expectation of your dreams and goals.

Surrender is bringing the power, perfection and peace of presence into your life and believing that there is a higher source who will take care of you. It's releasing the worries, anxieties, doubts and fears and knowing that all is well.

Meredith Hill, ex-President of Hills of Africa Travel, founded the Global Institute for Travel Entrepreneurs (GIFTE) to empower frustrated and struggling travel consultants by helping them to connect with their passion again, attract ideal clients, and build a business that makes a positive difference in people's lives.

In 2007, faced with a long-standing struggle of not having enough clients in her travel business, Hills of Africa Travel was on the verge of closing its doors. Instead, Meredith used her gift for finding the path to success no matter what the odds. Realizing they had to revolutionize their marketing, she and business partner, Sandy Salle, looked to other industries for direction, and began applying cutting-edge, effective marketing techniques for the small business, learning in the process, the importance of passion, mindset and support for entrepreneurs in travel.

Thanks to their determination and efforts, the company doubled its income within the first year. During three of the most difficult economic years in travel history, Hills of Africa quadrupled its business and was doubly proud of hitting a milestone in 2010, when they surpassed $1.6 million in sales.

Meredith has a never-ending love for Africa, but her deepest passion lies in empowering travel business owners who want to make a difference. She founded GIFTE after noticing many travel professionals alone, at a standstill, trying to navigate the unchartered waters of an industry experiencing major change. Meredith's goal is to revolutionize the travel industry by helping people connect with their passion again, adopt a mindset for success, get desperately needed support and build successful travel businesses that change people's lives. Meredith continues to use her gift to blaze new trails and guide her clients to their paths of success.

CHAPTER 23

Cinderella Success Strategies 10 Hidden Storybook Secrets for Success in Life and Business

by Donna Duffy

Once upon a time in a land far away, lived a young servant girl named Cinderella. It's likely that most of us are already familiar with her and her rags to riches story. But if we look more closely into her life, we see a tenacious, resourceful woman determined, against all odds, to live her WHY. Here are a few of her timeless wisdom lessons:

I'm a worm; I'm wonder woman.

As women, we vacillate between thinking we can conquer the world and then think, "What am I thinking?" We struggle with our worth, our weight and our wonder. We stack ourselves up against those who are more successful and think, "I can do that—I can never do that." In our quest toward excellence, we bump into our weaknesses and failures, but if we're true to ourselves and our calling, we'll embrace our WHY and purpose and use them to help bring our authentic message to the world.

Cinderella sidebar.

From the hearth to the ballroom, tell me she wasn't thinking—"Are you talking to me?" Fairytale or not, we all identify because we've all been there, and the truth is no matter what struggles or foibles we possess (worm), we also possess some pretty incredible strengths and gifts (wonder woman). Embracing ourselves as we are, the good, the bad and the ugly, gives others the courage to be just as authentic as they pursue and realize their own success.

Make the best with what you've got.

You don't have everything you need and most certainly not everything you want but you have what you have, so work with it. Waiting till we've acquired everything will be too late! The world is changing much too fast and we have to step up to stay in the running. So look at what you have in your hands right now and make the most of it. Use it to grow yourself and your business and more will come. What you're walking toward is walking toward you, so trust that you'll have all you need every step of the way and do your best to learn, grow and evolve in the process.

Cinderella sidebar.

With no shopping mall in sight, she had to resort to using what she had in her hand and right there around her. I love that everyday things were repurposed to position her in the right place at the right time. She didn't take herself out of the running because she didn't have what everyone else did. She made the best of it and in the end was prized more than all the rest.

Things aren't always as they seem—believe beyond the moment.

Think of where you are right now and where you want to be. The truth is the potential and possibility you offer the world are already within you. Sure, you may need to work on your mindset, get your marketing together and make your way in the marketplace, but the good news is that your passion and your purpose are the very things that will fuel you and keep you going in that direction every day. You've got to see yourself in it, trusting that the thing you're meant to do, you'll be equipped to do.

Cinderella sidebar

Now take a look at the girl. At first glance, does she look like she's headed anywhere special, let alone going to end up being the princess? I don't think so. We quickly size up this little waif and easily write her off as not having what it takes to even show up; forget wowing the prince and living happily ever after. If she didn't believe, she would have been finished. Only as she saw herself beyond the place and circumstance she was in, could she elevate her thinking to bust out of there and write another chapter in the book of her life.

Live your dream in the moments in between.

None of us has the luxury of completely pushing the pause button while we pursue our dreams. In fact, dreams lived apart from reality are illusions. There is much to be done in the plain mundane of life. There are things we put our hands to every day that help us become excellent at what we do, and with our dreams and purpose woven in between, we impact and influence those around us and we are changed in the process; our dreams are realized.

Cinderella sidebar.
Cinderella was no slacker. She has her scary, overpowering stepmother and hateful stepsisters to deal with every day. She didn't trot off to the meadow to journal and ponder about her dreams. No, she got on with the tasks at hand, faithfully serving and doing, but in her heart she was preparing for something better. In between the chores and demands, Cinderella grabbed snatches of time to prepare for the ball. In fact, she was so good at what she was doing; no one even noticed that she was taking time for herself. But when her moment came, she emerged and realized what she thought at the time was her dream. Little did she know there was something even greater that would soon come her way.

Never forget where you came from.
None of us got where we are today by ourselves, and our stories and paths that it took to get here are not always pretty but here we are. That story, your story is part of who you are, and believe it or not, it can be mightily used to bring shift and change into the lives of others. You can't hide where you came from. In fact, sharing it with others as you rise in success helps them know that their stories are not deal breakers, disqualifying them for the race—just the opposite. It's your story, your personal path of pain and struggle, your journey of victory and triumph over adversity that makes you so much more powerful. Seeing what you had to overcome and endure infuses others with hope and the courage they need to pursue their dreams.

Cinderella sidebar.
When I think of Cinderella, one of the first words that comes to mind is humility. No pride, no ego. She knows where she came from and steps up anyway. Good for her that she didn't talk herself out of it and head back to her chores. Despite her circumstances, she stepped up when the opportunity came and went from a lowly, unknown servant to headline news.

Embrace your unique gifts, talents and strengths and use them to bless others.
You are you! Take that in for a sec. Soak in the truth and the knowledge that who you are is totally one-of-a-kind, and the message you have to bring to the world is for those who need to hear it. That's what you were born to do. Are you doing it? Are you busy about it or are you sifting through your gifts and talents, not sure what to do with them? Ask! Then sit and listen to the answers that come. Watch who appears in your life; the opportunities that are before you. Open your eyes and see! This is your moment to live and be; your time to put into action the gifts you've been given so you can bless and be blessed.

Cinderella sidebar.
Only what she had in her hand; that's all she had to work with—her tenacity, character and dreams lifted her up and out to a whole new place in life. She knew who she was and took charge using the gifts and talents that she possessed. Not waiting to be better equipped, she took imperfect action and stepped out. That is what we need to do as well and soon we'll see the ground as magically grown under our feet.

Don't waste your energy on payback—the Universe already has taken care of that.
I don't have to waste one minute plotting and planning on how to get back at those who have done me dirty. Call it what you will—karma or the law of reaping and sowing. What I know is it's not in my hand. It's not for me to worry myself over or spend my energy on. My life should be about creating, growing, serving and equipping. Building up, not tearing down; focused on positive things, not negative things. Use your energy to impact the world for good, steering clear of the things that pull you down. The world is far better served that way and so are we.

Cinderella sidebar.
I don't recall my Grandmom ever reading me the part of the story where Cinderella takes revenge. That's because she never does. She didn't waste her time setting up the nasty stepfamily for harm, but instead, kept intent on making herself and her circumstances better. That little lesson alone could save us so much time, energy and heartache.

Get by with a little help from your friends.
It takes more than a village if you ask me. Think of the support you

have around you from your family, friends, colleagues and fans—they're everywhere and so it's meant to be. If I learned anything from my years living in the Middle East, it's that we are here for one another. Life is richer, better and more bearable because we do not go it alone.

Cinderella sidebar.
Try to imagine where Cinderella would be if not for her amazingly talented furry friends, her fairy godmother and that magic wand! I'm going venture a guess that a good bit of her tenacity and triumph came as a result of her peeps whispering in her ear. Just knowing that they were there to help her through her transformation made the sheer task of it so much more bearable. I can't imagine where I'd be today without those sent to me as gifts to tell me to keep running forward and never give up!

Remember that nothing is wasted.
This is so good for us to tuck away in our minds and never forget. Every thread; every experience, person, trial and joy is woven together to make up the fabric of your life and who you are today. What may seem like setbacks in your life are actually stepping stones to success.

Cinderella sidebar.
Did the fact that fate had left her tethered to her dysfunctional family stop her? Did her rag bag clothes and need for an extreme beauty makeover stop her? Did her complete obscurity and one-in-a-million chance of making it stop her? We know the answer—she pressed on, and with everything hurled at her, every setback, she was undaunted! She finally makes it out, the clock strikes 12; it seems that all has failed. Beautiful dress back to ratty old clothes, carriage back into a pumpkin, glass slipper lost. You'd think she'd just call it quits. After all, she already tried and seemingly failed. Why try again? Because that's all there is! Getting back up, trusting, believing and working until our change comes.

Trust in the One who can truly make things change in your life.
For me, this is where my hope lies. To know there is One greater than me, looking out for me and working things together for my good is uplifting, inspiring and empowering. I am NEVER alone. The things I'm hoping to do in the world were planted in my heart to do before I was even born. The purpose and passion that drive me come from within

and from beyond and help me know that it's not just my bright idea that I'm pursuing but something I'm truly meant to do. With that knowledge, I equip myself daily for the task at hand. I give it my best and my all, even on days when I'd rather just quit. I'm in a Universal partnership with One greater, higher, wiser and stronger as well as with those poised and purposed for greatness and the change they'll bring to the world. I wouldn't have it any other way.

Cinderella sidebar.
Here's a girl who looks like she's found her lot in life—to serve and slave for every whim and whining of her unloving, unkind family. But that's just how the story starts; it's not how it ends. In fact, she was being groomed and prepared for her place in the world all along. Deep down, she knew it. That's why she never settled for a life at the hearth. She was to serve a higher purpose than for three greedy, selfish women. In the end, all that was lost was restored. The slipper fit on only one person and it was her. The task, your dreams, your glass slipper—they are yours, for you to do. One greater than you has intended it and now it is up to you to live it!

And they all lived happily ever after who did what they were born to do and walked in the gifts they were given to bring blessing to the world!

Along with 3E Marketing Solutions, Donna Duffy is the co-owner of two other small businesses, Academic Connections Tutoring and Memorable Milestones Event Planning. Her passion is to build community and help others realize and develop their potential especially in the area of events, education and entrepreneurship.

Donna has led weekly 3E Women's Circle meetings, helping local entrepreneurial women become more enlightened, equipped and engaged as they pursue their passion and purpose in the marketplace. She also leads workshops and seminars that help women work through their Marketing MRI—Mindset, Resources, and Identity.

As a member of her local chamber of commerce, Donna has led

networking meetings for event professionals and teaches classes in their Chamber Academy on affordable marketing strategies and solutions. She enjoys a grassroots approach to networking and has led a kitchen table, breakfast mastermind meeting for small business owners in her own backyard.

Donna and her family returned to the U.S. and moved to Delaware after living in Nazareth, Israel for many years, where she was instrumental in heading up educational and community projects, including a school for Arab-American students.

Recently divorced, Donna has experienced the pain, the lessons and the gifts of transition and starting over. She is now helping and coaching women as they move through their trials to transformation on the pathway of transition. Her mission is to help women learn to live out their WHY and she is excited to see the change and impact they are making in large and small ways in the world around them.

Donna's quest for authenticity and wholeness is coupled with a sincere faith and heartfelt desire to bless others with the gifts and strengths she's been given and she enjoys doing that through coaching, teaching, writing, and speaking.

CHAPTER 24

Embrace Your Luxuality to Become a Blissful Entrepreneur

by Kate Navarro Fessler

Starting your own business when you've been an employee all your life can be like going to a foreign country without knowing the language. It's exotic and beautiful and you really love the food, but it takes awhile before you understand how to navigate your way around, much less are able to have any meaningful communication with the natives. And there are a lot of things you need to learn before you can live there comfortably.

When I started my journey from employee to entrepreneur, I was unprepared for the obstacles I would encounter. I had pretty successfully navigated corporate America, and I considered myself to be fairly intelligent—how hard could it be?

My husband tells me I could sell a block of ice to an Alaskan in winter. I can certainly be persuasive when there's something I really want. But when it came to selling my services—actually enrolling clients—I choked. I thought all I needed was a little guidance about marketing—ezines and sales pages and such. What I discovered was that I needed so much more than that.

If you're like me, you've gotten pretty far doing what you do. And if you're like me, you're a little skeptical when presented with new ways of thinking. My subconscious was working overtime trying to sabotage my plans. Confusion reigned. My body rebelled. I had no energy. I was depressed. I compared myself to others and came up lacking. My confidence level was frighteningly low. I thought I had made a big mistake.

Maybe I should just forget about this dream and go get another job!

No. I wouldn't do it. I hadn't come this far to retreat, and I knew getting a job would not be postponement, but the death, of my dream. I felt like it was now or never. I wasn't getting any younger. I had to figure it out!

I sought out mentors and programs. I learned about how to build an email list. I learned how to craft my signature talk. I learned how to do teleseminars and an ezine, and what not to put on my business card. I learned the copywriting buzzwords that would have my clients falling all over each other to work with me. I even learned my life purpose and my life lesson. And, of course, turning your passions into work you love was my area of expertise!

The mentors were fabulous. The programs were the best.

But it wasn't working.

At a laser coaching intensive with one of my mentors, who is very direct, I was asked to write down the completion of this sentence: I am [blank]. I wrote down a couple of things, and I got stuck. I was embarrassed to write down complimentary things about myself. And I was appalled that most of the answers coming to me were negative. I certainly didn't want to share that with the group!

The problem was that even though I knew my material, I lacked confidence in my abilities. And as confirmed through this exercise, I was a little low on self-esteem. This mentor reminded me of chapter 14 in the *Science of Getting Rich*, which talks about how to be successful in attracting clients, you must convey to them the "impression of increase."

So I had to cultivate this "impression of increase" so that I could attract clients. But how could I do that? I had bills to pay. I *seemed* desperate because I *was* desperate! I was sending out vibrations of neediness because I needed income and I needed it now! How could I become serene and confident and project this impression of increase when I was experiencing anxiety and lack?

I discovered that I had a "deserving deficit." Deep down inside, I didn't really believe that I deserved to be successful, or that I really could create whatever life I wanted for myself.

All the marketing and sales techniques in the world, no matter how well they worked for other people, weren't going to help me.

At some point, in order to truly grow, I had to surrender to the paradox. I had to start living my dream before I could help others to live theirs. I had to uplevel my own life before anyone would believe I could help them create a better life for themselves. I had to feel successful before I could be successful.

I had to become the star of my own movie, the queen of my own life.

So I made that my mission. I figured if I was struggling with this, maybe others were, too. Your greatest challenge usually turns out to be where your "gold" is. In searching for a solution to my greatest challenge, I turned adversity into opportunity and found my unique message.

I even coined a term for it. I call it embracing your "Luxuality," and it's based on three core principles that are essential to success, particularly for a service-based entrepreneur: self-worth, self-care, and self-expression. And then I turned these principles into a process I could share with my clients that would guide them on the journey from deserving deficit to blissful entrepreneur!

The process is called the Queen Rules, a foundational blueprint for luxurious living. When I use the term "luxurious living," I'm not talking about conspicuous consumption or an excessive lifestyle. I'm taking about an authentic life of freedom, choice and prosperity. It's about doing what you want, when you want, and with whomever you wish. It's about serving your clients at your highest level and helping them to transform their lives in ways that only you can because you're fully showing up in the world and sharing your extraordinary gifts.

My personal and professional growth has been phenomenal since I've put these principles into action, and my clients have reported similar results. You may not want a high-priced lifestyle, or you might want to amass billions, it doesn't really matter. The foundation is about choice.

It's about knowing you deserve to have what you want, to take extraordinary care of yourself without feeling guilty, and really being grounded in who you are and what you have to offer so you can fully express your brilliance—and yes, everyone, I don't care who you are, has brilliance inside of them that someone, somewhere is waiting for you to let shine.

Here are a few tips from the first part, the QUEEN portion of the process, that you can apply right away, to embrace *your* Luxuality and become a blissful entrepreneur!

Quality

You deserve the best. Period. There's an old saying that "living well is the best revenge." Forget revenge, I say, 'living well is the best!"

William Morris, a leader in the Arts & Crafts movement in the 1800s said "Have nothing in your house that you do not know to be useful, or believe to be beautiful." I would expand that to your entire life, including your relationships, your thoughts and behaviors, and anything or anyone which you choose to bring into your world.

I usually ask my clients to do an inventory of their life, to rank everything on a scale of 0-10, with 10 being you are completely delighted with it, wouldn't change a thing. One woman was so overwhelmed by how much she was tolerating that didn't support her that she broke down in tears. The good news is, this is just a baseline and it's always best to know from where you are starting when you embark upon an unfamiliar—but very rewarding journey. And the rest of the process is designed to get you to where you want to be, regardless of where you begin.

Upgrade!

You can't live like a queen if you treat yourself like a peasant. And you can't deliver 6-star service to your clients if you're living a 2-star life. Anything that ranks five or below on the scale needs immediate attention. Take it slowly at first and build momentum. You'll soon find that it's a joyful process to continually attract better and better things, people, experiences and opportunities into your life.

Another client was so relieved when she gave herself permission to want to be surrounded by beautiful things. She had been operating under the false belief that true service meant personal sacrifice. She immediately saw an increase in not only her enjoyment of life, but the quality of client she was attracting!

Let go of the myth of self-sacrifice. It doesn't serve you or your clients. Be open to receiving, and accept opportunities to upgrade in everything, from the way you communicate to flying first class when you travel. Remember, you deserve the best!

Environment

Where we live, the conditions in which we work, and people with whom we surround ourselves, our daily thoughts, behaviors and rituals are all important in supporting us on our journey.

Your environment should feed your soul and fuel your creativity. Clear out clutter and surround yourself with things and people that uplift your spirit.

My office used to be filled with piles of stuff. Books, papers, workshop manuals, magazines I wanted to read, mail that needed to be opened. Of course I knew where everything was. But finding things wasn't the issue. All that clutter left little room for my creativity to flow. I was so used to it, I hardly noticed, except when one of the piles fell over, cascading across the floor! Once I started to really see it, it felt like a prison. Clearing it all out made me feel physically lighter. And guess what? Now that I can actually set a vase of fresh flowers on my desk, new ideas come to me more easily, too.

Energy

Being an entrepreneur takes a lot of energy, and you'll want to guard your energy and use it wisely. Your outer world is a manifestation of your inner world. If you're stressed or exhausted, people will notice, no matter how well you think you're hiding it.

Cultivate self-care practices. Take good care of the vessel, and be sure to refill your internal cup on a regular basis. You can't serve others if you let the cup run dry. Engage in activities that keep your mind, body and spirit energized daily.

Stop struggling! Success doesn't have to be hard. Don't get caught up in negative thoughts or surround yourself with negative people. Don't indulge in gossip or speculation about anyone else.

Align your energy with your purpose, your passion and your desires. When we are in alignment, things flow. When we are out of alignment—well, you know what that feels like. Incorporate rituals of clearing and alignment into your daily routine.

Nurture

Your journey to a being the queen of your life may be a fragile thing at first. Like a newly planted seed, you must give it care and feeding and protect it from destructive influences.

Take good care of yourself, listen to your inner guidance and cultivate your creativity. Put your best self forward and show up in the world as the unique and impressive being that you are.

Be open to new opportunities that will come your way. Nurture a new image of yourself as a beautiful, confident, and brilliant, blissful entrepreneur!

There's more, of course, but if you put these tips into action, you'll start to notice a difference immediately. I hope it will help you to become not just comfortable, but joyful, living in the land of entrepreneurship. After all, you don't want to create just another job for yourself, but a wildly successful business that enhances and supports your blissfully luxurious life!

No matter whether you're a minimum-wage employee with a big dream or on your way to owning a billion dollar enterprise, you deserve to treat yourself like a queen, embrace your Luxuality and have the life, and business, you desire!

Kate Navarro Fessler is a former-employee-turned-entrepreneur, coach, mentor, speaker, and now a published author! Her mission is to inspire and empower women in transition to reinvent themselves and create blissfully luxurious lives of freedom, choice and prosperity.

With her unique Embrace Your Luxuality program (www.myluxurious-life.com) and her signature QUEEN RULES process, she empowers women to break free of the myths of struggle and self-sacrifice and create lives of abundance, beauty, grace, ease and elegance. Through the Blissful Entrepreneur (www.blissfulentrepreneur.com), Kate provides training, tools, resources, and business mentoring services to help women create meaningful, fulfilling businesses that enhance and support their blissfully luxurious lives.

Kate lives in Seattle with her husband, James, and their chocolate lab, Freyja. She is an avid traveler, and food and wine enthusiast, and she often incorporates these passions into her programs. She is currently working on the full book version of the QUEEN RULES. For more information or to pre-order see www.queenrules.com.

CHAPTER 25

Do What You Came Here to Do!

by Peri Coeurtney Enkin

"Everyone has a calling and your real job in life is to figure out what that is and to get about the business of doing it." —Oprah

So many times I wanted to throw in the towel. I wanted someone else to take over for me. I wanted relief from overwhelm and struggle. And I didn't understand why I was working so hard for so few results.

It took me a long time before I understood I was not alone with these feelings. I thought other people had this "entrepreneur thing" easily figured out. It appeared that way on the outside and it confused me. I was bright, creative and passionate about what I was doing. What was I doing wrong? I was sure there must be an important ingredient for success that I was missing and I wanted to know what it was.

As I talked with other passionate people who were up to big work in the world I discovered that even the most successful among them had periods of doubt, worry and frustration. They got overwhelmed and experienced stress, too. Many had burnt out, gotten back up and started over. But here is what I learned also. The entrepreneurs who were successful had each discovered and put in place their own personal practices for meeting challenges so they could move through them quickly. Sure they got stuck but they weren't going to stay there.

Nurture Your Spark

One savvy entrepreneur takes a full day away from all technology each and every week. No computer, no phone, no Ipad and no email.

Another has her massages and pedicures at her home so she doesn't have to drive in heavy traffic.

For years I've shared a monthly spa day with my women friends. I have a regular journal writing practice that helps me get right with myself and with the Universe. When I feel unsettled or confused about my business, the first thing I do is pull out my journal.

I make sure the dance classes I love are on my calendar and appointments get scheduled around them. And I read a lot.

There are days when I can't stand to sit at my desk a moment longer. And I live in Hawaii! So I take my audio programs, journal and books to a quiet beach and I work from there. There is nothing more recharging than a day by the ocean or somewhere in nature. I make sure I do it often.

Writing, reading, movement, good friends, and beautiful environments all nurture my spark. What nurtures yours? If you don't know what it is make a decision to discover it. If you do know, I encourage you to make room in your schedule for whatever lights you up and do it regularly. Self-care increases our reserves. It gives us stamina for the long-haul, and as entrepreneurs, we aren't in this for a quick fix.

Declare and Commit

Ordinary thinking tells us to commit after we see results when it's actually commitment that sets the stage for our success. Right out the gate this is often a key missing ingredient that must be put in place. It's something I ask of my clients before we begin any mentoring relationship. They have my full commitment and they need to have their own.

One foot in and one foot out the door with sneakers on does not cut it. We can't muster our full energy if we are not fully in the game. Big changes happen when we declare our purpose and commit to it. Energy we didn't know we had carries us through days when we don't think we have it in us. We tap into resources that were previously out of reach. And the Universe truly does organize around our commitments. Unexpected opportunities and support shows up as if by magic. It's not magic. It's the power of our commitment that attracts and makes us magnetic.

Trust Life

I knew, from a very young age, that invisible forces were guiding me and helping me. Still, it took me a long time to realize I didn't need to figure it all out before taking action. I had lessons to learn and skills to develop.

If I were to put it simply, I'd say I had to get on board with transforming myself into an instrument for the fulfillment of my calling. I had to get out of my own way. I had to do my part in my partnership with something greater than my self and I had to be willing to get on with the business of doing what I came here to do in the first place.

This may sound easy but of course our human stories are much more complex than what I've described above. We are creatures of habit and change is not something we embrace easily. When faced with letting go, transforming ourselves, doing something new and out of the ordinary most of us hold back. We resist. We dig in our heels and refuse to move forward. We get stubborn. We hit walls. We build walls. We tear down walls. We climb the walls. Sometimes we bounce off the walls!

Eventually, as we open ourselves and learn to let ourselves be supported, we discover we are connected to a wise and loving life force. The bumps in the road that once stopped us from expressing our potentials now help us reveal and polish our brilliance so we can achieve our goals and help others achieve theirs also.

Be Yourself

Most of us have moments when we compare our lives with others. Usually our life comes up short. Once I was convinced I would be much more satisfied with my best friend's life. She had babies while I was buried in paperwork writing my thesis. She bought a house while I was designing workshops and scrapping to pay my rent. She drove a brand new BMW while I had an ancient patched up Audi that kept breaking down on the highway when I was alone.

She was having great sex every night with her husband (I know this because we are women and we talk!). I was dating weird characters that came out of the woodwork to complicate my life. Her life looked a whole lot easier, and more attractive than mine.

At the same time, she thought my life was much more exciting than hers and she feared she was missing out on the grand adventures I was having. We laughed about it together but deep down we questioned our own choices. Had we taken wrong turns? Who had made the better decisions? Why did we take the path we did? What motivated us and more importantly what would we choose for our futures?

You know those movies where the actors switch bodies and experience someone else's life for a period of time only to end up returning home and appreciating what they once took for granted? If we had been identical twins I think we might have tried a switch ourselves—for a day or two. Deep down, I think that's all it would have taken for us to realize how closely our lives were aligned with our personal values and nothing was wrong in her life or mine. I like those movies. They remind me to stay true to my bones—and to be grateful.

Comparing ourselves to others is counterproductive. It slows us down and stifles our creativity. And it's a signal that we've gotten disconnected from the truth at our own center. Instead of looking outside for validation it alerts us to turn inward with self-acceptance, self-respect, and honor.

I remember hearing Oprah busting the notion that it's wrong to be "full of your self."

"If you are not full of your self *who* are you supposed to be full of?" she asked shrugging her shoulders with that wise revealing look in her eyes that those of us who admire her grew to love and respect. "I mean really—who should you be full of if not your self?" Her words make big sense to me.

Listen to the Whispers

When we watch children play we get glimpses of their unique callings. It's easy to see budding scientists, artists and entertainers. If you are not clear about what you came here to do, you'll find clues by reflecting on both your childhood delights and disappointments.

Dreams, desires, interests, talents, gifts and quirks appear early on. They are like rivers of truth that run through us highlighting our preferences, defining our uniqueness and making us precious and magnificent. They are bigger than our small minds, larger than our personalities and they guide us to genuine happiness IF we listen to their messages and heed them.

I love this story told by Alan Cohen.

> *When a woman in a certain African tribe knows she is pregnant, she goes out into the wilderness with a few friends and together they sing, chant, and meditate until they hear the song of the child. They recognize that every soul has its own vibration that expresses its unique flavor and purpose. When the women attune to the song, they sing it out loud. Then they return to the tribe and teach it to everyone else.*
>
> *When the child is born, the community gathers and sings the child's song to them. Later, when the child enters education, the village gathers and chants the child's song. When the child passes through the initiation to adulthood, the people again come together and sing. At the time of marriage, the person again hears their song.*
>
> *Finally, when the soul is about to pass from this world, the family and friends gather at the person's bed, just as they did at their birth, and they sing their song as a part of "being with" them at the very end.*

In our culture it is more common for the first part of our life to be a time when we get filled up with other people's ideas of who we should and shouldn't be. Our work, as we grow and individuate is to listen deeply for our own song, to embody it and to sing it.

Values and soul intentions evolve slowly over the course of a lifetime but the core of us stays steady and unchanged. Our potentials get revealed and refined as we claim our power and choose our purpose but they are in us from the start just like the acorn carries the potential to become the oak tree.

Don't Give Up

Yes, there is hard work to do. Yes, it takes time and energy and focus. But here's a question I've asked myself when fantasies about doing something else caught my attention. What else are you going to do with your precious life that will be more meaningful than fulfilling your calling? What could be better than doing what you came here to do?

When you are on purpose you know it, your body knows it, your friends know it and it feels good on you.

The truth is these are great gifts we give ourselves: This choice to lead our own lives, to champion our own purpose and to go for our dreams. Many people don't. In fact, many will tell you not to. But if you relax about it, and settle in for the ride, you will get there. There will be bursts and breakthroughs but I have found steady, consistent action creates the way. It takes as long as it takes. Along the way, you build skills and stamina. You need both of these things.

The Universe supports your success and wants it for you. Really it does. Sometimes we forget this. Partners are everywhere. I, for one, celebrate you and your unique calling and encourage you to keep shining. Bravo! You are here. You are on your way to fulfilling your calling. What could be better than that? You are Magnificent!

Peri Coeurtney Enkin is an author, success mentor and the Founder of Creators Choice, a company dedicated to helping Spirited Entrepreneurs who are passionate about fulfilling their calling with practical systems for creating their unique projects and enriching the lives of those they serve.

Her book, *Love Letters From Your Higher Self* and the accompanying workbook *Dancing With The Universe* lovingly reminds us that we have access to all the resources we need to fulfill our calling and that we are not alone in our journey to do what we came here to do. She has developed a successful and innovative business helping others create and package their unique content into programs so they can take them to the world. Peri has over 25 years of experience facilitating programs, seminars and live events, and brings her passion and devotion to her mentoring of others as they choose and design the containers and signature systems for their own core messages.

She taught at Vancouver Community College, gave seminars in England

and Switzerland, and now custom-designs programs for private clients around the world. Her programs include:

- The Turnaround™
- Whole Person
- Aware Entrepreneurs™
- The Core Experience
- Create Your Own Seminar, Program or Retreat & Take It To The World™

Through her VIP private mentoring, life purpose strategy sessions, global immersion training and retreats, Peri supports passionate people to:

- Transform defeat and hopelessness into confidence and exhilaration
- Build strong creative muscles and stamina
- Make Empowered Choices that place them on a trajectory for the fulfillment of their deepest yearnings
- Design practical systems and structures for easy expression of their unique and specific talents and gifts
- Anchor into their value and worth to attract their tribe of clients and customers
- Align their Human Lives with their Spiritual Intentions
- Enjoy being Aware Entrepreneurs

Peri makes her home on the Big Island of Hawaii. You'll find the spirit of Aloha infuses her work like a tropical breeze reminding you of the value of relaxation in the ongoing creation of your greatest life. Visit her at www.creatorschoice.com.

CHAPTER 26

Joy Beyond Your Dreams—It's Absolutely Possible!

by Kelly Epperson

As I ripen into my true self, I feel constant love and gratitude. Every day I wake up feeling thankful. I say the words, "I love my life."

It astounds me how many women can't say that.

I've created a life I love, and I'm no magician. I'm not "special" "gifted" or "lucky." It's the old cliché that if I can do it, anyone can. My mantra has become: Never say never. If a former IRS agent can become an agent of joy, anything is possible!

The "former IRS agent" title is now a tidbit folks use when introducing me at speaking engagements. It gets a laugh and shows that you can make a 180 in life.

I used to be like the majority of the American population, terrified of public speaking. I also used to be like many women, living on autopilot. I had the requisite husband, job, kids, dog, and minivan. In society's eyes, I had it all. So why did I have an ache inside? Why did I think "*What's wrong with me?*" I wasn't even sure what it was I wanted, and yet I felt guilty for wanting it.

I let the quiet nag of an internal dissatisfaction be silenced beneath all the Shoulds, Duties, and Obligations (SDOs). Taking care of everyone and everything else is what a "good" woman does. But something in me knew there was more.

Most of us get gradual chunks of awakening. That's how it works for me anyway. Digging through old journals, I found three straight pages of "I am so sad. I am so sad. I am sad." I chalked it up to a bad bout of PMS, but this grabbed me: "I don't let my real self out much."

The SDOs had taken over, and I'd allowed myself to get cut off from my real self, my Inner Voice, my IV. We all have an IV, and it truly is our lifeline. If we get unhooked from it, we shrivel up and our real selves go dormant.

When I began listening to my IV, my life started to change. I tapped into "me" again. Now my IV and I are constantly in the flow, and when an occasional kink happens, I feel it. I feel it physically and emotionally. I get back on track and keep joyfully exploring the path ahead of me. With hand on heart, I proclaim that my IV has NEVER steered me wrong.

Think about it. When you know something feels right, or for that matter, absolutely wrong, you feel it, you feel it in your veins. Your IV is telling you what to do.

Tune in to your Inner Voice every step of the way. Mine has led me here and I'm singing "I've only just begun."

So how does an IRS agent become the "Joy Fairy" teaching other women how to live joyfully? Well, I do in fact have sparkly fairy dust and a magic wand, but my journey has been one of baby steps. I used to chide myself for baby steps, but baby stepping is still forward motion.

One thing I did to start creating this life I love was to leave my cushy government job. Many people thought I was nuts to leave Uncle Sam and financial security, but my IV told me to step out.

It was scary, but I did it.

Another thing I did was leave my cushy 20-year marriage. Many people thought I was nuts to leave my husband and financial security, but my IV told me to step out.

It was scary, but I did it.

I don't want to sound glib about divorce. Becoming unmarried was gut-wrenching, sad, and difficult. It was a long time coming, a culmination that led to that point. As painful as divorce is, my IV was right and letting go of each other was the best thing for both of us.

The key words are letting go. Letting go is the hardest thing we humans ever do. It is in the letting go that we let in the space for what our souls really want. Letting go of the SDOs, letting go of other's opinions of us (we cannot control that anyway), and letting go of (fill in your blank here) is a huge step.

So what is my guidance for women seeking to find fulfillment? Quit your job and dump your husband? Absolutely not. That was part of my journey, and in retrospect those seem like big leaps and not baby steps after all, but the heart of the matter can be summed up in one very old saying: To Thine Own Self Be True.

Life is meant to be lived, joyously, fully, deep and wide, and with a bit of whimsy. We can skate across the surface and fulfill all the SDOs, or we can take a journey full of adventure. There is nothing more adventurous or more fun than being able to wake up every day and proclaim: "I love my life."

My career path led from IRS auditor to ESL instructor to joining the staff of a local non-profit agency that teaches adults how to read to going solo as a full-time freelance writer, and now author/speaker/happiness consultant.

Every decision stemmed from asking my heart what to do and following through. ("Follow Your Bliss" is very good advice.) The advice may be simple, but the acting on it is not always easy.

In my times of transitioning, I learned that it was okay to get the support of others. I had always been the uplifter, the listener, the encourager, and to accept help from others was new and different. A quote that spoke to me at the time included the phrase, "Pears cannot ripen alone, so we ripened together." Those words are still painted on my dining room wall.

Using the wisdom of others who have traveled the path before me makes me stronger. Now I know the value of investing my time, energy, and money into me and my business and into my very soul. The dollar cost may be an "expense" for me, but my entire life benefits. The return on investment is immeasurable.

Loving life is what we are all meant to do. Honing in on one's passion, your dream, and taking leaps or baby steps to live that life is not for the somebody elses of the world. It's for all of us. Spreading that joy and teaching that JOY means the Journey of You is my mission, my WHY.

A quote on my desk states: "To love what you do and feel that it matters—how could anything be more fun?" Katherine Graham hit it on the head. I have that fun life and I get to help others live their fun life. Pinch me!

Working with women these past five years has shown me that we females often lose our self-confidence somewhere along the way. When you learn how to be unabashedly you, you light up and the music of your heart starts to play again. Your IV wants you to dance!

Your joy is within your reach. Please, never say never. I've got a gazillion examples. For starters, I overcame my fear of public speaking. Long story short: Because of my newspaper column, I was asked to talk to a group. I was nervous (that's an understatement), but my IV said go for it. There were 12 sweet retired guys sitting around a breakfast table. When I stood up to speak, I froze. My mind went blank. My prepared sentences became awkward rambling. It was awful.

In my newspaper column the next week, I wrote about what a train wreck it was. Someone else invited me to speak to their women's group.

That baffled me, and tickled me, so I tried it again. It went much better. Baby step by baby step, I kept getting speaking invitations and now I love it. A room of 350 folks laughing and more importantly taking the message to heart brings me joy one hundredfold. Becoming a speaker is a testament to the "Never say never" mindset. There are abilities inside of you that you never thought possible.

We all know to be scared and do it anyway. One of my fave quotes is: *"Anything I've ever done that ultimately was worthwhile initially scared me to death."* —Betty Bender

Right here, right now, make a vow to tune into your IV, to be unabashedly you. What are you waiting for? You don't have to quit your job or ditch your husband. You have to believe in you, even when others don't "get" you or your business dreams.

You have to know that you sparkle when you let your real self out. (When I did my first vision board, the word sparkle/sparkly appeared several times.) When you regain your self-confidence (you may not even realize it has taken a vacation), you begin to make your decisions based on what brings you joy. Listening to your IV is the best thing for your physical, mental, emotional, and spiritual health.

Pinky, promise right now that you will start to do these small tips. Upping your happiness quotient reaps positive long term rewards. FYI—No matter what your inborn internal happiness set-point is does not matter. You can increase your happiness, your confidence, your joy with these steps.

Your choices will no longer be based on the SDOs. Your business plans and your daily life will flow more smoothly because you are operating from a place of internal calm instead of a frantic desire to succeed.

As you proceed on your path, your business will grow and you will have more choices. You will know to stop and take a breath. You will ask your heart, because your heart knows. I am continually having to say no to good opportunities because although good, they are not aligned with my joy. You will get "in the zone" and be able to make clear decisions, because you feel it in your veins if it is right or wrong.

These initial tips are simple. Some folks originally scoffed, then were amazed at the results. Truthfully, all the tips you ever need to know are simple; they just require action.

1. Start a JOY Journal. All the self-help gurus will tell you that a habit of thankfulness can change your life. The American Happiness Association (it exists and I'm a member) states that gratitude is the #1 happiness booster. Simply grab a notebook and at the end of each day, jot three things that went your way, made you smile, or didn't totally suck. You can be brief or you can write pages. This one tip will start a whole new pathway in your brain. It's a fact: We can train our brains to be happier and optimistic.

2. In your JOY Journal, also write three things you like about you. Do this every day. (A lot of women groan at this one.) The more you start to like and love yourself, the more confident you will be in your choices. You will make your decisions based upon what brings you joy. Remember, your IV never steers you wrong.

3. Talk nicely to yourself and about yourself. Lose the negative slams and self-effacing comments. Look in the mirror and say out loud the things you wrote in your journal. See yourself as a real person, a sparkling vibrant being who emits love and happiness. When you love yourself and are happy with yourself, you attract the right people into your life.

Kelly Epperson, a former IRS agent now an agent of joy, is the author of *When Life Stinks, It's Time to Wash the Gym Clothes* and *365 Days of Joy—How to be Happy Every Single Day,* plus she has ghostwritten many books for others, including a New York Times best-seller that has sold over three million copies.

Founder of the Happiness Club of Loves Park, Kelly presents humor and happiness keynotes and trainings to a wide variety of national and regional corporate, private, and philanthropic organizations, and also coaches individual clients. She writes a weekly newspaper column, weekly "Live the Joy" ezine, and blogs at www.kellyepperson.com. Kelly is the creator of the "Joy Beyond Your Dreams" Life Mastery Program, and is a mentor to women (and men) who want to step up and live life—full and deep and wide.

By living what she teaches, Kelly has made profound, and subtle, changes in her life. She receives daily confirmations that "this happiness stuff" really works.

Recent honors include being a judge for the Erma Bombeck National Essay Writing Contest, and YWCA Woman of Achievement for mentorship: for having a major impact on the personal and professional development for women, for teaching, guiding and inspiring women in ways that have changed their lives.

A member of the American Happiness Association, the Association for Applied and Therapeutic Humor, and the National Society of Newspaper Columnists, Kelly knows that a person's true credentials are our life experiences.

Kelly also knows that it's all not worth a darn if we don't have fun.

She currently resides in Loves Park, IL (city with a heart) with her Prince Charming, and two teenage sons. She loves her life, and loves teaching other women that they, too, can love their lives. To get a free copy of Kelly's "7 Steps to Becoming Happier Right Now!" go to www.kellyepperson.com.

CHAPTER 27

Play to Learn, Learn to Play

by Dr. Sarah David

This journey of discovering my WHY started many years ago. It actually started when I was a child during playtime. I loved to play "teacher." My sister and our childhood friends would be the students. I remember bringing home extra homework activities from elementary school so the other kids could do the homework that I, of course, would assign as the teacher. I remember the satisfaction and joy I would feel playing "teacher." Well, today I don't play teacher any more…I teach for a living. Teaching has become a way of life in my service to others. Teaching has also sprouted into other areas of service such as coaching and counseling. Looking back, my life's work stems back to my love of helping others. Teaching others how they can pursue their dream career; teaching others about how to understand themselves better through assessments; teaching others about resources to empower themselves; teaching others how to connect with one another; teaching others how they can translate their talents and strengths into work they love.

We are all given an inner compass to guide us in the direction of our calling. I was determined to identify mine so I set out on a quest to experience as many vocations and jobs as possible to see what I enjoyed.

I sampled a handful of careers over the years. The first time I was bitten by the entrepreneurial bug, I was in high school. My father was in the Air Force and we were stationed four years at Kadena Air Base in Okinawa, Japan where I started my first entrepreneurial endeavor. As most young teenagers, I did a lot of babysitting. I actually had a summer job where I worked at the child development center on the base. I had such a blast with the toddlers it did not even feel like work. We laughed, played and snacked together. If I could have gone down for a nap when the toddlers did, it would have been perfect. Unfortunately, as in any typical job, employee siestas were not allowed. Parents at the child development center began to ask me if I could watch their children outside of business hours in the evenings and weekends. The word spread and other military parents begin to contact me to babysit their children. Before I knew it we had a full-blown babysitting service running out of our home on the base. I had to hire extra help. My younger sister Pam was a great assistant. Now I had gone and done it! I had gotten a taste of entrepreneurship and I loved it! I was hooked. From there my career exploration continued.

When it was time to go to college, I remember feeling so lost during orientation because I was struggling like many students to identify a major. I was not sure how to match my interests and who I was with a career that would allow me the opportunity to be me. I made my way to career services to speak with the career counselor and she helped me explore my options and develop a plan. It was not that I did not have a direction. I knew where I was headed but the path to get there wasn't clear. It was because of this experience with my career counselor and my personal career exploration that I knew I wanted to help others match their gifts with work they love.

As I continued to explore, I tried a variety of opportunities from professional jobs to entrepreneurial endeavors that included department store cashier, telemarketer, cosmetic consultant, wardrobe consultant, sales associate, direct sales associate, marketer, recruiter, consultant, career coach, voice-over artist, actress, residence director, career counselor, college professor, assistant dean and program director.

What I found out by sampling all of these opportunities is what I liked and just as importantly what I did not like. What I learned through this exploration was that I was an entrepreneur. I loved the creativity it gave me to do things I loved, the opportunity to do a variety of things that generated multiple streams of income and that I discovered that I liked to work in spurts and the time of day I liked to work when my energy was the highest. For me, entrepreneurship is a way of being and a mindset. It really defines the manner in which I love to work.

With this revelation, I focused on developing my skills as a counselor, business and career coach so I could assist others in their entrepreneurial career discovery, advancement, transition or reinvention. Because I discovered who I was I have always supplemented my professional 9 to 5 income with my entrepreneurial opportunities to give me the variety and creativity I needed.

Why We Do the Things We Do

I am so blessed to have the opportunity to live my WHY every day by helping others identify their WHY. I love what I do because I get a chance to serve others by empowering them to create their dream careers. Nothing pleases me more than to see someone get excited because they finally had a "light bulb" moment when it all comes together. When your inner being has connected with the world of work and you realize how you will infuse who you are with what you do and contribute to society in a meaningful way, you'll be doing what you love!

I am inspired daily to live my WHY because of the joy I receive in serving others. So many people share with me their desire to reinvent themselves, step out on faith and start a business or new career. I enjoy using a variety of career and personality assessment tools to help others identify strengths, show them how they are viewed by others through personal branding to identify their WHY and how they will present it to their tribe in the world.

My entire professional career as a career counselor, career coach and reinvention strategist has been dedicated to helping individuals identify their dream careers. The number one question I get from others is "How do I identify the business or career that is right for me?" Through living my WHY, I've been able to identify their strengths, passions and dreams and how to translate that into fulfilling work. There are three important factors to consider when deciding:

- What would you do if you did not get paid to do it?
- What is something that you do that others say you are good at doing?
- What is something that comes easy for you but is challenging for others?

Many people are walking a tight rope between their professional and entrepreneurial career dreams and an unfulfilling professional "day" job. This is the place where people may be working for someone else, confined by job descriptions and toxic work environments or they have not yet focused in on how to relate their skills to a business. They find themselves stuck in unfulfilling careers when they really want to break free and be what they have been called to be and do in life. They want to create a career that they love and structure it in a way that suits their life instead of the traditional model where most are fitting their life around work. I have found many people looking for career invention or reinvention are looking for options, whether they are aspiring or seasoned entrepreneurs, solopreneurs, coaches and consultants, professionals, leaders, educators or employees seeking career advancement.

Along the journey, I realized it was time to step up and live my WHY. Understanding that I am passionate about and what others say I am good at has become my mission and reason "why" that lead to the evolution of NICE –The National Institute for Career Empowerment™ where I have the honor to serve others in doing what they love by launching their dreams into businesses and careers. I just love business and personal development. I get excited talking about it, strategizing, creating and connecting with others. NICE is my opportunity to take all of my education, experience, expertise, talents, training and what I am known for, to teach others how to create or nurture their own opportunities through entrepreneurship in step-by-step coaching programs, teleclasses, tools, live events, philanthropy, and a worldwide community.

How to Live Your WHY

There are 7 strategies that I use in my coaching programs to help others gain clarity in discovering their WHY identify their strengths and how to translate their unique gifts into a dream career that is fulfilling.

1. Identify your mission in life. Whether your mission is to start your own business, work for someone else or volunteer for a worthy cause, the work around identification is very important to the process. Whether you have known your mission since you were a child or you are still trying to discover it, do the self-reflection needed to understand your mission in life.

2. Follow your heart. In counseling and coaching others, I have found that many people have delayed their dreams. They put them on a shelf. They go around the mulberry bush with other careers that may not be fulfilling but they pursue them because they are more popular or they pay more or because someone else thinks it is a good idea. I would like to share there is nothing wrong with doing what is practical but I have found that people always circle back around to their original dream somewhere down the path. Find a way to incorporate what you love into your career.

3. Trust your outrageous ideas. What makes it different from other ideas that are out there? One thing I have learned is that there are no new ideas. They come a dime a dozen. The difference is how do you take an idea and build on it to make it even better. You may also be thinking that what you are thinking has already been done before, more than likely it has but what extra twist, service or benefit can you add to a concept? What makes your idea uniquely different?

4. Know what you don't know and get the help that you need to move forward. The old saying "knowledge is power" is true but knowing what to do with that power is key. Continue to learn and research information regarding what options are available.

5. Identify your strengths, values, passions and goals and understand how these foundation steps are critical to identifying your business or career of choice. First, identify what you do well. There are several ways you can identify your calling. Some people already know what this is because it was a seed that was planted early in life. It may be that "thing" that you knew you wanted to be or do when you "grew up." For others it may be that "thing" that you have been mentored to do your entire life such as run a family business or continue with a craft.

6. Find your cheerleaders and identify your tribe—finding the support you need to excel will help you live your WHY. I highly recommend joining a support group of like-minded people. A coach can also serve as one of your biggest cheerleaders. Identify who you will follow and who you will lead.

7. Invest in yourself. If you don't then who will? I will forever be a lifelong learner. There are many things that I am excited to continue to learn throughout my entrepreneurial career. Many years ago, I realized the importance of education. I have invested in myself both formally and informally in addition to obtaining the wise counsel of trusted business advisors, mentors, coaches and consultants.

Live Your Dream Career by Doing What You Love

There are many reasons why people don't pursue their dream careers. The common excuses I hear are a 9 to 5 job, lack of knowledge or skill, starting over, limited finances, family, fear, doubt, mindsets or not knowing where to begin. What excuse are you using? What would make your dream career a dream? Creating your own schedule; profiting from your creative ideas; moving faster; creating your own income; generating multiple streams of income. What would doing what you love look like?

So how do you get started to discover what you love and put your plan into action to do it?

Here is my "D.R.E.A.M.print™ process I use with my clients:

D Determine what you love to do (passions, gifts, and talents).

R Research your options of the type of career you want to create.

E Evaluate your current skills to identify what other skills you need to obtain.

A Actionable steps are needed to create a plan and to take it from dream to reality.

M Monitor your mindset in order to position yourself for success.

Play to learn and learn to play while following your dreams and doing what you love. And always remember, life happens and setbacks will come but keep moving forward no matter how small the step.

Dr. Sarah David, Founder and Chief Empowerment Officer of NICE—The National Institute for Career Empowerment™, is a thought leader in the field of career, personal and professional enrichment. She specializes in facilitating creative ways to increase the success of others by equipping them to do what they love and create dream careers through entrepreneurship. She believes that people can take who they are…personality, values, abilities and skills and translate that into a fulfilling business or career that aligns with our dreams, goals, mission and passions. Sarah helps individuals invent or reinvent themselves, create careers in order to identify ways to generate additional income and achieve a work-life balance. She believes that God has given us all a calling and if we can determine what that is we can lead a more inspired and meaningful life.

Sarah is the author of *Jumpstart Your Career Now*. She is also a frequent speaker, trainer, and workshop facilitator for businesses, organizations, colleges and universities. She serves as a professor in higher education teaching career development and mentoring both undergraduate and graduate students. She holds a Doctorate in Higher Education Administration (Leadership) from the University of Texas at Austin, a Master's Degree in Education in Counseling from North Carolina State University and a Bachelor of Arts in Speech Communication from Louisiana Tech University.

What sets Sarah apart from many others offering career education is she uses over 13 years of personal, business and career development expertise as a national certified counselor, certified career management coach, business consultant and personal branding strategist to empower others to create dream careers through entrepreneurship through her coaching, consulting and mastermind groups. Sarah helps others invent or reinvent themselves, create careers to generate additional income and achieve a work-life balance. She also encourages and highlights those who are making a difference in our world through philanthropy.

With work-life balance being a personal priority, Sarah enjoys spending time with her family and is committed to taking time out for body, mind and soul renewal. She enjoys warm weather, salsa dancing and cultural events. She is the "entrepreneur's career coach," author, career reinvention strategist, world traveler and beach lover.

So what is your career calling? Sarah identifies a practical step-by-step career plan that marries who you are with what you do. If you have tucked your dreams away, high up on the top shelf in order to fit into a "box"…a job box, a practical box, a realistic box, a doubt box, or someone else's box, Sarah will inform and inspire you to break out of the "box" by connecting the dots to take your dreams off the shelf, dust them off and do what you love! Visit www.nicealliance.com for free tools to help you do what you love.

CHAPTER 28

Living With Freedom Of Choice, Purpose and Passion!

by Deborah Skye King

Freedom is a human hunger, a need so primal and deep that we seek it in a myriad of ways. We want it in our relationships, our finances and in our choices. When we don't have it, we get stuck and feel powerless. The entrepreneur seeks to create her own income on her own time and to live her passions in the pursuit of her freedom, her calling card to purposeful living.

Purposeful living enables you to have that freedom, but what if you don't know what your purpose is, how do you find it and cultivate it along with your passions? Being the author of *Discovering and Living Your Soul's Purpose And Awakening To Your Divine Self*, I have had thousands of women globally reach out to me and ask the simple, yet profound question: "How do I live my life on purpose when I have a family, a job, a career and I lack funds to do the things I really want to do?"

Many women feel stuck in a rut with no paddle to row to shore and the shore is so far off in the distance, sometimes it's hard to see. I get that, I really do. I understand how the human spirit has the ability to overcome obstacles that might seem impossible to breakthrough, but I promise you, if you do these 7 simple steps, your life and business will change and you will feel empowered by your choices.

1. One of the best ways to accomplish your goals is to get an accountability buddy. You can find one at a networking group,

online mastermind program or ask someone you know of who you admire and is pursuing their dreams and goals and seeking the same results as you. When two or more are gathered, momentum can begin, and a partnership can form that will deepen your passion for your work, clarify your goals and allow you to see your business from a new perspective.

2. Defining your goals for your business is best laid out when they are in direct balance to your beliefs and values. This is the number one tip that should run through all personal and business choices. When I get a new idea for Soul Therapy, I see how a new product or partnership would add to the business. Will the collaboration provided be a positive relationship to the overall mission of the company, and is it in alignment to my own personal beliefs and values? If it is not, I do not pursue it. I have turned away many business opportunities, media, TV and radio interviews because of this value system. If it is not in alignment to who I am or what my business represents, then I do not compromise. I keep it clear and clean within my value system. It will create longevity in your business.

3. I have a saying: "Show up for your business and it will show up for you." Like any committed relationship, your business wants to be loved and nurtured, respected and trusted, along with having honest communication. When I first received this insight, I was amazed at the results that I received in the first week of applying this philosophy. My business grew in leaps and bounds by applying this equality of myself and my business into my working relationship. It was no longer "the business needs this," "I need this," but the communication began with, "we need this in our business to flourish." A partnership formed that deepened the respect that I had around the energy of my company. It changed my life and my 'idea' of what my business meant. I respected the healthy boundary that was created by this one idea and it has made a huge difference in my finances, my vision and my heart connection to my business.

4. When you are crystal clear with whom you work, and what your outcome of your service provides, then you will understand who your target market is. When you get clear on this you will no longer be stuck in a situation with a client or a partnership that is causing

havoc in your life or to your business. Be discerning and recognize who is going to benefit from your company's long term vision and mission. It will save you hours of emotional headaches.

Get very clear on who you are speaking to, who your audience is, and what your perfect client looks like. How does she dress? Where does she shop? What is her lifestyle? When your desire is to live on purpose and live passionately, you will want to be inspired and uplifted by the world around you, and that also goes for your clients and customers. You want that energy to reflect back to you in who you attract to you! You will notice clients will be attracted to you *because* of your lifestyle and how you create a platform that truly serves your passions.

When you magnetically draw into your business your ideal clients, your work becomes effortless. There are particular stages and steps to creating this.

Step 1. Envision your client, her age, her income and marital status and her geographical location.

Step 2. Business development. What stage is she currently at in her business? Is she starting a new business? Is she a professional seeking to enter into a new career or is she desiring to advance her current level within a corporation or take a step outside of the corporate world to begin her entrepreneurial one?

Step 3. What goals does she desire to accomplish that you can personally and professionally help her with?

Question yourself in the same way you would question a new coach, contract or program that you want to enroll in and ask yourself why are you attracted to the person or program. What is it saying to you that you can say personally that will benefit your company or program?

5. Create a product or program as soon as you can! One of the best ways to live financially independent and experience the effects of entrepreneurial freedom is to create a product, ebook, CD, or MP3,

coaching program, certification training or membership site. Create a product that is downloadable and automate it through your shopping cart so that purchases are done automatically. Not only does this create passive income for you, but also shows your customer and future clients that they can return later and pursue a working relationship with you via your products and programs, which can deepen into a long-term relationship further down the road.

Always think long term when creating products, programs and free offers as one free offer can later become a long-term client. It happens to me frequently. It can happen for you, too!

6. You are gifted. You have talents, and you are unique in your own abilities and how you share your message and how it is delivered. Remind yourself daily that you are precious gift to the world and no one else has the same fingerprint that you do nor mind or heart as you do. You are unique, and your message matters to this planet. You have purpose and you can live passionately by claiming it. Breath deeply into that.

Love yourself and be kind in how you speak to yourself. It has lasting effects that show up in a myriad of ways. When you believe in yourself, others will believe in you. It is a very simple thing to state, another to live by. By surrounding yourself with people who reflect your beliefs and who stand for the same values as you do, it will encourage you to step boldly into your future with courage and conviction. Surround yourself with people you desire to emulate.

Trust is one of the hardest things for people to do, yet it is the basis of your reality. It is inborn prior to birth. It is there at the moment of conception, inherent in your DNA. It is your Spiritual connection that allows you to trust that place of innocence. It is time to reclaim that trust. It will enable you to truly live your passions and to live on purpose. I have seen it take shape and form for thousands of women. It is right here for you to claim and hold within your heart.

Spiritual freedom is at the cornerstone of personal success and financial abundance, it is a pathway that leads to a transformation of the heart and mind, unlocking the subconscious beliefs and opening up new realities for you to step into and claim as your own. One thing that I am sure of is that the life of the entrepreneur is a life of freedom based on your own choices and you get to decide how much you want to make, when you want to make it and in what market. There is no ceiling. There is no limit. So climb high and climb into the place I call your StarPower* because the journey of the entrepreneur will lead you to your greatness. If you ever need help or a support system, remind yourself that every woman here in this book is a rung on that ladder that is here to support you.

What I found out was that when the entrepreneurial spirit takes hold, it is a hard to return to the normal life, and the 'job' mentality or the idea of a regular paycheck, the commute through early rush hour, the not seeing the kids or husband, and most of all, not having the time to do what you really want to do, vacation and travel if that is on your list. It is for me.

It takes tenacity and personal conviction to follow your dreams till they are realized and manifested, so surround yourself with powerful, passionate and heart-centered women who will support you along the path to a life of your choice. Once you have fulfilled your dreams, they will grow and expand in direct proportion to how much you do, so dream BIG and I'll see you along the journey!

Deborah Skye King is recognized globally as the leading authority on Soul Therapy, and North America's #1 Soul Therapist. She is the CEO and President of Soul Therapy International, creator of The StarPower* System for female entrepreneurs, Director and Founder of the International Association of Professional Past Life Regression Therapy & Training School, Creator of The Divine Energy Matrix Connection and Spiritual Bio-Dynamic Healing.

Soul Therapy International offers certification training, online mentoring programs for women and StarPower* soul coaching with yearly retreats to luxurious and exotic locations for empowering women in an "unplugged" environment and Soul Exploration Sacred Travels to Ancient Sacred Sites and Maya Temples.

She is the author of *Discovering and Living Your Soul's Purpose and Awakening To Your Divine Self*. Deborah Skye lives in Nelson, British Columbia, Canada with her daughter Luminous.

CHAPTER 29

Productivity and Procrastination: Finding a Better Way to Live Our Big WHY

by Kate Kerans

Do you have a project that seems overwhelming? Or feels too big to tackle? Do you set your standards high, but always feel like you've failed? Could it be that as a brilliant entrepreneur you get in the way of your own progress?

We all procrastinate to some degree in our lives. How much we procrastinate usually corresponds to the level to which it can have a negative effect on both our businesses and personal well-being. Procrastinating causes stress, lack of sleep, missed deadlines, missed opportunities and unhappiness by creating guilt and self-recrimination in our lives. Looking at some of the tasks that remain outstanding on many to do lists, it's easy to see why they are avoided. Visits to the dentist, doing our taxes or even getting the oil changed in our car are tasks that need to be done but are often avoided which then sometimes become a much bigger ordeal. Or perhaps we only imagine it to be. But, still we delay. And of course, now it's much easier to make excuses that we don't have time to invest in such a large task. And we delay it further. Procrastination is a vicious circle, but one that we continue to engage in. Why?

Many people procrastinate in spite of the negative consequences that might come as a direct result of doing so because we are rewarded by our procrastinating. Here is the scenario: you have a task that for whatever reason you wish to avoid. You make excuses as to why you should avoid it and instead do something you enjoy, like watching television. This, in turn, leads to a higher chance of procrastinating in the future because you were rewarded by getting to do something you enjoyed instead of something unpleasant. Occasionally, if you delay long enough, you are rewarded by the task no longer being relevant or somebody else taking over and completing the task and lastly, you have made the task even more disagreeable now that you have put it off.

So, let's step back a bit. What leads us to avoid certain tasks in the first place? A familiar stumbling block is a fear of failure. Being a perfectionist means never doing anything less than perfectly which can be an impossible goal to achieve. Rather than risk completing a task less than perfectly, we fail by not completing the task at all. The paradox of perfectionism is that it is a never-ending self-fulfilling prophecy. The more we delay, the less likely the chance we have of doing justice to whatever task we want to be perfect. In the end, if we do finish the task, it will often be substandard because we haven't allowed ourselves sufficient time to complete it properly and our fear of failure is confirmed.

Fear of success is another fear. Why would we be afraid of success? If we are successful, we raise other's expectations and can be fearful of not living up to those higher expectations. So it's not really a fear of success, but rather a fear of the expectations that might follow as a result of that success.

While I was pondering the reasons behind my own procrastination, my research uncovered another possible reason. Control. If we don't do something someone else has dictated we do, for example a client or your spouse, you exert control over the situation by refusing to do it or delaying it. Kind of passive aggressive, but when I read this as a means of procrastinating, I was surprised to see shades of my own behavior.

So what can we do about procrastinating? Well, the first step to overcoming it is to recognize that you are doing it. This is probably the easiest step to working towards a better way of coping. It's also an uncomfortable one. Who really wants to face up and admit their fears, insecurities and less-than-admirable ways of coping?

It can also be helpful to figure out what triggers our procrastinating. One way of identifying possible triggers is to stop yourself when you find yourself delaying and keep a record of what you were feeling. What excuses did you use? Did you opt to do another task instead? What were you thinking? If you do this for a short period of time, you will start to see patterns to what you do and be much better equipped to do something about it.

Not all procrastinating is negative. We usually procrastinate with certain tasks but this can drive us to complete other less pressing tasks. And we might complete a lot of other pressing tasks. But, it is a deceiving process because while we appear to be accomplishing a lot, we fool ourselves into thinking that our functioning is higher than it really is.

So, what to do? A step in the right direction might include breaking down bigger projects into smaller tasks and assigning a set time to do a single task for 15 minutes. This allows you to view the magnitude of the project objectively rather than simply being overwhelmed by the size of the project. While this seems like a practical suggestion, it's one that I always have difficulty with. Chunking things down is hard for me because it forces me to look very closely at the very task I am trying so hard to avoid! But if I can push past that and find a small task to start with, it can be very effective. I have also found myself working beyond the time limit set which has given a sense of achievement as opposed to one of failure. I have also downloaded a neat little free tool called Cook Timer which is simply a countdown clock. The first time I used it, I set it to 15 minutes and was startled when my time was up because I was totally engrossed in the task by the timer went off. I immediately set it for another 15 minutes and was on my way.

Sometimes when we delay starting a task but have researched it endlessly, we are then faced with what I call 'information devastation'. There is so much information you have gathered you haven't a clue where you should start, leaving you in a state of paralysis. One way to tackle this particular issue is to approach it from a different angle entirely by writing down why it is that you can't do what are putting off. This can often lead to thinking about your project in a different light and allow you to at least start sifting through all the information you have gathered.

Another handy tool when dealing with information overwhelm is mind mapping. By laying out ideas or concepts visually, it allows your mind to focus more effectively. When I work on a mind map, I become drawn into working on the mind map and stop worrying about what other people expect or if this particular task is going to be a success or how it has to be finished in the next two hours! I also find it useful for creating new content because the way a mind map works helps to organize information but also leads naturally to creating fresh ideas. I use the free version of a program called XMind and find it can be of tremendous help when trying to sift through a mountain of information.

Mind mapping has had a positive impact on my business because I can continue collecting enough information to feel well-prepared for upcoming projects yet feel confident that it won't hold up my ability to move forward. I also enjoy the process of mind mapping and find it challenging to work through organizing and generating new content.

Another entirely different approach that might also help when dealing with procrastination is to put a picture of someone you love where you usually do your work. Having a visual reminder of who it is you are working to support can serve as a catalyst for just getting it done.

Finally, your path to change shall have a much higher chance of success if it is accompanied by an actual plan as to how one is going to make that change. Your plan must be specific. It must indicate exactly how you are going to make a change and when. And what are you going to use to replace that habit? Because our good intentions are never enough. For example, in order to spend time in the evenings working on your business instead of watching television, you must have a plan. So your plan could be that for two evenings a week—pick which days, you shall work on a task that you have identified as a specific step towards achieving your goals for no less than 30 minutes. If you do this successfully, you can reward yourself with 30 minutes of doing whatever you choose to do. It isn't enough to simply promise to make the change; you must design how you are going to make that change and what positive reward you will get to reinforce the new habit that replaces the old one.

It takes practice and commitment to change old habits, and if you backtrack occasionally, the ability to forgive yourself and move forward regardless is a necessary part of the process. We need to be kinder to ourselves and recognize that we would never treat a friend the way we sometimes treat ourselves. It is commonly accepted that it takes at least

21 days of consistent repeated effort to learn a new habit. It took years to develop these habits and changing them won't happen overnight.

Kate Kerans is a graduate of Red Deer College and Founder of The International Association of Virtual Business Entrepreneurs (IAVBE), a membership site created specifically for online entrepreneurs. Her passion lies in helping entrepreneurs generate more from their business through strategies such as creating passive income, lead generation and effective marketing techniques.

Kate is a seasoned entrepreneur having built a successful company providing online support for legal professionals. Her professional background has been with the legal industry since 1994 and she is a certified paralegal specializing in real estate conveyancing. Kate has been a contributor to *The FabJob Guide to Become a Virtual Assistant* and *How to Build a Successful Virtual Assistant Business* in addition to being interviewed by the Virtual Assistant Forums, Calgary's *Child Magazine* and *The Lawyer's Weekly.*

Throughout the adventures of developing her own online business, Kate has discovered a talent for coaching new and seasoned online entrepreneurs and has expanded on those skills to launch the IAVBE. The mission of the IAVBE is to provide a community where online professionals can access resources, support and global networking opportunities to exponentially expand their businesses. By providing relevant content, teleclasses, webinars, group coaching and ongoing support, the IAVBE creates a community of like-minded individuals who support each other while building profitable online businesses.

Kate lives in DeWinton, Alberta on an acreage with her husband and their two boys, five horses, two Border Collies and reigning cat, also known as Hailey.

CHAPTER 30

Keep Following Your Dreams

by Starla Fitch, M.D.

Some people would just say "Follow your dreams." The trouble is, there is truly no "end of the line" when it comes to your dreams. It is like a complicated highway system, with lots of intersections. There are detours, twists and turns. At each intersection, you must make a decision: left or right? north or south? Then, you reach the next intersection and must make yet another decision. This process is life long. It is heartwarming. And it is heartbreaking. Sometimes you will feel your navigation system has pointed you in the totally wrong direction. Sometimes you will feel you have reached a dead-end. But, just like a shark must keep swimming to stay alive, you must keep moving to keep your dreams alive.

Decide to Decide

How do I know this? Well, when I was growing up, the only career options for women (from my mother's perspective) were teaching or nursing. While these are both very noble professions, they didn't speak to me. Or, if they did, what I heard was screaming children? Sick patients with bedpan needs? Neither of these prospects seemed appealing.

So, like a driver without a map, I started college with an undeclared major. My first class, Introduction to Sociology, was fascinating. It was all about our society and the norms and values we hold dear. My professor was dynamic and I wanted to be like him. So, four years later, I finished up my degree in sociology (with a few bumps along the road, like a cross country move, a marriage, and a divorce).

Then, the question was: What next? One of my professors suggested graduate school. So, like a car in cruise control, I continued in school for two more years. When I looked up, I had a Master's Degree in sociology.

My first real job was driving around the countryside of Virginia. I would knock on the doors of selected homes and interview the elderly who lived there. This would be unheard of (and extremely unsafe!) in today's world. Back then, the only time I felt ill at ease was when I encountered large signs saying "Warning! Electric Fence!" or "Mad dog! Enter at your own risk!" I scratched those homes off my list!

Day after day, as I spoke to the sweet older folks that welcomed me, a stranger, into their homes, I became convinced that this was not my calling. These older people told me that, sure, they sometimes would go to the Senior Center for bingo. And, yes, they would use the Meals on Wheels program when they were sick. But what they really wanted to know was, why were they taking that pink pill their doctor had prescribed? Did they have heart problems? High blood pressure? They had no idea. As one dear lady put it, "Hon', my doc just doesn't have time to tell me what's wrong with me. He just tells me to take these pills, so I do."

Then Decide Again

After a few months of hearing this broken record refrain, I decided that I could do better by these folks. My heart went out to them. I didn't know what the pink pills were for, either. So, I started lugging around a huge book, called the PDR (Physician Desk Reference). It looked like the largest encyclopedia you could imagine. This was before cell phones and search engines. I would look at the photos of the pills in the book and match them to what the elderly people were taking. Together, we would discover, "Oh, this is for your tummy troubles!" "Yes, it looks like you DO have high blood pressure!" They were so grateful to be given knowledge of their own health problems.

As the weeks went on, I realized that I could do more. Much more. I started looking into going to medical school. With a major in sociology, I had not been focused on science at all. So, this would mean going back to school for three years of pre-medicine to complete all the anatomy, chemistry and math courses. Then, if I was lucky, being admitted to four years of medical school. This would be followed by a year of internship and a minimum of three years of residency. Then, perhaps, fellowship training for another year or so. Wow. I would be an elderly person myself by the time I finished my education!

Stay the Course

Undeterred, I enrolled for a few pre-med classes to test the waters and see if I drowned. It was a bit of a struggle, since most of my classmates were much younger and had been on the science track for a while. I spoke to guidance counselors, took some aptitude tests, and decided to go full speed ahead into my true vocation.

You would think that, at this point, my family would be doing cartwheels and sending me incentive checks for straight A's. Uhmmmm. Not so much. In fact, when I called my parents to let them know my plans, in a way that clearly stated I was not asking for financial help, just moral support, my dad said: "You are crazy. You have no idea what you are getting into. I think it's a terrible idea and we are against it." Gulp.

For some odd reason, instead of curling up in a ball and thinking, "Okay, maybe I can't really do this after all," it only made me hold on tighter to my dream. In fact, that was probably one of my dad's greatest gifts to me. Because if you tell me "No," I will say, "Oh, yeah?!"

So, off I went. With conviction and bravado (externally, at least!). I managed to make it through my pre-medicine classes and was accepted to medical school. After medical school, I landed a prestigious residency and fellowship. It wasn't until I was at my medical school graduation that my dad wrote on my graduation card, "Well, I guess I was wrong. You were able to do this."

Now, the moral to this story is: Along the way, on your path to your dreams, you will not always (sometimes NOT AT ALL!) find things easy. You will not always have a big cheerleading support team to help you. But, you must have that fire in your belly and keep stoking it, so you can lift yourself up.

Are We There Yet??

So, was that the last of my struggles? Was it Happily Ever After? Hah!

Not so fast, Grasshopper.

I landed my Dream Doctor Job in my Dream Location (with a few more bumps along the road: another move, marriage and divorce, and then FINALLY! meeting my perfect mate!). Then, I looked around and discovered that I was not in my Dream Environment at work. As the only woman in a sea of men, I was constantly feeling "less than." Each day, my work with my patients lifted me up. Each day, my interaction with my partners brought me down. For a multitude of reasons, going on my own did not seem the best option. So, I got out my compass, did some research, and looked for direction.

Maybe someone else had the wisdom to point me on the right path. Maybe other people had been in a similar fix and found the way. Maybe I just needed to stop long enough in my struggles to ask for help.

Follow the Yellow Brick Road

That's when I discovered that there is a whole group of Navigation System Specialists out there. They are called coaches, mentors, advisors. They are people who can look at what you have in your cupboard and show you how to make a delicious feast! They are people who are right there, whenever you pull over to ask for directions. They are nicer than the lady in the Navigation System machine who says repeatedly, "Turn right! Turn right!…Recalculating…." They are smarter that the guy at the gas station who says, "Go down to Smith's farm, about 60 yards east. Then, turn right at the old elm tree that Joe, Jr. ran into with his pick-up truck last winter…." They are your Dream Catchers. Your lifeline. They have your back when no one else does.

"You always had the power." —Glinda the Good Witch

Here's what happened to me. By unexplainable luck and grace, I fell into the path of a wonderful coach. Not only did this coach have amazing insight, but there were lots of other people just like me who were in various stages of challenges (In the old days, I would have called these "struggles."). I am only a novice when it comes to being coached. I am Junior Varsity material. But, what I can tell you is this. If you are even the tiniest bit lost. If you are the least bit unsure of your way. A great coach can make the difference between living your life and LOVING your life. A great coach can help YOU make the changes you need. You cannot change others. Don't try. It will only make you frustrated. You CAN make the changes you need. I promise. And when you do, it will open up a whole new world of hope and continued awesome dreams. It is like getting a passport for world travel when you have lived in a little country town all your life. It is like winning a First Class, Around the World ticket to EVERYWHERE! Honest.

So, here is my short list to take on your journey:

1. Follow your dreams.

2. It's okay if those dreams change.

3. It's okay if other people don't think your dreams are great. Their opinions are not your problem.

4. It's okay to slip through the clouds a couple hundred times as you walk towards your dreams.

5. It's NOT okay to stop. (Remember the shark!)

6. It's NOT okay to beat yourself up because of perceived inadequacies.

7. KEEP following your dreams! The magic is in the momentum.

Dr. Starla Fitch is a Board Certified Oculoplastic Surgeon. As the only female surgeon in a group of 24 physicians, she brings a special blend of gentle compassion and expertise to her practice.

Dr. Fitch graduated from Southern Illinois University School of Medicine in 1987, after receiving her Bachelor's Degree cum laude from University of Southwestern Louisiana and her Master of Science degree from Texas A&M University. She completed her internship at Baylor College of Medicine in Houston, and her ophthalmology residency at University of Washington in Seattle, where she served as Chief Resident her senior year. She went on to complete her Oculoplastic Fellowship at Eye Plastic Surgery Associates in Dallas. Throughout her career, she has received many honors, including election into the prestigious Alpha Omega Alpha, National Medical Honor Society. She has had numerous articles published and has been a speaker at national meetings.

Dr. Fitch joined a large multi-specialty ophthalmology practice in Atlanta in 1994, where she is the senior oculoplastic surgeon. While trained in full scope oculoplastic surgery, Dr. Fitch has a special interest and expertise in cosmetic eyelid surgery and eyelid reconstruction.

Dr. Fitch is married to Dr. Chris Vandewater, an oral surgeon. They have been fortunate to combine their love of travel with their desire to help others by participating in a medical mission to Africa. They enjoy special family time with many nieces and nephews, one of whom is following in Dr. Fitch's footsteps by attending Southern Illinois University School of Medicine.

CHAPTER 31

Visions, Harmony and Mystic Perspectives

by Dr. Rona Thau

I prefer to see similarities where there are differences. I think most people forget that the whole can be viewed from many different vantage points. Rather than picking one view as right or wrong, explore the ideas from a different point of view. When you alter your vantage point, it's like having new eyes to uncover a something new. Usually, the 360 view leads to the same point via a different method.

Looking for and finding these similarities promotes smooth connections, and minimizes discord. Harmony is far more uplifting than dissonance. That's the way I like to see it. It's a great eye-opener in relationships, beginning or shifting business strategies.

Seeing familiar things as if standing from a different vantage point enables us to find new routes to connect with our deepest self, with our business visions, and with other beings. Although differences exist, the big picture is a singular one represented by interconnected and interesting ways. Take a peek in to your life and business from a different point of view.

There's a children's book that illustrates this point incredibly well. Istvan Banyai's book, *ZOOM*. Banyai presents visuals as if from a zoom or far away lens to play with the mind's eye. With the turn of each page your perspective must alter to make new sense of the new picture. It's fascinating.

Similar although different to the way Harold draws with his purple crayon creating whatever he envisions as he dreams and creates. The teaching is that you can't always believe what you see is all that's there. There's a lot more going on than we realize. We just haven't fully trained our ability to see from all perspectives.

Perspective plays a major role in how we see ourselves and the many roles we play in life. It shapes how we choose to live each day.

The tips and tools I share here will open the depths of your mind and enable you to live, work and play in greater harmony with a broad foundation understanding limitless connections.

Knowing Verses Thinking

Knowing is more of a visceral sense, kind of like when you know there's a pebble in your shoe. It rubs you, it pokes you, your foot begs you to stop and remove it. That sense is different than thinking to yourself, "Oh there's a rock in my shoe I'd better stop and take it out." They're close but so very different.

Similarly in your life and/or your business you may have a sense that gnaws at you. Perhaps something that you've always wanted to do. You may have stuffed it away a long time ago, or it may be so close you can taste it.

The visceral need isn't necessarily a logical thought.

It may entail something you've always dreamed of, something you were praised or criticized for, or something you just can't stop feeling or imagining.

To create a life that mixes what you love and what you do for a living, it's essential to lean in the direction of these visceral senses and dig deeper to discover exactly what they are and how they can be materialized.

It can be scary to unearth some of these things as many of us have hidden or tried to bury our gifts and treasures throughout our lives. Yet if we wish to live the life we dream of, we need to discover our purpose on purpose.

We need to explore some pieces of ourselves that may be buried, neglected, or that were left behind long ago. These parts are essential soul parts and are different than old skins you've shed.

You may have to reach beyond limiting thoughts and beliefs to explore the visceral senses.

Take the time to explore your sense of self, how you operate, and discover what you know to be so. This exercise will be a compass to direct you towards your true knowing. It will nurture your heart and soul, and help you on the path to living and working from stable ground.

Serendipity

When we step outside our usual zone of comfort and take risks, amazing things line up and happen that we never could have planned. There's a Universal, spontaneous energy that synergistically sucks us in to things because we've stepped beyond a boundary of comfort. We shift. The Universe perceives our lowered resistance and increased ease.

When we muster up the courage to lead life in the direction we want to go, as strange as it sounds, the Universe senses the shift and hooks you up. Like energies attract. It's spontaneous. It's enormous and it can't be planned.

Making and Taking Time to Re-New You

You must make and take the time to renew your physical, mental and spiritual body and soul. This is a must. If your sharp edge dulls, ease becomes effort. Unnecessary effort creates exhaustion and needless failures. You must take time to rest, renew, revive, and reinvest to be your best. Body, mind and spirit are intimately intertwined. We need a balance of time to create, stay healthy and reflect. Some suggestions are:

Creative Time

Write, paint, cook, sing, play and make things up in your unique way...

Health Maintenance Time

Exercise. Eat properly. To make sure your body is functioning optimally, schedule regular preventive care such as acupuncture, gentle chiropractic, and whole-body integration methods to maintain your body's health naturally. Contrary to the current norm, we must realize that regular maintenance is an integral part of our health care. This is my field of expertise and I could write endlessly about this point. If possible, refrain from drugs and over-the-counter medicines as they merely create masks and more problems. Find a professional who can help you fix the source of any problems before they multiply.

Introspection Time

Yoga, meditation, Tai Chi, Chi Gong, running and quiet time to reflect and regenerate all help give you inner balance.

Remember the Connections

Remember, you are not alone. We are all connected as a part of a collective united kingdom of greatness. Although things appear stable, all things are in a state of constant flux, vibration and change. We are wired to interact and do good things with and for one another. Sow the seeds and harvest genius. Plant, till, weed, water and stay the course till harvest. Remain aware.

Being Selfish Isn't Selfish

It's not selfish to be selfish. Selfish isn't scrooge-like or hoarding your gifts. Being Selfish means taking the time to unravel the gifts of your unique soul and sharing them. In order to share the gifts of your soul, you need to be fresh, free, and focused, to be fantastic. To free that, you need time to review, renew and delve in to your passion, your health, your creativity, your spunk. If we don't care for our own needs, we minimize effectiveness in our lives and our ability to care for the needs of others. When you nurture your self, it creates health, stability, openness and maximizes abilities to fruitfully share your gifts with others.

Be Selective Not a Sponge

It's essential to learn how to block negative energies. This entails selecting the types of friends you socialize with and the crowd you surround yourself with on a regular basis.

Frequently, at the workplace, or in public, we encounter both positive and negative energies. The energy may be tangible like someone's bad attitude, or may be a more subtle vibe you can't see. Just because it is invisible doesn't exclude its existence. You sense it. Like air, it exists. As your sensitivity develops, you'll begin to recognize what energies you need to block and decide if you need to alter your core group of contacts.

Be careful not to be a sponge for negative energy. This is a good time to learn how to limit the amount of negative stimulus you surround yourself with. Choose who you keep company with wisely. To keep out negative energies that you don't want to soak up try: make an imaginary shield around your energy field. Try imagining a color bubble or an invisible mesh. Pick something that works for you or remove yourself from the situation if it becomes bombarding. I'm not encouraging you to leave discomfort, just learn how to deal with it and not absorb negativity from the surroundings. Being in the midst of it helps you learn what's yours and what's not and teaches you how to be stable and aware of your own space.

Remain True to Your Heart and Soul

Because I'm so sensitive to energy, practicing being comfortable in the uncomfortable, learning what's mine and what's not and learning to shield my personal space have been invaluable processes. Peer beyond the edges of what you see. Promote positive possibilities. Protect your self. Use all these tools to tip the scales to shift negatives to positives. Take a different perspective to create unity rather than opposition.

Shedding Old Skins

I know quite well that we get attached to our stuff. Our stuff includes all our ways of being, thinking and operating. It can be sort of like an addiction and a tricky thing to break free from. That said, it can be done and it can be fun. I recently came upon a poster that read, "It doesn't have to be fun to be fun." I really like that. In the long run, if we take the time to nurture and participate in making our dream life, the shear volume of joy we'll have to give and take becomes limitless, and timeless.

We get attached to stuff that has served us well in our past. A cozy snuggly baby blanket, or other adopted things that bring to my mind the analogy of a life raft. These life rafts have served us well or saved us some time in the past but now have outlived their usefulness. They serve now to weigh us down, create unneeded burden and slow us down. We believe that they're still of use because they worked before, but they're just unneeded baggage we need to drop now.

Imagine it this way: once upon a time this buoyant new life raft was there for you just when you needed it. It took you and saved you from falling in to the rapids. Awesome. You kept the raft because, after all, it saved you. You never did need to use the raft again. Yet you've carried that raft everywhere. It's tattered, torn, and could never float again, yet still, its part of your well-worn, old gear. It weighs you down, constantly reminds you of the past and keeps you from new rivers for fear of drowning in the rapids.

My point here is we've got things we hold on to (mentally and physically) because they served us well once. More often than not, the need for the vehicle that got us through the tough time(s) is useless now. It's time to drop the old weight and illusions. Take on new challenges, drop the old gear and step in to the present moment willingly, open to face what is here. Shed the skins. Keep the perspective and wisdom you've obtained, but drop the need for the safety blankets and tattered old life rafts.

Dr. Rona Thau, BS DC is passionate about health, nutrition, fitness, and healing. Her passion and knowledge in these fields has grown since her teenage years.

A true healer, Dr. Rona advocates easy-to-implement practices that promote radiant health. She has taught and assisted people to live healthier lives for over 20 years. Her intuitive gifts and talents have been received with praise. She uses methods that provide a solid foundation so wellness can emanate with great ease from within.

Dr. Rona works with young and old, in person and via distance, to help overcome and conquer unnecessary illness and disease that are, most often, the result of bad choices NOT bad genes or germs.

"I especially love to work with children and young adults. The results come quicker and can promote great longstanding impact in our society. The earlier we can teach and instill the ideas and knowledge that root out the source of most health problems, the faster positive results occur and can spread out to help the masses. Our children are our future. They deserve to be genuinely healthy. The time to help them do that is now. It's not brain surgery or

chemotherapy—it's HEALTH that we need to respect and preserve. People need help. They need help now." —Dr. Rona Thau

Dr. Rona provides education on whole food nutrition in addition to natural preventive health choices so all people can access their best health ever.

Dr. Rona has earned degrees in Theatre Arts, Human Biology and a Doctoral Degree in Chiropractic Medicine. She writes poetry, studies and teaches yoga and meditation. Her journey of self-healing and study of holistic medicine began early in life but mystically transformed her life after an accident literally propelled her in to the field of healing and transformation.

Dr. Rona offers workshops on a broad range of topics that include How the Body Talks, Self-Healing with Food, Mastering Moving Meditation, the Joy of Anatomy and Physiology for Humans and Yogis, and the Toolbox to Relieve Pain and Generate Health.

Dr. Rona's highly-trained yet intuitive style of teaching and healing provides you with lasting tools to assist you to be healthy and thrive throughout Life.

CHAPTER 32

Lessons from My Mother

by Camille Gaines

My parents grew up in the South during the depths of Great Depression. This fact affected the lives of my brother, Blake, and me, as it did so many others in the baby boomer generation. My mother was one of 11 children in a family that lived on a rice farm in Arkansas. Although she had four older sisters, she was the first woman in her family to graduate from high school. Travel to the school required a long walk on many dark and cold mornings along the isolated train tracks. My mother walked to school, anyway. She knew that she wanted to create a rich life for herself, a life beyond the minimum that was expected of her.

I paid little attention when my mother told this and other stories when I was younger. Being older and presumably wiser now, these stories not only have my attention, they grab a strong hold onto my heart. Not only that, I am now able to recognize priceless lessons that I learned as she raised me. I now see that these lessons have had a dynamic impact on both my financial and my life journey. I didn't know it at the time, but these lessons have been a warm and guiding light in my life.

I want to share some of Mama's stories with you, in the hope that you will find the precious value that I have found in them, as you continue along your life journey. If you are an entrepreneur, then you have likely already learned that your entrepreneurial journey and your life journey are sweetly intertwined in a way that goes far beyond money.

Lesson One: You Can Do Anything You Decide To Do

Mother wanted to learn new skills so that she could become financially independent, instead of simply living a life that was the norm, and thus, expected of her: to marry a farmer, and live the rest of her life in a tiny town (with less than 200 residents). It's not that this would have been a bad life, but it wasn't the life that she chose for herself. She devised a plan, as a teenager, to create the life that she wanted. She borrowed $50 from Uncle Vernon so that she could take the bus to Memphis to get a job; and that she did. She found a room in a boarding house, where she lived and supported herself for several years.

This lesson served me well later in my life. After living on the island of Bermuda for over 13 years, my husband's job, which had taken us there and given us an incredible lifestyle, ended. We knew that the choices for a similar type of position for my husband, the primary earner then, would be in New York City or Chicago. We really did not want to live in either city, especially since we had become very comfortable living on a beautiful, quiet island estate on Hungary Bay in Paget! Our children were young, so we knew we wanted to live in a safe and beautiful place near our families that was small enough to provide a quality lifestyle. We chose to "wing it" and move to Austin, Texas, where we had frequently visited my brother when we lived overseas. He owned a waterfront "cottage" (being very generous with the term cottage) abutting Lake Austin Spa Resort, until just before our move back to the U.S. (Wealth Note: Think hard before selling any waterfront property; but that's another book!)

We knew the life we wanted, and we took a big and scary leap into the first steps to create it, just as my mother had done. We had no idea of what lay ahead, and we honestly floundered for a few years. The blessing of this time period (years of "wandering in the desert," as we call it now) is that we learned about creating all types of income streams and alternative investments. Unfortunately, virtually all yields on traditional investments tanked during our "desert years," calling us to deeper exploration beyond our previous financial fields. We learned more about real estate investing, oil and gas trusts, entity structures, Internet-based businesses and option selling. Some of the lessons were very painful ones; some things worked and others did not. What we learned is that from those lessons, we are now better able to help others in our financial programs learn what we learned without them having to go through the same pain themselves. We also learned my mother's lesson ourselves; that you can do anything that you decide you are going to do if you pay attention to your money, increase your skills, create a plan and then work it with persistence, faith and determination.

Lesson Two: Take Advantage of Opportunities to Advance Your Skills

My mother learned that she was an excellent typist shortly after landing her first job in Memphis. This skill was highly in demand in the 1940s. Soon thereafter, however, she had the opportunity to learn to use the Vari-typer so that she could improve the design and layout of the news bulletin that was sent to the customers of her employer. (Marketing principles never change!) She embraced the chance to take on this additional responsibility because she was able to increase her skills. I still hear the pride in her voice when she tells me about acquiring this skill, which was very prized at the time.

Don't you feel awesome after you learn a new skill? It lifts your confidence and capabilities. This is one of the reasons why I love being able to help women increase their financial skills; it's empowering, and I hear it in their voices.

Higher skills increase your value, plain and simple. If you are unhappy with your income level, increase your skill set. This principle applies to both employees and entrepreneurs. If you think about it, this applies to everything in life, including parenting, networking, golf, and decorating. The increase in income is from life enjoyment and satisfaction. In the case of parenting, the outcome can be life-changing for your children, and even the world. Positive expansion just happens when we get better at something.

During the "desert years," I was called to seriously increase my skills. Before I embraced that expansion, I would awake during the night and feel empty. Even though life is less certain and often more challenging now that we are full-time entrepreneurs and investors, I awake happy and fulfilled. Now, those "middle of the night" wakeup calls are usually prompted by a great idea regarding something new that I have learned that I cannot wait to explore.

Lesson Three: Create a Spending Plan that Supports Your Life Vision

Eventually, my mom married my dad. Later, as a stay-at-home mom, she ran our household like a little business, putting aside as much money as she could, to grow. For example, she wanted a new set of furniture for my bedroom, so she ordered a kit and built a beautiful set of furniture that she "antiqued" off-white. Our living room became a workshop packed with unfinished cut wood, nails, and tools. Can you even imagine finding the kit you want and ordering it without the Internet? My mother, however, had made a decision; her daughter was going to have one of those beautiful bedroom sets, and the cost was going to be within my parent's spending plan. (I prefer this term over the "b word": "budget.")

The bedroom set was only one of many projects that required our living room to become a factory for various projects that my mother passionately pursued to provide an excellent quality of life, while spending smartly. Mama had discovered that by purchasing kits or materials and making things herself, she could provide quality items for our family at a fraction of the usual cost. She applied this strategy to furniture, draperies, and even an amazing stereo system! This allowed my parents to put aside more money to grow. She wanted to have the funds so that I could go to college one day, and have ballet, art and piano lessons in the meantime. She defined and created the life that she wanted for her family.

I also learned that, with savvy spending, my family could have a lifestyle that was far beyond adequate. Sometimes life calls for savvier spending than other times, but it always calls for conscious and wise spending. The lesson I learned is to be creative and have fun with your spending plan so you can have positive cash flow. Live within your means so that you can create the rich life you want. By doing so, you'll lay the foundation for more wealth in your life.

Lesson Four: Always Develop Some Marketable Skills

When I began ballet lessons in kindergarten, my mother created a little sewing business making the beautiful, detailed costumes required for numerous students in the annual dance recital. Once again, our living room was turned into a "hands-off" workshop every Spring for many years, and filled with lovely sequins, elegant trimmings, exquisite fabrics and colorful tutu netting. I now realize that Mama enjoyed earning "her own money" by using her talents and abilities. She thrived on sharing her gifts through that little enterprise with the creation of all of those beautiful costumes. I know now that she also felt more confident and financially secure at the thought of having marketable skills.

Lesson Five: Don't Do What Everyone Else Does

The largest crime my mom committed was requiring me to wear black patent Mary Janes year round, instead of providing me with white shoes for the summer months. I still recall feeling as though I was the only girl in the entire universe without white shoes each May, completely oblivious to the fact that there were millions of little girls all over the world who would have given anything for a pair of black patent Mary Janes. What I learned from that horrible injustice is that black patent shoes are appropriate year round. (This turned out to be a very valuable lesson as an adult with my long, skinny feet that look like surf boards in white shoes!) More importantly, I learned that you don't need to follow the crowd. If only I had known, then, the wise lessons my mother was providing that would serve me well for life that went well beyond shoe style.

Savvy Spending Coupled with Investing Basics

My father regularly read a few financial publications, and he became very capable at being able to recognize undervalued assets. His attention to investing, along with my mother's savvy cash flow abilities, allowed him to take an early retirement. My parents began playing golf when I went to college, and even built a house overlooking the course so they could drive their cart right onto it. Shortly before my dad left this world due to a brain tumor, he told me that it was really my mother's savvy spending that had allowed them to achieve their financial goals, more so than his investing skills. I think it was a combination of the two, which is why I like to emphasize both positive cash flow and investing basics. You cannot reach your financial goals without practice and knowledge of each.

I discovered early on that my WHY is to help women increase their earnings, and then monitor and grow their money so that they can have the life that they want. I love living my WHY through my programs at www.financialwoman.com. These lessons from my mother are both life lessons and money lessons; the two are intertwined, due to the enormous role that money plays in our lives, including food and shelter provisions. Your money deserves your respect and attention to create and live a life that is all you imagine that it can be; a rich life.

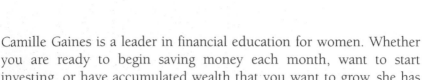

Camille Gaines is a leader in financial education for women. Whether you are ready to begin saving money each month, want to start investing, or have accumulated wealth that you want to grow, she has personally been right where you are on your money journey; she shares her simple and practical wisdom that can immediately uplevel you on the path to your financial goals. She has almost three decades of first-hand experience that provide a solid foundation for helping other women achieve financial success through her powerful and enriching programs at www.financialwoman.com.

She has been featured as a financial expert in numerous media outlets. Her award-winning blog and Financial Woman Radio Show allow her to share practical information in a simple and common language to which you can easily relate and understand. What sets Camille apart from many others offering financial education is that her experience has been on the investor side of the table herself, not selling wealth management products or advisory services; this allows her to have a completely unbiased and real-life perspective that puts others at ease.

A background in energy trading accounting, international corporate financial training, and commercial real estate laid the foundation for Camille's passion as a personal investor. She has invested in almost every type of financial product and worked with numerous financial professionals, giving her the ability to easily guide you through the maze of financial services and products to understand what makes the most sense for you, whether you want to personally invest or work with a financial advisor. Camille has successfully managed a simple and low-cost index portfolio based on a Nobel prize-winning strategy that requires only a few hours a year which she teaches to others who wish to invest their own money.

Camille's passion for investing began when she saw her father successfully time the purchase of tax-free municipal bonds, selling at deep discounts in the early 1980s. Her father's theory was that "the last thing to go out would be the lights." He was right; those bonds greatly appreciated and paid tax-free interest in excess of 20 percent over the next decade, allowing her father to take an early retirement and enhancing her parent's lifestyle. Isn't that what creating a nest egg is all about?

Following those early lessons, Camille lives her "savvy but smart" philosophy by finding value everywhere, from undervalued securities to designer jewelry online. While many may avoid financial topics, Camille asks what cannot be fun about growing your money when it provides so much, including food and shelter; it gives you the ability to change your life and even the lives of others. Camille would love to share what she has learned about money and investing to help you create the rich life that you so desire.

CHAPTER 33

Step Into Your Happiness Gap

by Carrie Strathman Ballard

Imagine…a new way of thinking, feeling, and action…a whole new way of being. Living your life on your own terms, taking the steps of living out the life of your dreams right now.

Does this describe where you are right now? Perhaps you are preparing to step into your next life chapter, but you feel afraid, unsure or how to make it happen. You have doubts and fears that it won't come true.

You so want more freedom; better, deeper, more loving relationships; more income; a healthier body; more knowledge; deeper faith; a career that inspires your passion. You want these, but are afraid that when you take that leap of faith, you'll fall into the abyss rather than step into your bliss!

Are you afraid or do you just not have a clearly defined vision of your passion and true purpose? You know it's there; you've felt it; you've glimpsed it in your mind's eye for a fleeting moment, but just can't quite describe it exactly. Let's take a moment to suspend fear and disbelief and catch a glimpse of your passion and purpose again.

Imagine living your life as you know you are meant to live it. You've been there before. Remember that perfect day, when all was in alignment.

Remembering that day, where were you? What were you doing? How did you feel? Most important, who were you being? Now suspend disbelief and imagine feeling that way again. Get the vision of it in your mind in deep, vibrant detail. Feel the feelings, the thoughts, the actions you were taking. You remember now, don't you? Yeah, that's it. That's the place.

Now imagine this place existing always in your mind. Keep it in the forefront this time. You can access it any time, any place you choose to. It only takes a moment. You have the time. Make the time daily, many times a day, to do this.

You know the saying by Gandhi: "You must be the change you want to see in the world." You are the change—you just need to choose it and choose it often. Others are wanting this change, too. There is already a major shift happening in the world—we just need to wake up to it. We need to learn how to take control of making the changes we want to see rather than just responding to circumstance around us and then asking, "Why isn't my life the way I dreamt it should be?

Do you feel you live a double life? Is there a disappointing gap between the image you see in your mind and feel in your heart, and the image you see and feel in the outside world? Hmm…what if you could close the gap between the two? You can, you know. It all begins with you. You are the common denominator here, you see. It's time to take control of your thoughts, feelings, and actions, and bring them into alignment with your vision, Does that feel scary? Don't know how? I bet you do. You just need to believe strongly enough and want it badly enough.

"And the day came when the risk to remain tight in a bud was more painful than the risk it took to blossom." —Anais Nin

Just take a moment and see yourself physically creating your world on the outside to be a mirror image of your world on the inside. Now take this a step further and imagine yourself doing this on a daily basis.

What if every morning your first thoughts were of what you intend to create for that day? What if these small daily actions taken over the period of a week, a month, or six months, could snowball into creating a new reality? What if these daily actions created a healthier body and stronger, deeper relationships with yourself and others? What if these actions created a career or vocation you are passionate about and you elegantly had more energy and more income?

Adopt a daily practice of creating your living environment, a living culture if you will, where everything is supportive of your creating and living your purpose; of living your WHY!

Do you have a Daily Success Formula?

1. Remember your purpose and how it will impact the world.

2. Create a compelling vision for how to carry out your purpose.

3. Find the knowledge from experts already doing what you want to do.

4. Apply these actions and knowledge.

5. Create the environment to keep you focused and disciplined to continue taking action daily. This is crucial. Remember that everything in this environment counts!

6. Share your success and knowledge with others for we are here to serve others.

7. Be grateful and appreciate what is.

"Happiness cannot come from without. It must come from within. It is not what we see and touch or that which others do for us which makes us happy; it is that which we think and feel and do, first for the other fellow and then for ourselves." —Helen Keller

Step into how this new world you are creating feels. Now imagine this for the rest of your life. Or not. Which feels better? Which feels right? If it feels uncomfortable, then good! It is right! It is the next step for you to take, isn't it? Remember, if you are not growing, you are dying. You know in your heart that is true. Which do you choose for yourself and for those you love?

Carrie Strathman Ballard is the CEO and Founder of Stop Waiting, Start Living Now! Since 1999, Carrie's life purpose is to support innovative, creators and thought leaders ready to step into their next life chapter. Learn to suspend disbelief, reconnect to your purpose and step elegantly into your best life now! To download your Success Map and Toolkit, and learn more about the transformation waiting for you, please visit Carrie at www.carrieballard.com.

CHAPTER 34

From the Shower…to the G-Spot

by Sophie Trpcevski

Little did I know that lying there on the bottom of my shower basin, 15 years ago, in my deepest moment of darkness, was going to be my greatest pivotal turning point of my life. Not being able to recall how long I had been lying there, and how I got there, was the most frightening experience for me, a mother of two children under the age of four, home alone.

I don't know whether you will be able to relate to this. However, I guess you may know someone who might...so I will share it with you anyway. I was one of those mothers who had to be in control of everything. Not only did I have to be in control of it, I also had to be perfect. I was living in a world of should—I should be much thinner. I should be more beautiful. I should be smarter. I should be a better teacher. I should be a better mother. I should be a better wife. I should be a better daughter. I should be a better sister. I should do this and should do that, and if I wasn't, I was riddled with guilt and beating myself up when I was being less than perfect. So how do you think that was working for me? Hmmm...not well! Finally my body shut down on me. I was not paying attention to any of the signs it was throwing at me, the anger outburst, the uncontrollable crying session each night as I lay down to sleep and the constant yo-yoing of weight gain and loss.

It was in that forced state of helplessness that I had time to reflect on where my life was heading. It came to me that if I wanted my life to change then I had to take 100 percent responsibility to create that change. For the next 10years, I embarked on a journey of self-discovery and professional development to discover "Who is Sophie Trpcevski?" and "What is my life's purpose?"

Fifteen years later, I now have a successful business, "The G-Spot For Women." G for Goal that empowers and educates women to love themselves from inside out, to live a magnificent and abundant life from their higher self. I have also developed online programs based on goal setting and team support.

In addition to the goal-setting process, I educate and coach women on their ***mindset*** and ***emotional intelligence***. I do this through webinars to assist them to eliminate their limiting beliefs around why they are stopped from creating great wealth and success in their lives, at the same time creating more positive and empowering ways of looking at situations which normally would be seen as challenges or fears. These women then realize that they can have choices which free them, to create new possibilities in their lives and businesses.

This business also allows me the freedom to work my own hours, around my family, using my skills and talents, creating balance and structure, while empowering women to discover their own strengths and passion that assists them to create success and happiness in their lives. I love the fact that it has taking me around the globe from the convenience of my living room. I can connect with all my clients via video, or live when—conducting workshops and seminars, giving keynote speeches and getting to know them on a very deep, intimate level in my retreat programs. I get to live my dream through my work... how blessed am I? All thanks to my dark shower moment some fifteen years ago.

I would like to take you on a mini self-discovery tour so that you can let go of "living in the world of should" by trying to keep control of things that don't need to be controlled,so you can focus on the things that are important and that matter to you, like activities that help you be more productive and successful in your business and life.

7 Secrets to Success through Goal Setting

"Goals give you a compass in order to direct your path through life. Goals focus your thoughts and actions on areas that have precise purpose and meaning." —Catherine Pulsifer

Values

Towards the end of my teaching career I wasn't enjoying my work. It was hard to get up in the mornings and I didn't find it fun anymore even though I loved the kids and I loved watching their growth and skill development as the year progressed. That light inside of me had died down to a tiny flicker and I didn't understand why until I attended a girlfriend's workshop on values.

It was when I did my own values audit, I realized what was causing the internal distress and therefore affecting my feelings towards teaching and my lack of motivation and energy at work.

I realized that I was not honoring my highest values and was not functioning from a place of authenticity, which was impacting on my performance, my vitality and well-being.

"Values" as defined by Anthony Robbins, "are private, personal, individual beliefs about what is most important to you. Your values are beliefs systems about right, wrong, good and bad."

Values are a guiding principle, an internal compass, by which we live our lives, shaping the kinds of experiences we seek out and those we avoid.

At the highest level, these are likely to be things such as security, joy, making a difference, financial freedom, integrity, respect, creativity, service, health or being loved. They are generalizations on what does and what does not matter.

If you know your values then you know who you are and what you stand for. Your life is owned by you and shaped by your terms! For example, Nelson Mandela spent nearly three decades in prison, and when he was released his convictions were as strong as the day he was jailed.

We all have values but few of us are consciously aware of this. Most people do not realize that their values are shaping their lives because our behavior flows directly from our values. If someone values fairness, they would also believe that people should be treated equally and act that way themselves. When they don't act that way, they would feel uncomfortable with their actions or with anyone else who has treated them unfairly.

To achieve fulfillment and success... true success...it is essential to decide what you value most in life and then commit to live your values every day. When you are clear about what is important to your life, you will be able to make effective decisions. Decision-making becomes effortless once you know what you stand for and what is most important, especially in the tough times.

Once you have a clear picture of what you want and the values that you are going to let drive you, you need to stay focused on the end result and what that is going to give you.

Motivation

Motive/Action. What is your motive for action? Why do you want to achieve it? The reason why needs to be so compelling and big enough to make you feel uncomfortable, and be stretched way out of your comfort zone, however, not so far that it will freeze you. It needs to be bigger than you. You do not need to know how you are going to achieve this, just why you want to achieve it. This energy and desire will start to attract the opportunities, the resources and people that will help you to achieve your goal. Your job is to see it, believe it and most importantly...feel it.

WIIFM (What's in it for me?) You must have a big enough WHY, otherwise there is not enough motivation behind it. It is generally to avoid pain. I am tired of not having any money, a near-death experience, loss of a loved one or it can be to receive pleasure. If I lose weight, I will look and feel fabulous and be able to attract a better partner. We tend to do more to avoid pain than receive pleasure. A good example of this is the avoidance of public speaking. People would work harder and more hours to attract clients instead of getting up to speak for an hour to a room full of potential clients that would generate ten times more business and leads due to their fear that they might not be liked or might appear somewhat less than perfect in their presentation.

Vision

Visualize the end result. What does it look like, feel like, sound like, smell like, taste like? Ignite all your senses and get emotionally connected to achieving the goal and visualize it as though you are there right... now in the moment. Your brain does not know whether it is real or not. So the more you visualize, the more the brain accepts it to be your reality.

"Your vision becomes clear when you look inside your heart. Who looks outside, dreams. Who looks inside, awakens." —Carl Jung

Plan

Set SMART Goals (Specific, Measurable, Action Based, Realistic, Time Framed). What, specifically, do you want to achieve? Break the big goal into smaller, achievable action steps with due dates to aim for. Plan for possible solutions and obstacles that might come up which may prevent you from achieving your outcomes. How are you going to measure your progress along the way? Be realistic on the outcome. Don't set yourself up to fail. Remember to stretch yourself, but not so much that you will freeze. If you go to my web site www.theGspotforwomen.com, you will be able to download, for FREE, a MP3 file of me guiding you through the goal-setting process as well as the Goal Setting Template.

Action

Take 100 percent responsibility for all your actions and do what it takes. Be determined and persistent in achieving the goal you set out to achieve. Be the 'cause' in your life—create what you want and not be the 'effect', laying blame and making excuses about what is going on around you. Keep in mind that there is no failure only feedback. Look for the lesson in each challenge. Be flexible because the journey has twists, turns and some detours in it. You will not be travelling on a straight road all the time.

Results

Celebrate your small successes along the way and then treat yourself to something special when you have achieved your goal as a thank you for a job well done. Spend a moment to reflect your journey and the learning. It is the journey and not the destination that grows you to be the person that really matters.

"Your success or failure in life will not be decided by the number of setbacks you encounter, but rather how you react to them." —Unknown

Accountability

Sharing your goals with another, allows you to stay focused and work harder to achieving them because someone else knows about them. You don't want to disappoint that person or look bad by not keeping your word. You could find a buddy who also wants to achieve the same goal so you can motivate each other or work together on it. Hire a coach who will keep you on track, challenge you and provide tips and tools to achieve your goal faster. Or best of all, you could join a team of like-minded women who will not only support you, they can assist you to achieve your goals.

Sophie Trpcevski, The G-Spot for Women Founder, is a leader in emotional intelligence and self-empowerment coaching in Australia.

Sophie has a passion for helping women from all walks of life to step into their power, discover their strengths and fulfill their goals while educating them on how to love themselves from the inside out. So they can live a magnificent and abundant life from their higher self. Sophie coaches women individually and through a series of goals groups that meet each month throughout Australia. She is the creator and facilitator of a very powerful transformational program "Loving Me Inside Out" which focuses on living an authentic life from your higher self.

After graduating with a Diploma in Health and Physical Education and a Diploma in Teaching Primary and Early Childhood, Sophie worked as both a primary teacher and tertiary lecturer at the Royal Melbourne Institute of Technology.

During her 20 years as an educator, Sophie developed a passion for the power of emotional intelligence awareness. This led her to undertake a Diploma in Executive Coaching, specializing in emotional intelligence leadership.

Sophie is also a Master Practitioner in Life Coaching and specializes in Cognitive Behavioural Therapy, Neuro-Linguistics, the GENOS Model of Emotional Intelligence, and Extended DISC Personal Analysis.

Sophie's own program, *Teen Personal Excellence*, has equipped hundreds of students, parents and teachers with the tools needed to help teenagers create alternate pathways to success and emotional well-being.

Also as the Director of Mindscollective, Sophie has helped leaders in organizations, through coaching and workshops such as Telstra, Alcatel Lucent, Sportsnet, the Victorian Education Department, and numerous local municipalities and medium-sized businesses to engage constructively with their people and ultimately build productivity and performance.

CHAPTER 35

Business: Living Art Form, Creative Process, Offering to the World

by Dr. Nalini Chilkov, L.Ac, O.M.D.

"Your greatest work of art should be your own life."
—Anais Nin

Visioning, growing and sustaining a business is essentially a creative process. Being an innovative, leading-edge professional or entrepreneur is not unlike making a great work of art. Real art moves us. Real art stops us in our tracks, gets our attention and curiosity.

Real art takes us to an edge, someplace new. A thriving professional life is a creative life.

Real creativity calls on all of our resources, life experiences and knowledge to meet the moment before us and birth an inspired original response. Powerful art is sourced from authentic experience. We need more than our business skills and professional training to go from ordinary to extraordinary. Every aspect of our lives informs our business and professional decisions.

When I started in private practice, I thought that I was supposed to play a "role" be the "doctor, the "authority" or some such "somebody." When my mentor, Deena Metzger, asked me, "What do you know about healing that has nothing to do with your training?"

I began to bring what I know from dance, high-altitude climbing, meditation practice, living in other cultures into the treatment room with my patients. My work and my relationships with my patients transformed, became enlivened, rich, and multi-faceted.

I began to really trust myself. I also felt whole and really enjoyed my days. From that place, I decided to tell the fairy tale of *The Handless Maiden* to a patient with over a year of paralysis in both of her hands as her "medicine." One week later, she returned, able to once again hold her child. I dared to make a creative original act and use story as healing salve, not at all part of my professional "training" or job description. This was a turning point in my career.

A creative process is alive, fresh and vital. This state of presence and flow seeds itself in a perpetual life-giving process. Creative, fully present and engaged, we find ourselves on the edge of giving life to something new, seeing from another perspective, meeting a challenge with innovation and originality with both heart and mind.

Joseph Campbell sees the function of the artist as the bridge builder, the one who takes us across the waters. The artist ferries us from the mundane and connects us to the sacred, to something greater than our small self. What could be more sacred than a true creative act of service as an offering to the world, to your community, to the client in need before you?

Living the creative life, requires full presence and awareness, full engagement and commitment. We must show up 100 percent, not 99 percent. My business associates and my patients many times, have held up a clear mirror to me, showed me where I needed to stretch, to grow.

The willingness to face myself with openness, curiosity, flexibility and radical honesty is essential. We must continuously "re-create" ourselves. We must have the flexibility to shape shift in order to serve more fully. We must be able to let go. In difficult moments, we must be humble and self-reflective rather than defensive and egocentric. We must learn to put the small self aside, exhale. However awkward or graceful, we must be grateful for the opportunity, if we are genuinely motivated to be of service, egocentric defenses fall away.

Willingness to hear the truth and allow radical honesty makes space for a creative reshaping of the self. When we embrace our full humanity as mere imperfect mortals, we also grant full humanity to others in the same breath. I hope I have made all the really big and many of the small mistakes and missteps by now...something tells me…there are probably more mistakes in my future.

To create and sustain our visions, we must ponder and redefine the real qualities of a "successful human being," not just a successful businesswoman. Real success is not about "What is my net worth?" "Am I famous and important and getting my ego massaged with recognition?" Rather, "Am I making meaning? Am I making a contribution and being of service?"

At the end of each day, can I say, "Today I made a difference. Today my words, actions, presence contribution made the world just a little bit better"? The real satisfaction and rewards are intangible. Real "success" is measured by whether our way of walking our path and standing in the world is truly life-giving. This capacity to give and nurture life are core creative qualities of the feminine.

When women are able to embody the feminine rather than attempting to fit into patriarchal values in order to "succeed"...then our true nature as vessels and gateways of new life is evident, and the ultimate creative act is available to us. We become ourselves, fecund, full of potential, carrying the fertile seeds, ready to birth and nurture, finding the delicate balance between holding close, guiding and pruning, being spacious and letting go so that our creations can blossom and flower and bear fruit. What could be more creative?

Just as in growing a garden, a professional life has weather and seasons, times to labor and times to be still. We must prepare the soil. We must protect the seeds and fruits from danger and predation. We must attune to the cycles, know when to act and when to wait, when to speak and when to be silent. We must have a sense of timing. We must cultivate authentic relationship. We must show up and pay attention day after day, notice what has changed and what is needed. We must bring energy and effort. Sometimes we rise early and at other times we see the moon rise, warding off the night stalkers who would dig up what we so carefully sowed and nurtured. Sometimes our crops fail and we must start again. If we have paid attention and stayed the course, we may harvest sweet fruits, and have in our hands, new seeds to sow for the next generation, the next cycle. We also honor the season in which we rest, reflect, go within, and count our blessings. We restore ourselves in preparation for the next cycle of sowing and reaping to circle around once again. This is a generative, creative cycle.

Having circled the sun and made the journey through all the seasons we find we will never be quite the same. We find ourselves transformed by living the process itself. We have made meaning and created value. We have remade the world and ourselves by offering the gift of our intelligence and energy, creativity and attention, tenderness and fierceness. No small task!

I really wish that someone had talked to me about the realities of the journey and the essential qualities needed to make my career and my professional life one filled with meaning and value.

I wish someone had asked me hard questions and caused me to reflect on these essential elements when I was young and starting out. Only later in my life and career, did I find true mentors. Instead, I went forward with the "by the seat of my pants" method, without a plan, without much guidance. (I don't recommend this method!) I had no rudder, but followed what engaged and enlivened me, not a straight line path, a circuitous, creative path. I have cultivated awareness and patience. Due to my intense passion and laser-like focus, I found my way, sometimes bumbling, sometimes skillful.

Now I am an elder in my profession and I can speak from experience. Over the last 30 years, I can remember only three or four times when I did not feel like going to my office. What I do has never felt like "work." My outer life is completely congruent with my authentic inner life. I have a good time. I enjoy myself. I make my own schedule. I created an environment that is not only healing for my patients but also nourishes me. A great place to spend the day.

I have continually followed what has interested and engaged me. I rarely looked too far ahead.

I was not motivated by money. Yet I have always paid attention, so that when a door of opportunity opened, if only for the blink of an eye, I was able to walk through it. I am the most surprised person when I look back to see where my path has led me and what I have created.

Not only that, I get to be fully myself and earn a nice living!

When we give our gifts fully, offering all that we are, the Universe acknowledges us with abundance and support. When we bring the most precious human qualities of generosity, integrity and authenticity blended with courage, the willingness to apply energy and effort, to risk, even to fail, coupled with intelligence, discrimination, caring and compassion, when we make meaning and create value, we are rewarded with the blessings of fulfillment and peace.

After 30 years of professional life, in the end, this is what really matters. At the end of my life, I will not be saying "I spent a lot of time at the office." (Even though I have!) Instead, I will be saying "My life has been a fulfilling creative process and I have made a meaningful and valuable difference."

If someone had told me when I was younger that this was the journey and these are the qualities required to both be fully human and make an act of power and compassion in the world, to be a "success"...I might have felt I was not up to the task.

Whatever we think or feel, life tempers and tests us and grows us into our glorious unique, eccentric selves.

May you, too, taste the sweet fruits of your labors.

Dr. Nalini Chilkov, L.Ac.O.M.D. combines her diverse training in traditional oriental medicine, modern biomedicine and cell biology with 30 years in private practice. Dr. Chilkov primarily serves patients with cancer and complex, chronic illnesses alongside her Optimal Health and Wellness practice. She is a respected expert in Collaborative Integrative Cancer Care, known both for her meticulous attention to detail and individualized treatment plans as well as her warmth and compassion.

Dr. Chilkov is a seasoned clinician and an innovator, building bridges between modern and traditional healing paradigms, and partnering with physicians to provide best outcomes for patients.

She has been a lecturer at the School of Medicine at UCLA and UC Irvine in California as well as many schools of traditional oriental and naturopathic medicine over her long career.

Dr. Chilkov is a regular contributor to the Healthy Living Section of the Huffington Post. www.huffingtonpost.com/nalini-chilkov

She has been recognized as a go-to clinician in Suzanne Somers' book *Knockout:: Interviews with Doctors Who Are Curing Cancer-And How to Prevent Getting It in the First Place*. Dr. Chilkov sits on the Scientific Advisory Board of the Mederi Foundation for research, education and integrative care of patients with cancer and chronic illnesses.

Dr. Chilkov holds a degree in cell biology and is trained in nursing, travel and wilderness medicine. She stays abreast of leading medical research worldwide. Dr. Chilkov has provided care in medically underserved regions and wilderness areas on several continents.

Dr. Chilkov has a lifelong involvement in creative and meditative arts and has studied dance and music in West Africa. An avid hiker, Dr. Chilkov has climbed mountains in Africa, Asia, Europe, and North America.

Dr. Chilkov has provided her patients with truly personal and individualized integrative care and brings a wealth of wisdom and expertise to her practice. She offers her unique approach to Integrative Cancer Care: The Healing Cancer Plan at www.alternativecanceranswer.com.

Brilliance is in the Balance

CHAPTER 36

A Life in Style

by Catherine Cassidy

Creating Your Life in Style

I loved my job. It had me flying to New York for Fashion Week, backstage at the fashion shows, creating the product assortment that would ultimately go into the stores, styling the lookbooks for our buyers to buy from and working with the owners of the company on the brand vision and strategy. It was exactly the job I dreamed of—a perfect balance of creative and analytical elements. It merged my love for business and strategy with Fashion and creativity.

There was just one little problem. I realized that wasn't enough.

Over time, the exuberance I felt for each workday, challenge and opportunity to create waned. Suddenly, I realized that instead of jumping out of bed as I was used to, I was hitting the snooze button a couple of times and downing two *bowls* of coffee (I'm not exaggerating!) and throwing on whatever sort of worked to just get my butt out of the door.

I was so torn. I truly loved my job by its definition, but I was so frustrated and I wasn't sure by what.

Then, the company started promoting its Malawi campaign in an effort to show its philanthropic side. This really made me consider the meaning of the work I was doing. Perhaps that was because I saw through the campaign as a way to align with the cause du jour for shameless self-promotion, not genuinely caring about the impact in

Malawi. Great that the company was at least doing *something* to help others, great that I had a big impact on the assortment that went into the stores and ultimately into women's closets to make them look and feel fabulous, but that wasn't enough. I felt like all I was really doing was adding to the company's bottom line and encouraging women to buy more clothes than they needed.

It wasn't meaningful. I wasn't fulfilled.

After many long hikes pondering my next steps, a year and a half researching other fashion companies to find one that would give me a more meaningful and challenging experience, and even an extension class at UCLA, I still didn't have a next step. I had no direction. I was just going through the motions.

Until it hit me! On just another hot summer day in LA stuck in traffic on my way to my regular facial, I got a call from my best friend. She had a crazy idea. It involved quitting my job. Perhaps it was that she was sick of hearing me constantly complain about how much I worked and all my frustrations or perhaps because she did see a potential that I couldn't see in myself at the time. She gave me a way to quit and strike out on my own.

Of course, I'd thought of this before. I'd had ideas of starting to style and offer personal shopping on the side as I'd recognized I had a knack for understanding women's sizes, shapes and personalities to find the best and most flattering clothes for them. Even then, that idea was boring. It's been done, so why do I need to do it as well?

And then it dawned on me.

I'd been working 10 to 12 hour days consistently, often weekends as well and witnessing the demands on my boss who had a three-year-old daughter at home and constantly had to make sacrifices on her time with her. I'd not had much of a social life, much less a dating life.

Giving women the tools to live a life in style

For me, it wasn't just about personal style or shopping for women. It was about balance. It was about empowering busy women to live their lives in style while taking one thing off their very full plates. It was about creating the company I wanted to work for that not only empowered our clients, but also our employees.

Aaahhhh....

Maybe that's why this time, finally, it hit home. Like a whoosh, I felt the certainty that this was the next step I was searching for. What is a seemingly impulsive decision from an outsider's perspective was actually perfectly well thought out.

After a week of considering my options financially and also to ensure that I really wasn't being impulsive, I put in my notice. My boss was shocked, to say the least.

I can understand why.

Heck, *I* was shocked! I couldn't believe I had the courage to do it. I actually quit my job!

What I realized in my car that afternoon was that I couldn't be the only woman struggling to find balance and *do it all.* And I definitely wasn't doing it all. I was working a lot, and getting in exercise, but at the end of the day I was pretty spent. And this is *before* family and kids...how do *those* women do it all???

I wanted it all! I want *you* to have it all, too!

Fast-forward three years later: I know I made the right decision for me. I have learned so much more than I ever would have at that job or at another company. It's been way more work both personally and professionally than I'd honestly anticipated, but it's also allowed me the most amazing relationships with such fabulous women—both friends and clients.

Living a life in style is what allows you to have it all and do it all. The catch is that you're not doing it all yourself. A life in style allows you space for each aspect of your life that's important to you—personal, professional, family, friends and health. This is all determined according to your personal needs, just as your personal style and wardrobe is determined according to your lifestyle and personality. Who you ARE! It's effectively a lifestyle by design.

In these last three years of building and growing my business, I learned that it wasn't just the last job that made me a workaholic. Even when I could set my own hours, I was working just as much. It turns out that I simply have that tendency. For instance, I used to jump out of bed and head straight to the computer and start working away. Now, I've created a morning ritual to ensure I start the day with self-care, not work. Taking that time for myself is such a decadent luxury.

It's the little indulgences and simple luxuries that create a life in style.

And isn't time the ultimate luxury?

How much time do you have to yourself? For your work? For your family? For your friends? How do you fit it all in? How DO you do it all?

You don't do it all yourself.

I've learned through my experiences and by observing my clients, many who are incredibly successful women (and moms), is that you can't do it alone. We would need more hours in the day! *We can do it all, we just can't do it all ourselves.* From part-time child care, personal trainers, business assistants, dry cleaners that pick up and drop off your clothes, car detailers that come to you, to girls' nights, mastermind groups and consultants, it really does take a village.

More importantly, if you want to have it all, you have to take care of yourself first. As women, we're programmed to take care of everyone else before we worry about ourselves, which often means we forget about ourselves completely. This doesn't mean you forget about others, but it does mean you prioritize yourself. Unless you'd rather simply burn out.

As moms, business owners, corporate women climbing the ladder to the top, we face a lot of tough decisions each day. Sometimes, sacrifices will have to be made. With the right support, those sacrifices don't have to be detrimental to us or those we care about most.

Your time is your most valuable resource, so how are you spending it? Do you take time to indulge in a book, go for a hike, take your kids to the playground, or are you working all the time?

If you're constantly in work or 'to do' mode, look for one thing that you could take off your plate that would free up your time. This could be your housecleaning, picking up your dry cleaning, shopping for an outfit for that VIP meeting, ordering in a healthy dinner, etc. How much time does that free up? And what could you do in that time? Taking these things off your plate that aren't meaningful to you means that you can focus on what is.

It was a big leap for me to hire my first assistant. It was scary. It was money I didn't necessarily have. But the beautiful thing of it was that she took menial things I didn't want to do and weren't the best use of my time off my plate. I had time to create new products and packages, follow up with potential clients and contacts and take time for myself to recharge. Amazingly, the money easily came for me to pay her.

Now, it doesn't necessarily mean hiring someone, either. How can your husband, boyfriend, roommate, children or best friend help you with something? Just don't be afraid to ask for help!

A life in style can be taking the time for a spa day with a girlfriend, indulging in one piece of chocolate (not five!), and making your health a priority as much as it means presenting the best version of yourself each and every day in presence and style. It doesn't have to all happen at once either. For my own morning ritual I mentioned, I started with just reading something inspirational in the morning since I was an avid reader and missed reading. Then, I added a bit of meditation to center myself for the day and find my inspiration. Finally, I added exercising for 20 to 45 minutes. As an added bonus, I've found that exercise actually enhances my meditation. The point is that I took it one step at a time, adding pieces to my day that were meaningful for me, creating my ideal day and my ideal lifestyle.

Of course, our style is reflected in your wardrobe, your presence, your communication, and your being. If you're overwhelmed and frustrated, chances are you're not caring about your wardrobe, you're not caring about your fitness or diet, you're tired and you're probably not communicating with those around you all that well.

Trust me, I've been there! And I've come out on the other side!

At my last job, all I bought was gray, black, camel and white. Pretty neutral. Pretty boring. However, in my own style evolution these last few years, I've noticed that I gravitate towards anything with color, specifically bright blue. I've always had that tendency, but I'd just gotten lost in the overwhelm. I was tired. I didn't care.

Now, anytime I feel a bit blah and not wanting to dress up, I add an accent of color to my look—whether it's the top, skirt, necklace or belt. Just a little something gives you that extra boost. By adding the color and accessories, you're also pulling yourself together both emotionally and physically.

***Style in its truest essence is simply confidence*: in your abilities, your intelligence, *and* your presence and image.**

This is one reason why what I do is so satisfying. Aside from seeing the excitement on a client's face thanks to a fabulous new outfit (likely sourced from her own closet), they find this inner confidence in their style. In knowing what to wear for their body type and how to create outfits that fit their personal style, they discover a new ease…with their bodies and their style. Suddenly, it's all a whole lot easier. It's a whole new meaning to 'just throw it on and go.' Yes, it's quick and easy, but that doesn't mean sloppy and boring.

For us busy, successful women, confidence comes from knowing that we've got it all handled (whether or not we do it ourselves) *and* we look fabulous! But looking fabulous is just the icing on the cake. Living a life in style is not just about looking fabulous, but feeling fabulous.

After working in the fashion Industry on the corporate side for Nordstrom, Robinsons May (now Macy's) and BCBG, Catherine founded U*styled in 2008 with the mission to empower busy women everywhere to find a life in style and balance. Catherine's corporate experience had her interacting with customers to identify and fulfill their needs, accounting for an advertising and marketing budget, working behind the scenes at Fashion week, styling the looks for the buyers and ultimately the brand's magazines, and working one-on-one with design to create a collection that supported designers' visions, the market trends and consumers buying habits. Now, with U*styled, she applies these skills to YOUR closet. The perfect assortment isn't about following the trends; it's about creating YOUR best style. Catherine helps time-starved professional women across industries streamline their wardrobes to reflect their lifestyle, personal style and brand image. You can learn more about U*styled at www.ustyled.com.

CHAPTER 37

My Big Miracle Breakthrough

by Joanna Garzilli

I remember sitting in our beautiful but extremely small 619-square-foot apartment in West Los Angeles with a sea of credit card bills scattered across our bed feeling totally overwhelmed.

Our newborn son Dominick was only a few weeks old and my husband Nick was exhausted from doing night shifts as a waiter at a luxury hotel. I felt ashamed that I had ended up in yet another financial mess, as I was already a successfully published author.

My parents were disgusted and annoyed by my situation. They didn't hold back on their feelings, labeling me "a failure," "pathetic," "odious," and a list of other degrading words.

In the back of my mind, I always thought I'd be taken care of because I was due to inherit several million dollars from my dad. I never asked him for any help but I had an entitlement issue. I had this toxic belief that because my dad had money, he should give me what I needed. I also had some residual low self-worth issues. This mindset was a large contributing factor to my business breakdown.

I had been a TV host and creator of a psychic TV show that aired across Europe back in 2004, and headed out to the U.S. at the end of that year to give it a shot at *The American Dream*. I approached Kate Mitchell, the owner of a high-end New Age store called the Aura Shop in Santa Monica, CA and asked if she'd take me on as a psychic. After a few weeks, she said, "Yes," and I began to see clients on a regular basis as a sole proprietor.

Another problem that lead to a breakdown in my business was when I made the switch to becoming a corporation. I deferred all responsibility for handling the financial affairs of my business over to a CPA I had just met, who wanted to understand the mechanics of Internet marketing. I'd already been studying Ali Brown's *Online Success Blueprint* for a couple of years and was successfully implementing it. This CPA looked at my numbers and was impressed. In less than two years, I was generating $65,000 a year.

She told me I needed to become an S-Corp and that she'd set everything up and run it for me in exchange for me giving her psychic readings and showing her how to set up her accounting business as a virtual business.

We also went on to create a social media product together that was a flop. Our agreement was for me to author the product and she would handle the sales and marketing. I invested approximately 250 hours of time researching and writing on a topic that was not my passion, while in the second and third trimester of my pregnancy with my hormones out of balance.

When it came time to market it, my new business partner dropped the ball, making the excuse that she didn't have time and asked if I could handle the marketing instead. Hmmm, with a newborn baby as well!

It was a tough lesson to learn. If I had been a Smart Woman I would have:

1. **Checked in with my core values.** I should have asked myself if this opportunity was in alignment with my life purpose.

2. **Done my due diligence before making a big change to my business.** There were many costs to becoming an S-Corp that I wasn't aware of which led to an audit by the IRS and late penalty filing fees because I didn't take responsibility for every aspect of my business.

3. **Not quit because of insecurity.** A condition of me going into partnership with this CPA was that I was not allowed to work on my business America's Intuition Coach, Inc. I stupidly agreed to her conditions because I was still a people-pleaser and I thought she was

much smarter than me because she had a degree in business and was a CPA whereas I was not nearly as qualified being a psychic and intuition coach.

That year, I only made $23,000 in my business, $42,000 less than I'd made the year before. It was an expensive, time-consuming and painful lesson but the blessings were many.

- I learned how to become a responsible business owner.
- If I didn't understand something, I'd find someone who could explain in detail what I needed to know and do.
- I realized that Spirit wanted me to continue sharing my gift of intuition and empowering people to connect to their spiritual purpose and passion.

I admitted at a business conference in front of 140 people that I'd had a horrible year financially and shared that I'd only made $23,000. Being honest was a huge relief and the biggest part of my breakthrough because the following month I made $30,000. That was more than I'd made the entire year before.

For the longest time, I held the belief that you are unspiritual if you are focused on making money. I am now at peace making money because it helps me take care of my family. I am able to pay my bills each month without using credit cards. I live in a beautiful condo steps away from the beach. My husband is in charge of TV production and marketing strategy for our business. He is also a stay-at-home dad with our son. I love that we don't have to commute to an office or spend long periods of time away from each other. We now own a multiple six-figure business. I say this not to brag but to make the point that if I can do it; you can do it, too!

I want to share with you how I live on purpose and in passion, so that you can apply these valuable tools to your own life and business.

Visioning and Strategic Planning

I get quiet and meditate on what I want and why. If your WHY is not strong, you will not have the passion you need to get through the tough times.

I visualize a positive outcome. For example: I see myself on TV giving guidance on how to tap into your intuition. I feel the emotions of success and the joy of helping others.

I write down an action plan of exactly what I need to do to make that a reality. For example:

1. Give a copy of my book *Unleash The Psychic In You: How To Trust Your Intuition for Successful Decision Making* to TV producers

2. Stay connected on social media

3. Network at Smart Women events

4. Post videos on YouTube

5. Join the organization Women In Film

Then I break down the plan even further by creating more steps. For example: post videos on YouTube action plan:

1. Brainstorm ideas that I'd like to talk about on TV that will help people tap into their intuition and develop their psychic abilities

2. Create a shooting schedule

3. Create a marketing strategy of how many times a week I will post on YouTube

4. Build strategic partnerships on YouTube with people who are aligned with my core values

I am a strong advocate of putting effective back-end systems in place to build a successful business.

After I had that first $30,000 month, I had another month at $30,000 and another but then I hit the wall. With a full intuition coaching practice, I couldn't expand upon my passion of helping people to trust their own intuition and heal the parts of themselves that were keeping them from living their spiritual purpose.

The way I broke through this block was I sat down and studied my income for the year. I entered my numbers into an Excel spreadsheet and converted it to a graph. I saw the pattern very clearly. I'd have three months where I was on fire, followed by a dip the following month because I had to refocus my efforts on marketing and then I'd have another stellar three months but it was frustrating for two reasons:

1. I could only work with a maximum of 10 clients one-on-one at a time because the process I take them through is very hands-on and intensive to help them get a spiritual breakthrough.

2. I wasn't getting my message out to more people because my time was limited even though I had a VA managing my calendar and admin but it wasn't enough.

Every time I sat down and tuned into my soul, I saw myself being recognized as an intuition expert at an international level. I knew I had to make a change to make this a reality. I asked my spirit guides for guidance and they told me to move across the country to Miami, FL and create a program that had already helped my one-on-one clients achieve successes in their businesses, personal lives and enjoy big financial breakthroughs.

The first things we did when we got to Miami was find somewhere to live. Spirit guided us to the most divine condo, which we found via Craigslist. Once we were settled, I went online and typed in a search for recording studios. There was a list of some very famous studios that popped up but Spirit told me which one to go for. Before I met Evangelos from Miami Beach Recording Studios, I already knew he was the one to compose the soundtrack for my product. I can admit that I went outside of my comfort zone by not taking on new private coaching clients and investing over $15,000 into creating *Big Miracle Breakthrough* but I knew that I had to do it if I wanted to have a successful seven-figure business and to reach the masses with my message of spiritual purpose and healing.

I made a commitment to pre-sell *Big Miracle Breakthrough* and got some sales right away. I had to decide a date that my customers would receive

the product and picked a date that I thought was realistic. This forced me into action, and every day, I was writing followed by going into the recording studio for long sessions. I'll admit it was intense but so rewarding. When I look back, I am blown away that I authored this program because if I'd known the challenges I was going to experience, I probably would have made an excuse as to why I couldn't do it. What drove me to be in a zone of peak performance and achieving my deadline was pure passion.
I had a deep burning desire to help people work with Spirit as their guide to manifest the life and money they desire because if someone like me who made zero income for five years can make multiple six figures, you can, too, if that is your desire.

If someone like me, who has a son and no business loan, can launch a business on credit cards, and create a profitable business, then there is no excuse as to why you don't have enough time in your day to get what you need to get done.

You have to make smart decisions every day and make sure they support your life's purpose and passion.

Here are some important Dos and Don'ts for your Life and Business:

Don'ts

1. Don't work on weekends
2. Don't stuff down your feelings
3. Don't rush
4. Don't take on other people's problems as your own
5. Don't live beyond your means
6. Don't make a commitment you cannot keep
7. Don't say "yes" to something if it doesn't feel right
8. Don't compare your business to other businesses (you don't know what's happening behind the scenes)
9. Don't allow toxic people to comment on your life choices
10. Don't make hasty decisions

Do

1. Do make time to go to your local spa, even if it's for a small $10 treatment once a month

2. Do have good food in your fridge
3. Do share your vulnerabilities with someone you can trust. If you don't already know someone, make it your mission to find someone.
4. Do only have clothes in your closet that make you feel good
5. Do plan your next day before you go to sleep.
6. Do exercise at least once a week
7. Do meditate for 5 to 10 minutes to clear your energy at least once a week, ideally daily
8. Do share your vision of what you want for your life and get an accountability partner
9. Do get out and have fun, especially when something is stressing you out.
10. Do pray. You don't have to be religious. The power of prayer is miraculous!

I hope you will refer back to this chapter often. There are many pearls of wisdom that I had to learn the hard way. Please learn from my mistakes. You are a Smart Woman and you deserve to share your gifts with the world. It would be a disservice for you not to!

British born and former London socialite Joanna Garzilli is America's Intuition Coach and author of *Unleash The Psychic In You: How To Trust Your Intuition for Successful Decision Making*

When Joanna effectively learned how to connect with her spiritual self, spirit guides and Source, she transformed her life from a failed relationship, massive debt, and low self-esteem to happily married, a proud mommy, earning beyond a six-figure income; helping people get unstuck to make hard decisions easily and quickly. She has shared her wisdom on radio and television with millions worldwide, showing them how to create a healthy and whole life.

Joanna is respected for her ability to help celebrities, politicians, conscious business owners and transformational leaders overcome their fear about the future and take confident decisive action in a fraction of the time with outstanding results and respect from their community. She has helped those who are ready to take full responsibility for their actions; and turn hidden paralyzing doubt, resentment and fear into decisive action, mind mastery and alignment with the genius part of themselves.

It is not uncommon for her clients to be offered TV opportunities, media attention and invitations to exclusive events with powerful and influential CEOs.

CHAPTER 38

From *Time* Magazine to Mavens and Moguls

by Paige Arnof-Fenn

When I was a young girl and people asked me what I wanted to do when I grew up, I'd put my hands on my hips and proudly announce I wanted to go to Harvard Business School and work in a bank just like my dad! I was an exchange student in France in high school and Italy in college, and by then, my dad had been promoted to president and CEO of the bank, so by graduation, my dream career had evolved into being the leader of a successful Fortune 500 business, traveling the world and being picked by *Time* magazine as the CEO of the year, following in the footsteps on Roberto Goizueta and Jack Welch.

Now in my mid-40s, my definition of success has changed quite a bit. As John Lennon said: "*Life is what happens while you're busy making other plans.*" I worked on Wall Street in the 80s, did, in fact, go to Harvard Business School, and even worked for the legend himself Roberto Goizueta at The Coca-Cola Company for the year before he died. But the closer that I got to what I thought I wanted, I realized along the way that these achievements did not actually make me happy. I knew I could attain them but the closer I was getting to these professional goals, the bigger the personal tradeoffs I was having to make in my life.

My dad made it to CEO of a big company and it always looked to me that he got so much pleasure on the journey. He was fulfilled by his work and really loved building the business; he was great at it and the work made him so happy. He did put on a lot of weight as he moved up the ranks and he and my mom did divorce though so I guess there were tradeoffs for him, too.

For me the tradeoffs came sooner. I married a wonderful person the year after I got my MBA. He's really smart, makes me laugh a lot and keeps me sane. He is truly my best friend and I adore him. My first job after business school was the first fork in the road of career choices. The headquarters of my company was in the Midwest but I asked them to transfer my offer to a regional office (realizing that meant less visibility at corporate) so I could live closer to my then fiancé who lived in that area. He and I both have strong preferences on places to live (on our honeymoon we determined there really are only five cities in the US we could agree to live in), so given the location of my new job and his, and based on the neighborhoods we liked, I was going to have to commute 56 miles each way every day. I got my driver's permit at age 14 (that was the law in Louisiana when I grew up) but never really liked driving much. I liked it a lot less as soon as I had to commute to work even though it was considered a "reverse commute" on four major highways on the congested East Coast corridor. I left home each morning at dawn and returned, frazzled after dark each night, road-weary and exhausted with no time for hobbies, friends or exercise. I gained 25 pounds the first year we were married.

That job lasted for more than three years and I happily found another job in an office closer to my husband's for the next three years, which was such a relief. I took the weight off and life seemed so much better and in balance. The next curveball came after almost five years of marriage when I was offered a dream job in another city hours away by airplane but in the same time zone. The offer was just too good to pass up and my husband supported my decision to take it. He knew I would regret it for the rest of my life if I let it pass me by, and, in fact, it was the game-changing career move I had hoped it would be.

I quickly realized that even though my husband and I both worked really long hours when we lived in the same city, we still ate two meals together every day even though breakfast was usually at 6am and dinner was after 10pm. When you live thousands of miles apart, it is just not the same sipping on a glass of wine over the phone to debrief your day. The commuter marriage experiment lasted less than one year before we both quit our jobs and moved to one of those five cities that we both liked and started our new adventure together again.

I am really glad we tried commuting. It made me appreciate what a great decision I had made in choosing my life partner and I no longer took anything for granted. Since then, we have both changed jobs several times but we will always stay together under one roof. Jobs come and go but good people are hard to find so if you are lucky enough to marry your best friend, then you move heaven and earth to make that the anchor of your life and the other pieces of the puzzle just work around that.

Ten years ago, my husband and I both started our own firms within a month of each other. Many people thought we were crazy and maybe we were but we both saw great opportunities post-9/11 in our respective fields and have never turned back. As a two-entrepreneur/no pet/no plant/no kid family, I can honestly say I have no idea how most people get anything done because even though we don't have much tying us down we still have no time to do many of the things we'd like to do most days.

I love running my own business. I work with and for people I respect and want to be successful. I have no tolerance for jerks or people who just want to suck you dry and not give anything back. I am so fortunate that I have been able to develop an ecosystem of great talent and meaningful work that energizes me every day. I am able to make time for friends and family, and most importantly, time for myself to enjoy the journey and stay in good health.

Sadly, my husband and I have both lost a parent in the last year, and that experience has also taught me a lot. Owning our businesses allowed us to leverage technology and be there for our families in ways that might have been impossible as an employee of a larger, publically-traded organization, managing a large staff like that path I had been on. Being able to spend time with our parents in their final years was such a gift to both of us and no amount of corporate accolades or recognition could ever replace that sense of peace the time together allowed, not even being on the cover of *Time* magazine. I know what it takes and the tradeoffs required to hold those positions and that is just no longer a deal I am willing to make.

I love sharing two meals a day together with my best friend, and as business owners, breakfast is more like 8am and dinner after 9pm, so we are getting better at managing our time I think. I love knowing that I built my company from scratch and my DNA is in everything that we do. Working for a large corporate machine, I always wondered how much of the success and growth was because of my contribution versus the inertia of managing a well-known brand that had been around for decades or longer.

My company is my platform to do the things I enjoy most. I love to write, speak at conferences, and serve on boards so I get to do a lot of those things as the Founder and CEO of a successful firm. I do not plan to ever retire in the classic sense; I hope to keep doing the work I love for the rest of my life. **Here are a few tips to help you on your journey to live a full life and find fulfilling work you enjoy:**

- **Be open to serendipity**
  You must do your homework and be prepared so that when those opportunities present themselves to you, you can recognize them and act on them. When you open your mind and your heart, you can see opportunities everywhere.

- **Surround yourself with smart, funny, caring and honest people**
  When good people gather, great things happen, plus you will have a blast along the way. These people are multipliers who create energy and make things happen. Life is short; let someone else deal with the jerks.

- **Create your own definition of success**
  The truth is that success is very personal and it is okay if what you want to make changes over time. You may achieve success and then develop a different definition or, like me, start to get there and shift gears along the way. Nothing is not carved in stone so just course-correct as you go and keep it relevant and meaningful to you. That is what makes life fun and keeps things interesting.

- **Treat yourself as well as you treat your clients**
  When I started my career and my business, I always took care of everyone else (my boss, my team, my board, my customers) before I focused own my own needs. I was tired, run down and frazzled most of the time. Then it hit me that if I do not feel good then I am not doing as much or as well as I could so I

need to start taking better care of myself. An investment in me is truly an investment in my company. I no longer looked at things like exercise, massage or even facials and manicures as a luxury. These activities are now considered part of what helps me achieve my peak performance. When I look and feel my best, the business thrives!

- **Put yourself out there**
  Do something every day that stretches the boundaries and makes you feel a little uncomfortable. It is only when you get outside your comfort zone that you really learn and grow both personally and professionally. Think big and dream bigger. Even if you don't achieve the ultimate goal, you will probably make incredible headway just giving it your all, and you will never know unless you try. So I give you permission to go for it. What are you waiting for?

Paige Arnof-Fenn is the Founder and CEO of Mavens & Moguls, a global marketing strategy consulting firm whose clients range from early-stage start-ups to Fortune 500 companies including Colgate, Virgin and The New York Times Company. She was formerly VP Marketing at Zipcar and VP Marketing at Inc.com before the company was sold to Bertelsmann. Prior to that, she held the title of SVP Marketing and was a key member of the IPO team at Launch Media, an Internet start-up that went public in early 1999 and was later sold to Yahoo.

Arnof-Fenn has also worked as a special assistant to the chief marketing officer of global marketing at The Coca-Cola Company and held the position of director of the 1996 Olympic Commemorative Coin Program at the Department of Treasury, U.S. Mint. Previously Arnof-Fenn worked in brand management at Procter & Gamble.

Arnof-Fenn is a founding board member of Women Entrepreneurs in Science & Technology and she is currently serving as Board Chair of the

Alumni Board of Stanford University. She is also the former Vice President of the Harvard Business School Global Alumni Board and the current Chair of the Board of Trustees of the Sports Museum at the Boston Garden. She holds an undergraduate degree in economics from Stanford University and an MBA from Harvard Business School. She is quoted regularly in the media, was a monthly columnist for *Entrepreneur* for several years, is on the IDC Technology Advisory Council, and is a *Time* Magazine Opinion Leader.

CHAPTER 39

Enjoy Your WHY: Build Awareness and Reduce Overwhelm in Your Biz

by Whitney McMillan

How successfully do you juggle overwhelm? In what ways does overwhelm weigh down your business? Ready to shift some overwhelm off your shoulders?

Although it often doesn't feel like it in the moment, the idea of "managing" overwhelm is humorous. Given the amazing power we have to manifest in our lives, we actually invite the situations that overwhelm us, and then we aim to manage these same factors. What are we doing!? It's like juggling boulders!

Focusing on three key boulders that could be adding to your overwhelm, let's explore some related techniques to build your awareness and reduce your overwhelm. It's time to enjoy the WHY of your business with greater clarity, balance and purpose!

What is Overwhelm?

Overwhelm, or its common partner in crime "stress," are a natural response to life situations, and can actually be a good thing. However, too much of it or the wrong kind of it can send your body, mind, emotions, energy, business, and life into a tailspin. The difference between overwhelm serving you positively and negatively is when it becomes too much of a bad thing—it becomes your boulders.

As an automatic reaction, overwhelm occurs in our bodies when there is a perceived threat. It may not necessarily be a real (actual) threat, but the sense or mere idea of a threat. When this happens, various physical functions turn on: muscles tense, heart rate rises, blood flow rushes, breathing quickens, adrenalin pumps, etc. We often call this the "fight, flight or freeze" response—a great thing in times of true danger!

However, most of our everyday overwhelm is not a life or limb debate. Instead, we live surrounded by deadlines, traffic, financial worries, endless streams of information, family responsibilities, perfectionist tendencies, a long list of expectations, social media overload, and so on. Growing layer upon layer, we become overloaded with the weight until it short-circuits our lives, leaving us stuck in the rut of overwhelm.

Certainly some aspects of overwhelm can help challenge us to grow and change. Yet, over the long term, ongoing excessive or even low-level overwhelm takes a toll, with a detrimental impact on our quality of life:

- Physical dis-ease/illness
- Mental overload
- Emotional fatigue
- Relationship breakdown
- Loss of self-esteem
- Business decay

It's hard to enjoy and thrive in your business when you feel buried under a boulder of overwhelm, unable to budge or breathe. Moments when everything weighs you down, slows your pace, numbs your senses, pulls you in a million directions, overwhelm forms the overall experience of stress—physically, mentally, emotionally and energetically. It may look and feel different to each person, but overwhelm sparks a collective understanding of stuck-ness: Yuck!

Your Overwhelm Story

Do aspects of your life reflect the holistic overwhelm of living full-on in today's complex, busy society? How does overwhelm appear in your business and/or your life? What does overwhelm feel like for you?

Consider your typical day. It may include work, school, children, romantic relationships, family, friends, exercise, meditation, hobbies, food, chores, errands, cleaning, emails, tweets, and so on. Envision your to do list—you may even have several lists! As you read down your list(s):

- Experience your physically being—feel your body respond as you read.
- Observe your thoughts—pay attention to where your thoughts go as the list grows longer.
- Feel into your heart—witness (without taking on) the emotions as the list consumes your day.
- Pay attention to your energy level—watching where is slows down, or even stops, frozen and numb.

Experience your sense of overwhelm from all or some of the items on your list. Sense what days upon days of this overwhelm feels like, wondering when or if will it ever end.

Consider that the seeds of your beliefs (on most topics) were planted when you were a child. Often it was loved ones (well-meaning parents, teachers, etc.) who shared and modeled their beliefs to you with the best of intentions. These beliefs live on in your adult life through your values, feelings, needs, desires, choices and actions. They are YOU! They feed your overwhelm!

When thinking about overwhelm, contemplate:

- What beliefs about work, responsibilities, time and success did you learn growing up?
- What activities were you passionate about and/or encouraged to do as a child?
- How do these beliefs and activities show up in your life now?
- How do you value your time, energy and passion now?
- How do you organize your many different activities?
- How do you factor in other people (i.e. children, partner, friends, employees, etc.)?
- How do you prioritize in your business?
- How does overwhelm show up in your business?

- How do you feel at times of overwhelm?
- What influences and adds to your overwhelm?
- How does your overwhelm serve you—positively and negatively?
- What do you want to change about your overwhelm?

Three Overwhelm Boulders

Ready to chat about the big three boulders weighing down your overwhelm? Knowing these boulders very well, both through my clients, plus in my own business and daily life, I walk the talk of taming overwhelm. You can, too!

In dramatic *reverse order* with a drum roll....

Busyness Does Not Equal Purpose

For some people, overwhelm is measured by busyness. How often do you tell people: "I'm sorry, but I'm busy?"

Some of us value being busy as a way to model a purpose in life. By doing so, busyness serves as a justification or evidence of our purpose on earth. It can create a sense of fulfillment. For other people, busyness fills time, looking for ways to avoid other responsibilities, fun, connection, etc. It serves as a tool to foster drama, excitement, and/or a sense of being needed. Still for other people, busyness allows distraction from more serious things in life: pain, loneliness, fear, etc. Busyness can be a wonderful emotional coping technique.

In almost all these cases, busyness keeps you away from what is most important: knowing your inner self. Whether as a justification, a drama or a distraction, busyness can safely keep your self-concept and inner wisdom at bay, protecting you from knowing and trusting your true self. The question is: what beliefs do you have about busyness? What function does it serve in your business and your life? Where does it have you stuck in a rut? How can you choose to shift it?

Certainly, you are busy—we all are. Busyness defines our everyday lives. Owning that it is part of your lived reality, you choose how much. Yes, you have the power to reclaim your time, your focus and your purpose! How? Become more conscious of the choices you make about what you do. Assess the importance of what you do and the value it brings to your business. Be conscious of what you truly want for your business. By focusing on what is important to you, you will find some activities on your to do list move down the list, or even fall off it! Ask yourself:

- Is this in my best interest or is it simply busyness?
- Is it in alignment with my vision, mission and purpose?
- Does it honor who I truly am?
- What is negotiable?
- What is NON-negotiable?

You will be surprised how much of what you do is 'busyness.' Now with this awareness, use your valuable time to focus on your dreams and align with your purpose! Seek clarity and discern what is in your best interests. Your time is a treasure—value it!

Should…No More

Do you find yourself living by others' expectations? Do you feel a lack of self-identity and self-empowerment? Do you know the "shoulds" in your life? Very often we aspire to live based on who and how we "ought to be," with a yearning to be liked and accepted. To be your true self, it's important to say "bon voyage" to your people-pleasing self and celebrate who you really are, starting by letting go of the "shoulds" of life!

Consider your "shoulds"

At the top of a sheet of paper, please write the words: I SHOULD… Now finish this sentence in five different ways with whatever comes to you. For instance:

- I should work only eight hours a day.
- I should follow up with clients more regularly.
- I should plan my project timelines more realistically.
- I should manage my social media time better.
- I should be more patient.
- I should…

You may have a hard time listing five, or you may want to write five pages! Please limit yourself to only five items…for now.

Personally, I feel "should" is one of the most damaging words in our language. Every time we use the word "should," we are making ourselves or someone else wrong—either we were wrong, we are wrong, or we are going to be wrong. Plus, we get clever with "shoulds," by disguising them with other words. Maybe you are like me, substituting my "shoulds" with "must," "need to," "supposed to," and "ought to"—all equivalents to "should." Being aware of how we get around saying "should" is important to no longer living "shoulds."

Moving away from "shoulding" on yourself, as if you are wrong, instead give yourself choice! How about changing every "should" to "could?" The word "could" gives you choice. In fact, with "could" you are never wrong, because you can always learn from each choice, and then make another choice.

Now write: I COULD… Write the same five previous items by replacing your "shoulds" with "coulds." For instance:

- I could work only eight hours a day.
- I could follow up with clients more regularly.
- I could plan my project timelines more realistically.
- I could manage my social media time better.
- I could be more patient.
- I could…

Review both lists and consider:

- For each "should," ask yourself: which of these can I let go of?
- For each "could," ask yourself: why haven't I?
- How does "should" feel different than "could?"
- How could you release your "shoulds?"
- How can you inspire more "coulds" in your business?

You Deserve

One of the most challenging aspects of living in today's overwhelming time is the disconnection from valuing ourselves, just as we are. For many people, this results in undervaluing or forgetting our worth.

Each of us deserves to experience our greatest and highest good—it's Universal Law for us to experience our true selves. But how do we when our ability to see, value and receive our deservingness is low? What is your deserve-ability?

Consider some questions:

- What meaning does the term "deserving" have for you?
- What were the messages/beliefs about deserving you learned as a child?
- What do you feel you deserve now?
- What stands in the way of you deserving more?
- How does your deserve-ability impact your business?
- How could it improve your business to claim your full worthiness?

Please know that living fully as you truly desire is your right—you do deserve.

Your business reflects your sense of your own self-worth—it starts with YOU!

Shift Your Overwhelm

Taking these three boulders into account, it's time to decide—ready to shift from your rut, or not?

- What beliefs about overwhelm do you want to release?
- What is keeping your ideal business success at bay?
- How does overwhelm benefit you?
- If you let go of overwhelm, what will happen?
- If you could change/release anything about your current overwhelm, what would it be?

Now, think of three choices you could make this coming week. They may be small (subtle), medium (manageable) or big (sizable) changes.

Focus on only three adjustments—do not add more to your overwhelm! Write these three choices down, and place it where you will see it daily:

1.

2.

3.

To focus intentionally on shifting your overwhelm easily, smoothly and gracefully, consider empowering yourself with positive affirmations, such as:

> "I let go of busyness that does not serve my business positively."
>
> "I embrace "coulds" in my life."
>
> "I celebrate my deservingness."
>
> "I chose my ideal life by releasing overwhelm."

If these affirmations are too bold for where you are at right now, tweak them by adding: "I am willing to…." Don't bite off more than is do-able for you—be gentle and respectful to yourself.

To live fully involves taking steps toward welcoming your ideal life, free of overwhelm. Your ideal business has the power to vastly enhance your quality of life. If you truly desire a life of clarity, balance and purpose, if you believe you deserve it, and if you are willing to accept joy and fulfillment, then you can realize your ideal life. YOU deserve to be free of overwhelm!

Whitney McMillan transforms overwhelm! She is an incredible overwhelm mentor, life success coach, workshop facilitator, intuitive, author and speaker based in Vancouver, Canada, and extending to the world. If you're a conscious woman buried under the weight of overwhelm, Whitney's workshops and personal coaching clear your fog, inspire your clarity, grow your inner trust and fulfill your life purpose. Align and thrive in the yummy vibrant life you REALLY want!

Whitney supportively guides you to manifest your BEST LIFE by embracing modernized Heal Your Life® philosophies and techniques of Louise L. Hay through personalized Heal Your Life® Coaching and Workshops. Whitney also offers Inner Wisdom Mentoring to develop and hone your intuition, and Reiki Energy Healing to balance and relax your well-being.

During her 20 years in Social Work (with her BSW and MSW), Whitney utilized a variety of techniques as self-care to heal, ground and guide her overwhelming journey. Having been trained in diverse healing modalities and counseling/coaching approaches, Whitney now merges these with her natural intuitive abilities and her sassy personality, offering workshops and one-to-one sessions, individualized to meet your needs.

Whitney's first book focusing on overwhelm will be published in November, 2011. Visit Whitney at www.whitneymcmillan.com

CHAPTER 40

Do You Have Trouble Saying No?

by Kay White

No. Such a small word but it makes such a big difference to your success if you're able to say it and mean it. Being able to say "No" in an assertive and respectful way makes the difference to whether you're able to truly live your life on purpose and in passion. It has to be—there's so much coming at us every day, so many opportunities, distractions, requests. Every time you say "Yes" to something you know, of course, that you're actually saying no to something else anyway and yet, more often than not, that something else is often what you actually *want* to do, know you *should* do or *need* to be doing. So why is it so hard for us to say that small, powerful word 'No'?

For women in particular it's a struggle, which often leaves us frustrated, overwhelmed and ultimately off-track. We think we have to please everyone and we're taught to be polite and be helpful so, by naturally saying "Okay, leave that with me," and "of course, I'll get to that for you." Well it becomes part of our hardwiring. It's a combination of fear of rejection, fear of hurting someone's feelings and, often, we think it's easier to say yes.

Well it isn't. The good news is too, that it doesn't have to be difficult. In fact, as a savvy and influential communication expert, one of the many things I show my clients—women in particular—is that you can say no, both respectfully and assertively, and the magical part (which is often described as Jedi) is that you often don't have to say the word 'No' at all.

As you start and grow your own business, there's going to be some "Hell

Yes" and more than a few "Hell No" moments to juggle. I've discovered my purpose is to show ambitious professionals how to use subtle language secrets and skills to make things happen, to get people into action and to be understood. The savvy and influential part is that most of this is possible without cajoling and pleading or the alternative, desk-beating and foot-stamping style, which shuts people down.

Founding my own business in 2006, after leaving my 25-year corporate career as a director in a global insurance broker, was a big but natural step. As a broker, I was based in London and had all but grown up being part of a mainly male, fast-paced, successful team. If you didn't stand your ground, stake your claim, set your boundaries, well, you got pushed all over the place and certainly passed over. I learned that very quickly, often by my own mistakes. What I also learned during that high-octane time, was that I could influence and persuade people, get people into action, without having to scream and shout. It was possible to get across exactly what needed to be said but to say it in a way that meant the person was actually happy you'd told them. That's what being influential is all about. It's about subtle distinctions, and they're all the more powerful because they're subtle. Saying no without saying it—it's powerful, subtle, and it's essential to your success.

So I want to share with you the actual words you can say and the way to say them so you can say "No" often without saying it but in a way that people understand and respect you. Before I do that though, I need to get into the why so that as you're able to comfortably get on with the business of your business as you start to say No more easily, more naturally and more assertively.

So, first, here are these 3 powerful mindsets.

Mindset One

Just because you're asked a question, doesn't mean you have to answer it

It's so easy, isn't it? "Can you do that by 5pm please?" Or "Are you able to sort that out before the end of today?" "Will you meet us there tomorrow with the report ready?" Now you'll notice, they're all closed questions, ones that request a yes or no answer. We hear those sorts of questions every day, and the subtle part here is to remember you can always answer a question like that with another question *first.* Find out a bit more before you say yes. By asking another question, you haven't said no, but you've responded by asking a bit more first.

How/What to Say: By asking some questions, you buy yourself some valuable time to think before you say yes and you also tell the other person, without actually saying it, that you're not just going to immediately respond to their request.

"Okay, so tell me a bit more about that?" (I'm not saying yes or no, I'm asking for more detail) or "When you say X, what exactly do you mean by that?" (Let me be a bit clearer first on what you're asking.) Or "Oh, that's tricky. Tell me where you're at with that." (You're alerting them that it might be tricky, and then rather than immediately offering to help, you're asking how they're getting on with it, i.e. not taking ownership of it yourself). The idea is to find out a bit more about the actual detail, deadline first. At the same time, you buy yourself this precious time to really consider what you already have on your plate, and what deadlines you're already working towards.

Now this is a great question to ask: "Okay, now tell me, what flexibility is there?" (Okay is agreeing so you're acknowledging the request and the word 'what' implies that there is some flexibility, you just want to know what it is.) You'll notice we haven't asked "Is there any flexibility?" That is one of those unhelpful, yes/no, closed questions. "What flexibility is there?" This buys you time both in thinking about the request and often in the flexibility that you get offered.

Mindset Two

People ask you to do things because they follow their path of least resistance

If you find a short cut home, you're likely to take it. If you find someone who's a bit of a pushover you're more likely to ask them to do something than someone who is a bit more assertive. If you always say yes to people, they'll keep asking you and they'll keep assuming you're going to keep saying yes to them.

To be able to help people and to stay on track yourself as you build and grow your business, you'll need to set some boundaries, and at the same time, this will help people help themselves.

How/What To Say: "Yes, now that's tricky." (You're subtly positioning here that it's not a yes, and yet you recognize they need help.) "Yes, now that's tricky. I'm full-on until at least 4 o'clock. (That's a subtle way of saying not now) So can you call me after then?" (That's your YES—what's possible) "We can discuss it then."

Now notice you've said "*can you call me*" so the responsibility of following up *is with the other person, too,* and the task is not suddenly added to your to do list. You've given them the gap that works for you i.e. not right now but later. Now what you find is that *if* it truly is an emergency, people will tell you and, more often than not, because you've not said no but you have given them a boundary and told them you will help them later, nine times out of 10, they'll go off and either ask someone else or they'll sort it out for themselves. Just this phrase alone starts to position you in that short sentence as someone who's prepared to help and someone who's also committed to what she's doing at the same time.

Mindset Three

It's a disservice to all those who follow your fortunes to keep saying yes to everyone

Now this third mindset piece is so very important, it's probably the *most* important because if you're reading this you either have teams of people working with you and for you, and you have businesses which rely on your productivity and how you succeed. We all have people who rely on our success—people both at home and at work, who—as I say—follow our fortunes.

Well I put it to you, it's actually a disservice to you, to your business and why you're in business, to your team *and* it's certainly a disservice to your family to keep saying yes when you really mean no, or not now. So many people follow your fortunes, and if you're committed to growing your business and making a real difference in the world but are so busy helping, rescuing or sorting out what everyone else should be doing before you really focus on what you need to be doing, then I put it to you that it's truly a disservice to all those people who are relying on your success. Now this can boil right down to the money you make as you grow your business to that time you have free to be at home with family and friends, the time you have to exercise or just hang out and relax. So this part I call 'Mind your Gaps.'

How/What To Say: If someone asks: "Can you help me find the information on A,B, C?" If you're right in the middle of something and you come from the angle of keeping your own commitments in mind, you could say "Yes, happy to help you *when* I've finished this project (i.e. not right now), so give me a call in an hour if you still need me." (This implies the word *still* even though you didn't say it. It's likely they might find the answer themselves by the time you're available.)

It's like a lot of things you've tried, practiced and learned. A bit tricky, wobbly and uncomfortable at first (I only have to remember my first driving lesson to know this to be true) and then, gradually, with practice, it becomes easier, more comfortable and eventually, it's just what you do naturally.

You don't have to sing that famous line "I'm just a girl who can't say no" from *Oklahoma!* anymore. In fact, your business and all those people who follow, and will follow, your fortunes are relying on you being able to say no in respectful, subtle and assertive ways. They're relying on your getting on with the business of your business. Yes or No?

Kay White, Founder and CEO of Way Forward Solutions Ltd. and Author of #1 best-selling book *The A to Z of Being Understood*, shows ambitious professionals how to get noticed, promoted, appointed and rewarded by using savvy, influential communication skills.

Using Kay's own unique branded 7-step LINKING-your-Thinking® system combined with powerful exercises and techniques, people understand how their language, their angle of approach, the feedback they get and give all combine to influence and transform their results.

Working around the world, virtually and face-to-face, with groups and one-to-one with corporate and private clients, Kay's clients include investment banks, national healthcare organizations, private healthcare companies, insurance brokers and underwriters, and law firms, as well as many small business owners and start-ups.

The principles Kay teaches are as powerful to large organizations as they are to solo entrepreneurs—what you say and how you say it is directly linked to your profits and your prosperity.

Kay's own career background includes over 20 years at Willis plc—the leading global insurance and reinsurance broker, working to director level. As part of a fast-paced, mainly male team, Kay was responsible for the marketing and negotiating of multi-million dollar global insurance programs. She also worked in Paris as liaison between the two offices and speaks fluent French.

Married for 10 years, Kay and her husband Snowy plus their three rescue hounds live close to London in the UK, close enough to London for fun and the bright lights, and far enough away for open countryside walks and quiet pub lunches!

CHAPTER 41

Secrets of a Successful Life

by Suzy Manning

A favorite quote of mine on success is by Marianne Williamson. *"Success means we go to sleep at night knowing that our talents and abilities were used in a way that served others."* We come to the planet to impact quality of life. There is a time in our life when we shift our thought process from 'it's all about me' to an understanding that it is about serving others. However, before we reach this realization, we have usually bought into societies' subtle brainwashing that if we are just the right body weight, if we drive the most prestigious automobile, live in the perfect geographical location, have 2.35 kids and a pedigree family dog, a highly visible career, a handsome, driven husband and on and on, we will be happy.

Life has a way of waking us up to reality. I remember sitting on my bed one sunny afternoon going over an aerobic routine to teach an exercise class when I heard a huge booming voice proclaim, "Let Suzy Out!" That day, that moment, woke me up to my journey to find out who Suzy was. Who was the authentic Suzy? I realized that I was a sister, wife, daughter, lover, exercise teacher, friend, and a mother. These were all roles I was playing. Who was the Suzy underneath these roles who needed out to impact the world? The message was multi-dimensional. Not only was it about the roles in my life, it was about an unhappy marriage. I was in an unsupportive, verbally abusive marriage that I needed out of for my own growth to be healthy in mind, body, and spirit.

Every one of us will have "a ha" moments that attempt to get our attention to wake us up to the magnificent, powerful, wise, sensuous, beautiful women we are. It is in these moments that we discover that success is not accumulation of material goods, achievements, or financial status. Success is being of service, but the critical piece is to be of service as our authentic self without concern for what others think. Too many of us are relinquished to living lives of quiet desperation attempting to be liked by everyone while fitting into someone else's definition of who we should be. There is a magnificent divine being in each of us wanting to blossom to gift our uniqueness to the world.

If you are feeling frustrated, bored, restless, or like there has to be more to life, congratulations! There is more! This is the start of your journey to discover and embrace your authentic wise woman who is within you. Trust what you feel. Your wisdom is your intuition—a body knowing that is dead on. You are stepping out of the mediocrity of a programmed life to create a life that resonates with your heart and soul. Once you start on this journey, there is no going back.

There are huge multi-dimensional shifts happening on the planet at this time. Grandmother Earth is trying to balance. We, as women, are impacted by the energies of a female planet. By 2013, 50 million women will have achieved menopause. Menopause is a natural journey that wakes us up at a cellular level to own and experience our magnificence to step into leadership. One in four women is depressed. Under depression is anger. We, as women, are ready to stand up and speak up to create a more humane world that works for all. We are angry at the untruths in the world. Heart disease is the #1 killer of American women. On an energetic level, we need to live what brings our hearts joy to be well. We need to live on purpose with passion. Women are discovering, embracing, and owning their divine femininity. All of these factors are contributing to the huge movement of women creating businesses that introduce feminine qualities into personal lives and into business. We are saying no more to meaningless, manufactured lives.

What resonates within you? What do you engage with that you lose all track of time? What would you do even without pay? What do you have a strong emotional tie to? If you tear up over an idea, it is your inner child coming to the table to get your attention. Are you inspired to do something? Inspiration means 'of spirit'. Spirit will not give you an idea without a way to manifest. The plan is already there. We need to trust the process, go with the flow, and our eyes will be opened to the how. A great teacher once told me, between birth and five years of age, we got too much of something and we want less of it or we got too little of something and we desire more. This is your life purpose.

My mother lost a daughter in childbirth when I was two years old. I remember my mother's pain, her isolation, the deafening silence in our home, and the devastation to all of our lives. I wanted to comfort her, but was kept away as I was too young, they thought, to understand. Women instinctually perceive others pain. Growing up, I was told by my father, even though I graduated with a Master's degree, that women could not think or do business. None of this made sense to me. I knew in my core that I could succeed in business and impact lives.

What is your story that literally compels you to make a difference in people's lives? I am extremely sensitive to women's issues and the ways we sabotage ourselves in this patriarchal society. It is time for us to step into leadership whether in our families, communities, or on the world stage. What is your WHY? It is an internal knowing that energizes your life.

Knowing and feeling this purpose at your core is what will sustain you, propel you forward, and ignite creativity for a successful life both personally and professionally. We are not just stepping forward creating a business that is of service; we are creating a new way of being and serving on the planet. We are introducing feminine qualities to join with masculine qualities to co-create together. We are redefining new ways to foster relationships and to engage in fulfilling businesses. We are shifting the paradigm from exclusivity to inclusivity. As we change our consciousness, other shifts automatically fall into place. We then move from fear to love, scarcity to abundance, competition to collaboration, power over to power within, hierarchical leadership to leadership in a web, linear thinking to circular thought process, and spiritual starvation to spiritual fulfillment.

It is our time. We are the leaders we have been waiting for. The more we are grounded in our core with our purpose, the more we own our feminine qualities, and the more we know "this is who I am, this is the reason I am on the planet, and this is what I choose to do," nothing will stop us. People do not like change, so any time we are moving people out of old ways of thinking and out of their comfort zone, our intentions will be challenged.

What do we need to do to be in balance to successfully lead?

To achieve balance, you need to make sure you meet your needs in all of the categories: physical, mental, emotional, spiritual, and sexual. Achieving balance creates a solid foundation in your life which translates in to more wellness, more energy, and smooth transitions with less stress.

Physical

We were created to move. Movement will energize your body, give you more clarity and focus, and boost your mood. Feeling depressed, unmotivated, unclear on a decision? Move. You will be amazed what a little movement will do for you. Pick something that you like to do. Walk, bicycle, dance, yoga—it does not have to be intense or competitive. Enjoy the activity alone, with a friend, or with a group. Turn on your favorite music in the privacy of your home and move your body. Have fun, be creative, and celebrate you moving! Movement will get you out of your head and into your body. You will begin to make decisions on how your body feels, not what the ego wants.

Mental

Write an affirmation on who you would like to be in life. Write it in the present tense like you are already that person. Make it an 'I am' statement. For example, I am a powerful business woman. I am lean and healthy. I am attracting what I need into my life. I am prosperous. Post it everywhere: on your computer, on the dashboard of your car, on the refrigerator, on your mirror. Repeat it daily. Repeat, repeat, repeat. Create the life you want with your thoughts. Your thought process creates your reality. Your affirmations will drown out the committee in your head that wants to sabotage your success.

Emotional

Emotion is energy in motion. We are like a battery. We need to take care of ourselves to store energy in our bodies in order to give energy to nurture family, friends, and businesses. Nurturing is one of our great qualities. The problem is we nurture everyone else first and ourselves last, if at all. If we deplete our energy with too much giving and do not replenish our energy, we become tired, depressed, and sick. List five things that give you pleasure and energize you. Make the time each day to enjoy a guilt-free pleasure: a massage, a bubble bath, reading a good book, exercise, yoga, meditation, pursuing a new career.

Spiritual

Make the time every day to notice the good in your life. Life is good! What we think about is what we attract into our lives. If we focus on what we don't have, we get more of what we do not want—lack. Each night, make a grateful list for the day. Don't negate the obvious: your life, good health, a roof over your head, food, friends, someone who listens to you, someone to love, a pet, your garden. Notice that when you are truly grateful for what you have in your life, more will appear in your life. The Universe is abundant.

Sexual

Our sexual/soul force energy catalyzes our life. It is our ability to give unconditionally with an open heart with no expectations or attachments.

Pay it forward is a great example of giving without conditions. Give to or do something for a stranger and accept nothing in return. Put extra money in a parking meter, pay the toll booth fee for the car behind you, pay for a stranger's coffee, or pick up an extra meal and give it away. It is the flow of Universal life force energy.

Only when we honor the gifts within each one of us and claim them as our birthright will we experience our true shining. We find our inner strength by going deep within ourselves and claiming ourselves as powerful leaders. Women are resonating with this movement worldwide in all walks of life. It is a vital healing movement originating at a cellular level. There is an inner knowing that we have gifts the world needs. Embrace this journey! It is one of enormous energy! Energy that is shifting the planet!

Suzy Manning is the CEO of SIZZZL, *Powerful Women Who Ignite the World*. She is a transitional coach, speaker, and author. Her expertise is helping transitional women create a solid foundation within them to design lives and businesses from inspiration, inner wisdom, and a place of service. Creating and living from this inner knowing anchors you so nothing will repress you. For over 30 years, Suzy has dedicated her life to transforming women's lives through her own fitness program, seminars and retreats, coaching, speaking, her international selling inspirational gift book *Wise Women—Circle of Wisdom*, and her BlogTalk Radio Show, SIZZZL—Women Living Inspired Lives.

Suzy holds a Master's degree in Agency Counseling from Siena Heights University. Continual immersion in her own self-growth and evolution allows her to connect with others with authenticity and impeccability. Her studies have included shamanism, reiki, massage, enlightened warrior training, train the trainer, millionaire mind intensives, investment and business building, inner wealth creation, and 4T prosperity.

Her personal intent is to empower women to own their magnificence, to ignite their dreams, and to illuminate their beauty, power, sensuality, and wisdom into authentic leadership in their Sizzzl years of 50+. There is a powerful energy at a cellular level in women as we embrace our 60s, 70s, and 80s. It is not a time to be invisible, but a time to be seen and heard. We are the change agents ushering in a new relational consciousness.

CHAPTER 42

What's Love Got to Do with It?

by Caitlenn T. Ainnsley

I entered the coaching field relatively early and using my marketing background, met with success, quickly having signed 32 clients in the first four months of starting my practice. I began making six figures as a coach in my second year in business.

I enjoyed the one-on-one and group coaching over the phone and was grateful to be doing work that offered such flexibility and didn't involve a commute. I came from a space of what do my clients need from me and I would morph into someone who would provide what they needed. I knew I was impacting people's lives positively.

Bliss didn't last long though. Five years into my career as a coach, as I heard my colleagues boasting they were pulling in seven figures by launching products, hosting large-scale live events and running high-end mastermind programs. I started to feel like I wasn't successful and by doing one-on-one work I wasn't helping enough people. Worse still, I felt like some of the coaches I'd mentored were passing me up. I felt "behind" in a profession in which I was once a pioneer.

That's when it started. Although I really prefer connecting with people in person, I put a $5,000 course on Internet marketing on my credit card, convinced the material would get me caught up to my colleagues. Instead, it left me confused, overwhelmed and needing more information and support, so I purchased program after program. I hired specialists and VAs and web gurus. I attended live events and teleclasses searching for the "how" of taking the highly intuitive coaching I did and bottling that in some saleable way.

I got some good information and some bad advice. I did launch two products, but one didn't even make back even half of what I had spent to develop and promote it. Even though I considered myself a hard-working student, I never found the magic pill or the secret sauce that would produce the results those in the testimonials said they were achieving.

In fact, six years later I was almost $100,000 in debt, miserably trying to launch and manage and be an affiliate for products associated with my business coaching practice. I was depleted, frustrated, and depressed. I was working more hours than I ever had. I had more staff on payroll than I'd ever had, yet I was making less after paying for all the people and systems to support the Internet engine that wasn't selling the millions many had promised it would.

I blamed myself. I believed that I was doing something wrong. I thought I'd chosen the wrong market or hadn't hired the best copy-writer or had launched at the wrong time of year. I even wondered if I had some messed up mindset about money that kept me from making a bunch more of it so I signed up for programs around that topic. Throughout the process, and despite repeated failures, it never occurred to me that maybe the programs and advice I was getting was either flawed or missing important components.

Then my wakeup call arrived. You might think being $100,000 in debt or feeling depressed, depleted, and frustrated might be a wakeup call, but they weren't for me. I was driven and kept pushing forward ignoring all the red flags. My wakeup call came in the form of an illness.

The stress of working so hard trying to implement plans and programs everyone else was telling me to create had completely run my system down. The business expansion that I had started to increase my income and give me more time off had become a time and money sucker of epic proportions and now it was literally taking me down.

I heeded the wakeup call and shifted my focus to finding out what was causing all my health issues. I let all but my bookkeeper go, pulled down all my websites, resigned from all the things I was doing to promote my products and focused only on my one-on-one clients. For a year and a half, I didn't invest in a single business program. I put myself first. I only worked three or four days a week and often times only three weeks out of the month. Though I knew I was doing the right thing, in the back of my mind, I couldn't help but to think that I was getting further behind my colleagues. I loved my one-on-one clients, but I even wondered if I should just quit and get a job.

After almost a year of testing, I was finally diagnosed with Hashimoto's disease and set myself on the road to recovery. Unless I wanted to end up in the same place, I couldn't go back to how I was working or the levels of stress I had endured.

Instead of seeing the gift my body was handing me through giving me a chronic illness that required me to get ample sleep, eat clean food and stay away from stressful situations, I was angry. I felt that my body was limiting me from having the success I knew I could have if I got back to work full force.

Anger is a hard emotion for me to hold, and the more I journaled about it, I noticed that it turned into sadness. I wrote about feeling sad that I wasn't as strong as others in my field who seemed able to work relentlessly to create massive cash flow.

Around this time, I reconnected with a coach who I thought was wildly successful following some of the same programs I had purchased. I wondered if she might be willing to let me apprentice with her so I could figure out what I had done wrong in implementing my Internet marketing plan. At this point, I was still thinking that I just needed to figure out the way to do it right.

To my surprise, I found out that she was suffering from a different stress-related illness and had a similar experience to mine. She also revealed that she had been in contact with many others whom I had envied and they, too, weren't getting the seven-figure returns promised, and some were experiencing emotional and physical symptoms because of the time, energy and effort they had expended trying. Some were also facing financial hardships.

I couldn't believe it—we'd been sold the modern-day snake oil and it was making us sick and broke!

This awareness precipitated a remembering in me. I began my coaching business to help and inspire others. In chasing what I thought I was supposed to be doing, I lost sight of my true WHY. I had disconnected from my passion in the growth area of my business because I was listening to others instead of myself.

When I reconnected with my WHY, an amazing thing happened—I started hearing my own inner voice again. The insight it gave me was that the way for me to evolve my business was to listen to myself and allow the business to reflect more of who I am, what I stand for and what I want for other people.

What a simple, yet profound message!

Along the path of pursuing success at all costs, I had forgotten who I was, so I started there. I began by asking myself the question, "What do I love?"

The usual answers rolled out of me first—dark chocolate, the ocean, traveling, scuba diving, hanging out with friends, connecting with people. I filled pages with life's little, and big, pleasures.

Then the question popped into my head, "What do you *really* love?" I paused. This was a different question. It pushed me to go deeper. I relaxed and the answer appeared: I love being love in the world.

Though the answer was poignant, I didn't know what to do with it, so I kept exploring. Using journaling, conversations with enlightened friends, meditation and reviewing the many assessments and readings I had done over the years, I came to see that at my, core I had always stood for love—both promoting the importance of self-love and loving others.

For the first time in my life, I was crystal clear that my purpose was to teach others to love both themselves and others. I also understood that I had to start with myself and my business.

The third question I asked myself was, "What do you love to do that could benefit others?"

I was surprised that the answer was, "Partner with them—not just your clients, but other professionals." For over a decade, I had been running my practice as a one-woman show. While I hadn't felt like I needed someone else to work with, I often yearned for the dynamic brainstorming and creative musings that comes from collaborating with others.

Armed with this answer, I decided that I wanted to partner on projects and elevate other professionals by bringing the love component to their passion. Though I didn't share this insight with anyone, within a week of owning this new vision for my business, I manifested three fabulous partnerships that have flowed easily and effortlessly.

LIFEspaSTYLE was created on an impromptu road trip with former mastermind partner turned close friend, Diane B. Hilton, who runs a business called My Lifestyle Organizer. We created LIFEspaSTYLE to provide experiences of relaxation, self-love and luxury that can be done every day, not just when you go to the spa. www.lifespastyle.com.

O-Love Circle was conceived after former client and sought-after public relations firm Olive PR Solutions and Pimento Fine Art gallery owner Jennifer B. VonStauffenberg and I attended a Oneness Blessing and decided that a monthly spiritual gathering in San Diego would elevate the vibration of the professional community. www.o-lovecircle.com

Heart and Soul Journey emerged from a powerful connection between me and Shaman Harry Paul. www.heartandsouljourney.com

Ironically, all of these collaborations have Internet marketing elements, and I have re-hired a team to assist me in managing and implementing what needs to be done. In contrast to before, I am approaching all business decisions organically and am allowing my intuition to guide the next steps I take rather than trying to follow someone else's steps to success. I have signed up for programs that really feed my heart.

My business life today involves coaching one-on-one three, sometimes four, days a week, doing some speaking, writing, and having fun collaborating with other professionals, including my team. I have abolished deadlines, though I still meet those set by others to make things happen in a timely manner. I start each day asking, "Of the projects I have on my plate, which one(s) am I most aligned with today?" I no longer feel depleted or frustrated by forcing myself to do things that aren't resonating with me. Lastly, I keep ample time in my schedule for connecting with others, be it a phone conversation, grabbing some tea or taking a walk on the beach.

I am running my business from a place of love. Love for myself. Love for my clients. And love for all of those around me.

The result is I feel lighter, energized and happy. I no longer push to make things happen or work past when I feel inspired or worry about where I am in comparison to my colleagues. My health is improving quickly and I am confident I will be able to get the disease to go into remission.

Even though I'm not pushing and exerting monumental effort, opportunities are always presenting themselves and the money is flowing with them.

I have learned that as long as I listen to myself and stay true to being love, coming from love and doing what I love, the business works and life, overall, is easier. For me, that's what love has to do with it.

Intuitive Caitlenn T. Ainnsley teaches people how to love themselves and others so they can experience more happiness, health, intimacy, and success.

Caitlenn integrates many processes and techniques to assist her clients in breaking though barriers and developing a loving relationship with themselves and their businesses. In her speaking, she strives to engage the audience in going within themselves to hear their right answers.

She is an ICF Master Certified Coach; a Certified Neuro-Linguistic Programmer; a Certified Emotional Intelligence Practitioner and a Certified Oneness Blessing Giver. She has been published in three books, numerous magazines and blogs, and has appeared on TV. She is a long-time Faculty member at CoachU.

Caitlenn is Co-Founder of LIFEspaSTYLE, www.lifespastyle.com; O-Love Circle, www.o-lovecircle.com; and Heart and Soul Journey, www.heartandsouljourney.com. Though she is a native of Colorado, Caitlenn runs her life and business coaching practice from her home in San Diego, California where her adorable mutt, Sage, chews up everything she can find.

You can learn more about Caitlenn and her current love projects as well as receive a special gift at www.caitlenn.com.

CHAPTER 43

Leap. Learn. Lead.

by Veronica Tomar

In one way or another, surviving difficult times has been a part of all our lives for the past few years in light of the economic downturn. For many of us this has meant having to reinvent ourselves, taking a look at best practices and failures and juxtapose these in the context of what we can learn from a historical perspective and perhaps do it better the next time around.

I am Veronica Tomor, the author of the *L.E.A.N Guide for the Business Traveler*, and as the title implies, a seasoned traveler due to the nature of my work. I have traveled to just about every state in the U.S. and accrued all the enviable elite status' of most airlines, hotels and car rentals due to my mileage with all. I have always viewed life as an opportunity. One day as I was delayed in an airport in the middle of nowhere at around one in the morning during a severe winter blizzard and after starting my day at around five in the morning the previous day, I decided to start writing the book. It turned into a conduit for self-expression for something that has always been a big part of my life (eating conscientiously and exercising). Writing became an outlet to share my experiences, anecdotes and research with others. Most importantly, it became a great mental outlet and good use of idle time at airports in the midst of my anguish and time away from home and my family.

During the time the book was conceived, I was in a very high management position with a pharmaceutical company. Life was good, albeit the trade-off was that I was allowed to work from home as long as I commuted to work in a plane every week or as many times as the demand and my responsibilities called for it. I never really worked from home, as with the level of my responsibilities, I could never have a dog barking in the background on a conference call, or my two-year-old crying or someone knocking on the door. I decided to rent office space in a commercial building, which gave me the structure of an office, and the separation of "church and state" meaning I could separate myself from work as soon as I left the office. The only caveat was that meant even more time away from home after being gone for a few days each week. In any event, it did channel my work into very productive outcomes. Amazing how, with modern marvels of technology these days, we manage to get so much more done than we used to with all the conference calls, gadgets and web-based software while working remotely.

What I did not realize at the time is that my second office was the airport since I spent so much time there and in different cities watching so many people. I observed how many people were overweight and the patterns of "grabbing and going" while satisfying the hunger demons or eating defensively when time for a meal can be so unpredictable. Furthermore, I realized that so many travelers, not just business travelers, were stressed from travel and resorted to eating and drinking (alcohol) as an emotional bandaid.

Factors that can cause self-sabotage are sheer stress from the travel factor itself or stress from high-powered jobs and the loneliness/guilt of being away from kids and family so much. This outlet can very easily become focused on food and is much more pronounced for travelers who have little to no control over the timing of meals or the preparation of meals. Thus, this became the topic of the book. My own struggles with weight, which became the most challenging ever. The mere factor of living an incredibly fast-paced life i.e. living on the "go" all the time much more than with a 9 to 5 job, but eating in elegant restaurants and hotels for business related functions and having food all around me for most events as well as the lack of time to exercise which compounds the problem tenfold.

What I learned from all this, is that you can to incorporate portability into your eating, and **choosing** the right foods becomes a weapon to guard yourself against fattening and calorie laden foods. I invested a significant amount of time and money to find out what the airport, airline and hotel industry have done to help the consumer stay at an optimal weight and incorporated these findings into the book.

My purpose in life became different; it was not so much about improving outcomes for the company I worked for, but actually to help others through my findings and research. How ironic, now I found myself looking forward to all I was learning in life's classroom at the airports and taking every opportunity at restaurants and hotels to gather information. The tables had completely turned as what had been a routine and a burden (the travel) was now becoming a tool for my business (the book). In all, I spent the latter part of my last year focusing on writing, researching and making the book happen, all while working a full-time job with high visibility and responsibility within the organization.

By December of 2010, after missing so many deadlines and readjusting the calendar for book submission so many times, it finally went from being a dream to a reality. I hit the submit button in my computer and the formal editing at the publisher began. This phase of editing began in January, 2011 and 20 versions later, I finally had a finished product. The book was in my hands in May as the final version!

After that milestone, I ended up quitting my traveling career and started with a company where I was given a director-level position with little to no travel. This, of course, was a joy to my kids (three boys under the age of 10) and to my conscience for being away from home so much in the past and to my husband who had been so supportive of me during all these years. I rejoiced with the new opportunity that would also allow to me to see my parents more often as well.

Nevertheless, as things go and as the saying goes, when something sounds too good to be true it usually is too good to be true. Long story short, I hated the job, and ultimately had three bosses I reported to and all very inexperienced. This was a true reality check. I had left an incredible job with a solid company (over 80 years in business and rated top 25 employers by *Fortune* magazine) and I left it for this! I must have been crazy, I thought to myself. I needed to put my family first and I did. I needed to spend more time at home, and this job had less flexibility than I formerly had but overall less travel. What I did not anticipate was the nature of the work and the fact that I was miserable going to work every day. It did not take me long to make a decision.

Hard as it was because I had been the main breadwinner for my household, I made the decision to quit. In the midst of a weak economy, having to pay the mortgage of a house we bought a year ago and no health insurance since I was the carrier, I still went through with it.

It was four months, seven interviews later with five major companies and I finally got a job offer in the midst of July, 2011. We live and we learn.

Throughout the process, I learned many of life's pearls of wisdom. I have not regretted leaving my second company. I pursued my dream of seeing my book to completion, getting it published, doing the marketing, being on radio shows and magazines and the opening of doors I never dreamed of. Nevertheless, I also put my family through a financial hardship and we went through the thick and thins of only having one income in the house (my husband's) during a weak economy. I also was fortunate, that we had no significant health issues other than my middle son cutting his chin open and having to go to urgent care for stitches.

In any case, I look at this as the one and only opportunity to finish what I started and launch it well, when I would have never had the time with my former job. It is a truly a dream come true. I will embark in a new chapter in my life as an entrepreneur, but in the meantime will have to balance work life in corporate America with that of running my book business and my household.

Was all of this worth it for spending time with my kids at home for almost four months. Absolutely! I feel proud of myself for putting my family first and making the decisions I made. As I see it, I still have a another 25 years before I am eligible for Medicare, so my time to pause, reflect and focus on my priorities has led me to re-invent myself while allowing me to enjoy a little bit of me time today in the moment as opposed to always looking at the future and projecting myself into a time horizon.

This is the greatest pearl I share with you. As scary as some of these moments have been financially, you stop and smell the roses. Life is short. Play hard but play smart if you want to be successful. Taking chances to live a life with passion is better than wondering how you could have lived your life, and hopefully you can make a difference in people's lives by sharing what you have learned throughout the journey.

Veronica Tomor is a busy woman always on the go. At the time the book was written, she worked for the pharmaceutical industry and spent the last three years in the health outcomes division of a major company in the realm of diabetes. As fate would have it, she realized that although her role involved outcomes research, her own health was talking a toll through the stressful, fast-paced living and reduced time for healthy eating and exercising, plus being on the road up to 75 percent of the time. This drove her to re-focus and prioritize her health by exercising amidst all obstacles and eating smart on the go, something she learns about every day.

As a healthcare professional, Veronica has worked in hospitals, health plans, the pharmaceutical industry and almost every aspect of delivery of healthcare. She has had the privilege of speaking to Congressmen and Senators on Capitol Hill regarding the Diabetes and Obesity epidemic in the U.S for three years in a row (2007-2009). She is an active member of IHRSA (International Health, Racquet and Sports Association), serves on the Women's Leadership council, and has represented the association on Capitol Hill speaking with Congressmen/Women about the need for more education regarding nutrition and physical activity in the general population.

She also contributed to Michele Obama's LET'S MOVE open forum to the public in providing input to areas of deficit pertaining to physical fitness and nutrition in children and youth. She has been a liaison for the WeCan® program—a National Institutes of Health-evidenced based, nationally recognized program—to fight childhood obesity in the U.S and has led several community awareness programs in Florida. Finally, and most importantly, Veronica is a wife and mother of three young boys.

Section Five

Big WHYs Lead to Big Growth

CHAPTER 44

Facing the NAKED Truth

by Tania Usher

We're running slightly over time as I address 150 women at my annual event 'Women Planting Seeds of Change'. Nonetheless, the energy in the room is intoxicating and vibrant, the audience captivated. "If you want to create a BIG life, then you need to have BIG dreams, take BIG leaps and you'll reap BIG rewards." I'm sharing the importance of thinking BIG in order to create a juicy, dynamic and rewarding life.

I'd arranged to meet my then three- and five-year-old daughters by the lunch buffet. Then a flash catches my eye. My darling girls are at the foot of the stage waving up at me. "Excuse me for a moment," I announce to the crowd as I stoop to listen.

"I don't feel well mommy," cries Mia.
"I want a cuddle," announces Rhani.

"Up you come." They waste no time racing up the stairs. For a moment we're wrapped in a three-way bear hug. My youngest reaches up her hands and I scoop her up onto my hip. Mia's clearly sad and stands with her arms wrapped around my leg. I feel her relax into my side.

I'm closing my pre-lunch presentation…

"You'll reach your dreams when you climb step-by-step…eventually. Instead, trust your instincts, believe in yourself and start leaping…you'll learn to soar. Step off the cliff and know your wings will grow on the way down…then up you'll climb."

I'm in heaven. Sharing possibilities and inspiring women to live a bold life is my passion. And despite jumping many hurdles along the journey, I've created an international business doing what I love, with my daughters at my side every step of the way.

There's no apologizing to the crowd for the disruption. There's no stressful juggling of priorities. My roles as mother and businesswoman have become seamless.

It wasn't always that way…

After living in Europe and Asia for 10 years, I left the action of corporate jet-setting and returned to Australia with visions of embarking on an excited new chapter of my life, motherhood. I never imagined that within five years, I'd bury a baby, become the sole provider of my two young daughters, a victim of emotional and physical abuse, get embroiled in a draining legal battle, witness escalating credit card debt, and be served home repossession papers.

My Battle with the Baby Gods

From the moment I held Mia in my arms, I knew I could NEVER return to the bustle of the corporate world. Despite loving the excitement and energy, the prospect of placing my young daughter into long day care so I could re-kindle my executive career was heartbreaking. Motherhood was my catalyst for entrepreneurship.

My baby boy Tate was the first of my children to teach me motherhood's most powerful lesson on which I'd draw frequently…resilience.

I watched his chest intently, willing it to rise and fall. He would start to breathe any second now. He'd sing his first vocal soprano. He'd wriggle his way to the comfort of my breast. He didn't. He lay there motionless, caught in an eternal sleep.

I'd had 10 weeks to prepare for this moment, if you can ever prepare for the death of your baby. At 28 weeks, I was presented with an incomprehensible announcement that Tate suffered from a rare genetic condition which was "not sustainable with life." After learning this tragic news, I carried Tate, until he was full term and it was 'safe' for me to give birth.

Despite the immeasurable pain of losing Tate, he bestowed upon me some of my greatest gifts.

The gifts of…

- Belief
- Hope
- Surrender
- Strength
- Determination
- Unconditional love

Victim or Victor the Choice Is Mine

In February, 2000, just 13 months after Tate was born, the Baby Gods blessed me with a healthy 9 lb, 13 oz daughter! Two years later, Mia's feisty little sister Rhani was born. I never imagined how much motherhood would reshape me from the inside out.

Despite the success of my events, I was beset with anxiety. Women were looking to me for guidance, encouragement, optimism and hope. So while our incredible events were touching the lives of thousands of women, my personal life was in turmoil. I couldn't believe that I'd got myself into a situation where I was living a life of emotional and physical abuse. My fairytale family dream had transformed into a nightmare. Every dream was being trampled, every goal condemned, and my soul crushed.

One of the pivotal turning points in my life came one violent morning in May 2004 when my young daughters witnessed the two people they love most embroiled in yet another conflict. For my safety and the well-being of my young girls, I made an oath to never put myself in such a violent environment again.

Despite the emotionally draining exhaustion, I knew I had to make a choice. Was I a victim or a victor?

I chose the latter.

Warm Breath on My Cheek

Forward seven years…

Each evening as I tiptoe in the dark, I'm comforted by the muted sounds of exhaling breath. Kneeling down beside each bed, in turn, I rest my head next to my sleeping babe. In that instant, I'm transported to a world of absolute clarity and knowing. As their warm breath caresses my cheek, I'm reminded, without a doubt, that Mia and Rhani are my most powerful WHY.

Knowing my WHY, embracing my passions and honoring all the facets of my life frees me to live on purpose. It's through facing challenges head on while juggling motherhood, self-care and entrepreneurship that I learned my 5 most powerful WHYs.

1. WHY: Martyrdom Crushes Authenticity

It's tough taking steps to change the direction of your life, especially when you're a busy mom, organizing the kids, getting them off to school, rushing to get groceries…only to return home where it all begins again, i.e. emptying out lunch boxes, sifting through paperwork, making sure the kids do their homework, preparing dinner and rushing through the laundry.

And the scary part is it seems like everyone depends on you to get things done, like the whole world is riding on your shoulders.

In the months that followed the violent separation from my daughter's father, I adopted what I refer to as my 'Martyrdom Mindset.'

"I'd show him, them or anyone who doubts me that I can create an amazing life for myself and my girls," became my mantra. I'd puff up my feathers and tell myself I didn't need help. That despite no money, no support, no plan, no man…NO IDEA what to do next…all I needed was determination to forge ahead.

I was wrong. One day I woke up and couldn't walk. I'd ignored the signals to slow down. So the power of our amazing Universe made me.

While flat on my back recovering from a herniated disk, I realized that I'd been wearing my "I can do it all myself" Martyrdom

Mindset as a proud badge. I wasn't driven by authenticity at all. My actions weren't coming from my heart. Instead, I was motivated to prove a point. Ouch! Admitting that stung.

So I decided to get help.

I found an online au pair service which connects families with young women looking to help care for children in exchange for food and lodging. Our first au pair was a delightful Japanese girl. Having someone to help with the hectic day-to-day activities was a huge relief and the girls love their 'big sisters.' Over the years, we've had a number of wonderful au pairs from Japan, Korea, Germany, and Canada.

The next decision I made was to pull out my credit card and hire a coach who encouraged me to think differently. Instead of treating my business like an expensive hobby, I became aware of the qualities and skill sets I needed to become an entrepreneur.

I was able to discard my Martyrdom Mindset and reacquaint myself with my authenticity.

2. WHY: Chaos Kills Creativity

Being forced to 'pause' for three months, led to a second epiphany that was invisible when I spent my days running a constant marathon.

It's impossible to find clear direction amidst chaos. When life is a constant whirlwind of activity, it's very easy to get dizzy and start spinning out of control. Once I stopped (or was forced to stop), I realized that creativity comes to you in the pauses. And it's very difficult to 'see' these pauses when your head, home and office is in a frenzy of clutter and chaos.

Stopping enabled me to experience the powerful connection I have with my environment. While resting, I'd look around my home and see 'stuff' that was draining my energy. I'd listen to exhausting chatter in my head. And I'd feel either positive or negative energy radiating from things around me.

So starting with my mind, I began extracting overgrown weeds, thoughts, beliefs and ideologies. As my body grew stronger, I'd move throughout my home, culling anything that didn't fit my criteria...

- Had a useful purpose
- Was something I love
- Emits positive energy

I discarded 70 percent of my belongings.

Slowing down, shifting my mind, re-evaluating my priorities and redefining my focus lifted my forced incapacitation and I was 'given back' my physical freedom. It was a powerful experience reminding me that what's happening on the inside will be reflected on the outside.

3. WHY: I'm My Most Valuable Investment

One minute shares are hot, the next minute it's property.

One financial 'expert' screams "buy!"... another yells "sell!"

So with the zealous intrigue of a detective I began searching for answers to how I was going to provide for my young girls. I studied some of the world's successful businesses and discovered that there's only 'one sure thing' in which to invest.

Yourself!

Investing in myself through education, mentoring and personal growth paved the way to a secure future for my family.

When you enhance your enormous potential by building inherent value in yourself, doors begin to open, irrespective of what the economy is doing, irrespective of the beliefs others may have about you, irrespective of the self-limiting beliefs you may have about yourself.

Self-investment pays off over, and over, and over.

4. WHY: Commitments Keep You Honest

Your life mirrors your commitments. Being honest about the good, the bad and the ugly in your life and business will reveal exactly what you're committed to.

Outcomes don't lie.

- If you say you're committed to being fit...then you'll honor your daily fitness regime, no matter how busy your schedule.
- If financial freedom is a priority…you'll make the switch from trading your hours for dollars to creating passive income streams.
- If a loving relationship with your partner is important…then the harmony in your household will reveal the truth.

When you make a commitment to your goals, you experience true freedom. You no longer have to wrestle with the decision about how to spend your day or which priorities to set. If you make a 100 percent commitment to answer emails within 24 hours…then that's it. The decision is made. You don't have to think about it again. Life becomes easier and simpler. Your commitment keeps you focused and frees up energy that would otherwise be wasted grappling with internal debates…should I…shouldn't I…I'll do it tomorrow. When the commitment's been made, you then have energy to pursue your creative achievements.

5. WHY: Nurturing Is More Powerful Than Networking

Nurturing relationships is the true essence of a strong, supportive and sustainable business. You can attend all the business networking functions in your area, collect hundreds of cards and yet be doing very little to connect deeply with like-minded entrepreneurs.

When you nurture relationships by taking a personal, authentic interest in someone's life, you're creating potential lifelong friendships. It's these relationships that are an asset to your business, not your huge collection of business cards.

It costs nothing to share your challenges and triumphs, or to ask about another's industry or occupation. Yet by showing your interest, you'll be making a connection that could prove immensely valuable to your business in the future.

Success is not a solo project. It needs to be shared. Working together with others, you'll accomplish far more than working separately. The success of your business lies in this ability to surround yourself with the right support. And when you do, you become energized, encouraged and empowered.

Tania Usher, often touted the "Queen of Connection" is internationally renowned for her get NAKED philosophies for uncovering your authentic success mindset.

After years of living and working abroad, winning numerous international awards and building a successful executive career, Tania tamed her wandering soul and returned to Australia in 1999 to start a family. Within five years, Tania left the jet-setting corporate world, lost her firstborn son, gave birth to two healthy daughters, become the sole provider of her family, witnessed escalating credit card debt and was served home repossession papers.

Tania's dreams of balancing work with motherhood were shattered. Frustrated, alone, exhausted and desperate to find a way to secure the future for her young family, Tania took a leap of faith towards entrepreneurship.

When her youngest daughter was just three weeks old Tania Co-Founded and directed the Whole Woman Festival, an annual International Women's Day Festival that brought together hundreds of women to share their wisdom on a host of topics, including business, relationships, finance, health, sexuality, parenting, environment, and general well-being.

With no budget Tania, together with a team of volunteers, took the

Festival from a half day celebration to hosting 14 sell-out events in nine days. By leveraging the power of free publicity, she was able to generate over 83 media 'grabs' in just three weeks. All while balancing the needs of her two young daughters who accompanied her to media interviews, sponsor meetings and often onstage.

An unstinting faith in her own ability, coupled with a hefty dose of courage propelled Tania to take huge leaps. In just five years, her creative communication ideas lead to over $5 million in media coverage for both her and her clients.

In 2009, when she launched her daring ezine, 'get NAKED...with tania' which reveals raw and uncut strategies for creating a dynamic life…hundreds of people from around the world signed up within hours. Thousands of people follow Tania online and her events have touched the lives of over 100,000 people from a variety of industries and nations.

Living on purpose, Tania's vision is to inspire heart-centred women around the world to create a dynamic life doing what they love…while having lots of fun. "Boring is out," is Tania's motto.

Featured regularly in the media, including recent appearances on the Today Show, Tania believes that nurturing relationships and making soulful connections is the key to success.

It's this ethos that led her to launch the Women Igniting Change interview series and accompanying book which celebrated 100 years of International Women's Day in March, 2011. Tania interviewed 30 prominent women from around the world and dared to ask powerful questions that cut to the core of creating a soulful life.

The tenacious Tania believes the only thing stopping people from reaching the success they crave, is their own self-doubt. "Entrepreneurship is one of the most powerful self-development journeys on which anyone can embark. When you couple the success mindset with powerful masterminding, insightful mentoring, and taking action… amazing things happen."

Tania's authentic, heart-centred approach to business will continue to inspire women around the world to take big leaps that will lead to the positive transformation in the lives of millions of people worldwide. Visit Tania at www.taniaysherinternational.com.

CHAPTER 45

Are You Ready for Financial Freedom?

by Linda P. Jones

What do women need to know about investing and building wealth that will make them interested to learn more? Well, frankly, that investing is very different from what you think, or how you've been taught. It's not boring, number-crunching stuff, it's creative and flowing and right-brained in many ways.

The financial industry, which I was in for 25 years, didn't teach women about investing in a way that made it interesting to learn and it also didn't address a woman's needs. Women are intuitive, spiritual beings. We want to take care of our families and friends. We are social and nurturing. And we like jewelry and shoes!

The financial industry has left women out of the equation. It hasn't addressed our issues or how we are different. Dealing with money seems left-brained, and spreadsheet-like. Sometimes we've been talked to in undecipherable jargon, talked-down-to, and even ignored. No wonder women haven't been interested in dealing with their finances!

In my opinion, women need a new way to learn about investing and building wealth and they need to learn about it from a woman.

The challenge I gave myself was to create a new financial solution for women—one that addresses women being intuitive and spiritual, social, and wanting to take care of our families and others. It had to address specific issues women have, such as whether they are worthy and deserving of wealth, what their true worth is and how money and spirituality are related, as well as how to get into the conversation about money without giving their power away to their spouse or financial advisor, so they can gain financial confidence.

To figure out how to engage women about wealth building has become my life's purpose. I didn't always know that it was my purpose. In fact, I didn't learn that it was until my husband collapsed unconscious from a brain aneurysm and I was sitting beside him in Intensive Care.

It was then I heard a loud voice inside me say, *"You're not living your life's purpose. You're meant to teach other people what you know."*

Say what? The voice seemed to come out of nowhere. Somehow I knew after Roger's death, my life would be about teaching others what I knew, but I still wasn't immediately clear about what that was. It took a few years and several mentors to help put the pieces together and see the whole puzzle picture.

Now, of course, I can see it all very clearly. And, I can see how I was meant to do this from an early age. Because even as a child, I was curious and wanted to know, "Why are some people rich?" And further, I wanted to know "HOW do you get rich?" Because if there was a choice, it sure looked like more fun to me than being poor! I also reasoned, if I was only going to live once, then I was surely going to have a full life and experience all the possibilities and to do that, I reasoned, I'll need a good amount of money.

From a young age, I was fascinated with how money grew and I wanted to understand it. I read *Think and Grow Rich* when I was 10 years old. Then I started reading biographies and autobiographies of millionaires. Hundreds of them. And I began to see a pattern of steps that they took to become rich. There were eight steps.

In the meantime, I thought perhaps getting an education would teach me how to become rich, so I took college courses and got a business degree from the University of Washington. But all that did was teach me theories, not practical information. Then I reasoned if I became a Certified Financial Planner®, I would learn the practical financial information, like about tax laws and retirement plans and investments. I did learn that, but that still didn't teach me how to build wealth. So I went to work for a large stock brokerage firm thinking I'd surely learn how to invest and build wealth there.

I did learn to invest, but mainly they taught buying mutual funds (groups of companies that are managed by a professional manager), and holding onto them for your lifetime. At an average long-term return of eight to 10 percent, I'd be lucky to have barely enough to retire some day. It didn't seem like it would make me rich. So I started reading about how to invest in stocks—companies that are publicly owned that you can invest in. I began to have a lot of success. Then more success.

I remembered the eight steps I had identified millionaires used. I followed them and, at age 38, I became a millionaire. At age 39, I made a million dollars in one year! I was hooked on investing. But I also noticed that what was working for me to build my wealth was often the opposite of what the financial companies advised.

They said "buying individual stocks are too risky." Hmm, not what I found. They also said, "Diversify." Actually, I had found not being diversified was what grew my wealth. I began to see that perhaps there was a place for someone to educate people about how to build wealth and that it was important that that person not have the conflict-of-interest of investing the money.

After Roger's death, I could never have imagined the process involved in settling the estate: the multiple lawyers, the sorting of stuff, the endless paperwork. I reasoned if I was a financial expert and I was experiencing being talked-down-to, bad advice, and frankly *wrong* advice, what was it like for women who had no financial experience? Knowing that the average age of widowhood is only 56, I reasoned many women would be having these bad experiences and worse, be taken advantage of.

That's how I became a wealth mentor. Now I teach women about investing. I founded the Global Institute of Wealth for Women and Wealthy & Smart. I show women, and smart men, how to grow and invest money and create your legacy. I love what I do and I can't call it work. It's pure fun! I love it when my women clients light up and they see it's fun, too! I enjoy talking about spirituality and money, self-empowerment for women, and how to have financial freedom.

What's different about me is I start with spiritual principles and then I teach the practical financial information. I believe all wealth begins with your mind, your thoughts, and belief systems. Like Napoleon Hill said in Think and Grow Rich, "Both poverty and riches are the offspring of thought."

Beyond that, I stumbled upon some profound information connecting the Universe to the economy and even the stock market! It happened when I bought some very expensive research from a stock market analyst I saw on TV. He mentioned the stock market didn't move randomly, that it was controlled by cycles that seemed to repeat in regular intervals and therefore was predictable in advance. What was controlling the cycles I found out, was planetary movements, their alignment to one another, and even sun spot activity.

I learned there was a direct connection between the Universe and financial markets. I had never heard that when I worked on Wall Street!

I explored the concept that celestial activity impacted us here on earth. For example, when sunspot activity on the sun was high, the economy was good (remember "irrational exuberance" in the 90s?). When sunspot activity was quiet, like in 2008 and sunspot activity was the lowest in 100 years, the economy was bad (financial crisis). In addition, the alignment of the planets in relation to each other impacted financial markets on earth. A researcher in the early 1900s named W.D. Gann, reportedly made himself a $50 million fortune by using planetary alignments to trade commodities. I found a few billionaires already knew this. It was then that I began teaching some secrets of billionaires to my clients.

The Universe also began to teach me other things. That we create our lives and we would get what we believe we get. It goes beyond the law of attraction. You actually create your life based on your belief. It's kind of like this: If you believe in God like I do, I believe after we die and meet Him, He will ask, "Why did you create the life you did?" Most people will say, "What do you mean? I lived the life you gave me." And God will say, "I would have given you anything you wanted. Why did you choose what you did?" In other words, it is given to us according to what we believe.

Most of the time, our belief systems are so faulty that we have a hard time believing that we can have what we want and that we create our reality. We have to replace those limiting beliefs we learned in childhood and during our lives with new beliefs about what's possible. What we believe in our subconscious is what we manifest in our lives. Once we change the limiting beliefs with new beliefs that agree with what we want, our lives change for the better.

Are you ready for financial freedom? It's not only possible for you to have it, it's possible for you to make it happen. You don't have to do anything extraordinary or be a genius. After all, Martha Stewart became a billionaire by cooking and Oprah became a billionaire by talking. It isn't rocket science. Currently, women are starting businesses at two times the rate of men. It's time for women to create the wealth they want for themselves. The wealth you want is within your reach…if you believe it is.

Linda P. Jones has been called "America's Wealth Mentor." She is CEO and Founder of the Global Institute of Wealth for Women, for women and smart men. Linda's clients learn how to get started creating wealth, and Live Wealthy & Smart. These entrepreneurs also learn where to invest and build wealth so they can have their money working harder for them and not have to work so hard. The principles Linda teaches involve the spiritual and financial in a fresh, new way.

From a young age, Linda searched for the answer to the question, "What makes some people rich?" She devoured books written by millionaires, identified a wealth building pattern they used of eight steps, followed them, and earned her first million dollars at age 38.

From there, she recognized there were patterns of investment cycles that reoccurred and peaked in bubbles, learned they were tied to celestial movements and sunspot activity, (something billionaires have known and used to invest successfully).

Linda's mission is to educate and empower her clients so they feel self-confident making financial decisions by themselves or with their financial advisor. Because she does not manage or invest peoples' money, Linda is free to focus on teaching techniques and strategies to become smart with money, invest, and build wealth.

Linda had a successful career in the investment industry and for over 25 years, represented many of the industry's best money managers, where she was responsible for an 8-state territory with over $200 million of annual investment sales. She graduated with a B.A. in Business from the University of Washington and is a Certified Financial Planner (CFP®). In addition to running her businesses, she donates her time as a member of the Board of Directors of SightLife, an international non-profit that is a leading organization for sight restoration through cornea transplants worldwide.

She lives in Rancho Mirage, CA and Seattle, WA with her two beagles.

Get to know Linda and learn The 8 Steps to Wealth at
www.wealthforwomen.com.

CHAPTER 46

Cracking the Ego

by Melanie Benson Strick

The Big Idea Catalyst

I felt like I was in a dream. Someone else's dream actually. I woke up in the Ritz Carlton, looking out over the beautiful Pacific Ocean, listening to the birds sing in the trees and hearing the waves crashing against the shore.

I got up and shuffled around the living room in the suite looking for my tea (I always travel with my own special jasmine tea.) I brewed a really big cup of hot water, dropped my tea bag in to steep and nestled into the couch, staring out over the water.

Damn I love this place.

Then, the feeling sunk in. I knew that my life was never going to be the same after today. Reality was finally kicking in. I wasn't ready to feel sad yet so I called up my friends and joined them for a day of playing at the pool.

Tomorrow. Tomorrow I'll deal with it.

The truth is that I was stringing a lot of tomorrows together trying to deal with it. Trying to deal with the reality that the million dollar business I had worked so hard to build for the last seven years was quickly falling apart.

I felt lost, confused, angry, shameful and most of all, baffled.

What did I do wrong? Why is it not working?

The event I hosted over the three days prior was supposed to be my golden egg. It had been carefully designed to enlighten the entrepreneurs in my industry as to why they weren't able to achieve seven-figure successes. Instead, it was a financial debacle—the concrete anchor that sank my business.

Pretty much everything went wrong, like a perfect storm. I probably could have overcome one issue but so many things went wrong it was like an out-of-control snowball where I just had to get out of the way and let it play out.

We spent months determining the best positioning and venue for the event to attract the caliber of people. I knew I had to go high end all the way. That's what everyone said you did when you want to leap. Hire the best. Invest at the level you want to play at. So hired the most expensive event planner, a top notch marketing manager and picked out the Ritz Carlton for our venue.

It all started as we rolled out our marketing campaign in late November. My high-priced marketing manager had a family emergency. Everything got pushed back, the sales materials were rushed, didn't really convey the right message and ultimately did not attract our desired attendance.

A small voice rose up in my head and said, "*Something's not right.*" I responded with, "*Go away, you are just my fear and I won't let you win.*"

As I pushed past the fear, I had to sign the contract with the Ritz. Within a few short weeks our economy took a HUGE nose dive, where over 50 percent of people who had been investing in personal growth discovered their credit lines had been slashed. I begin to panic as I realized no one was signing up. People weren't investing in ANYTHING, let alone a program designed to run a successful seven-figure business.

In February before the event, my long-time collaboration partner decided this wasn't the direction she wanted to go. We had planned to offer a $45,000 and $80,000 level consulting program to help people implement these strategies. I now have an expensive event, which was largely their vision and expertise, without a clear vision of what to deliver as a next step. Because we had always agreed to compensate her on creative direction and coaching time, it sinks in that I'm completely on the hook financially for this event. I now realize that the little voice I kept hearing was right…*I'm screwed.*

From the few people who did enroll we quickly realized we had another big problem. The hotel was a luxury even at the outrageous low price of $225 for a Ritz Carlton. They were doubling up or staying off property. I was on the hook for over 50 room nights…and we had only a fraction spoken for.

There is a saying that I lived by. "Put on your big girl panties and make things happen." I decided to put my best foot forward. I scrambled to come up with an enticing next step that would be attractive to my current clients and new participants. Deep down inside I was doubtful, disengaged and scared to death. My current platinum clients felt it. Each and every one of my $15,000-a-year clients decided not to re-enroll.

Looking back, I realized there were multiple times in which I intuitively knew that things should not continue on this path. I felt that there was a better way to draw in our participants but my idea got dismissed because someone else didn't agree. Because I was so afraid of being abandoned I went along with the consensus. In the end, I still lost the people I so desperately was trying to win over.

So by the time I closed the event, I'm over $80,000 in debt, with no great program to offer to cover my costs, I'm completely depleted of all my energy and experiencing a ton of guilt and shame. Not one to give up, I set out to follow some sage advice that I had heard many years ago, "think bigger than the debt." My ego was not going to let this situation get the best of me. I would beat my situation with an even better offer! As a matter of fact, I was so determined to rise above this that I attracted in my dream guy within a few weeks—a guy who so believed in me and my work that he quit his job to help me turn things around and build the business back. Even though things were stressful, I had my rock. I started to feel that invincible feeling again.

What I discovered over the next 12 months of desperately trying to turn this situation around transformed my paradigm of life, business, success and who I was being on this planet.

Cracking My Ego

Understanding why I crashed and burned took some digging. I had very carefully followed the advice and used the wisdom of some very successful mentors. So why was it not working for me?

I thought I was doing what other people who had successful seven figure businesses did. Why was I struggling and they were thriving? Why did everything they touch turn to gold but I worked my butt off to get a mediocre result?

I soon began to realize that I wasn't the only one agonizing over this question. Clients, friends and colleagues began to confide in me that they were struggling to understand why they couldn't sustain their big leaps either.

I realized that I was facing these challenges because it was up to me to shift the way our industry was mentoring people. I've always been a big believer in turning lemons into lemonade. My life was an incubator for other people's success. Everything I face, deal with, learn from and succeed with becomes the life blood of my client's success.

What I knew was this: *the old paradigm strategies were not sustainable for the masses. A new way of doing business needed to emerge.*

For a year, I pursued a new way of doing business. I tried one product launch after another. I focused intently on revising my marketing materials so they better educated my marketplace. I listened to what my clients wanted and created unique group programs to serve them. I felt a pull to collaborate with others so I opened myself up to creating joint venture programs.

Everything I focused on got dismal results. I began to realize that I was still using old paradigm strategies (I just put a twist on them.) So no wonder I still felt stuck.

Then I hit another low. I honestly thought that I had hit rock bottom and was on my way back. I had already lost 50 percent of my client base, had to let go of everyone on my entire team, phase out my coach partnership that I had grown to depend on, fire my bookkeeping company and drastically change my standard of living to deal with the financial blow of last year's failure. What else could possible happen?

One night after hosting a call for my members, the man I believed I was building my future with and was totally in love with walked in, sat down on the floor with a ghastly look on his face and said, "I'm out." It took a few minutes to sink in that what he meant was we weren't getting married in a few months—he was ending things. This wasn't just a personal loss. This was the man who I thought was going to run my business with me. This was my rock.

I had always thought I was a strong person. When I was born the doctor looked at my mother and said, "You'll never have to worry about this one—she's a fighter." What little strength I had left collapsed. I had finally hit total rock bottom and really began to question what my life was supposed to be about.

After three months of the greatest anxiety and depression I'd ever felt, a small crack of light seeped in and a new awareness formed.

What if my ego had been holding on so tight to my identity as a mega success story that my genius couldn't be revealed until I shed everything I was erroneously attached to?

I was attached to being wealthy.
I was hugely attached to having a man in my life.
I was very attached to what people would think about me.

I finally realized that everything I had pursued up to this point was to look good for others, to prove something to the world, and to fill a deep longing inside my heart to fit in and be accepted.

I had stopped living in my WHY and started living for other' people's why.

When we have an awakening, an awareness of our truth that has been abandoned and is now reconnected, every cell in our body tingles. It's like our brain instantly begins to rewire itself to accept that truth and shift into living it.

Awakening the Genius

Gay Hendricks, author of the book *The Big Leap*, explores the concept that each person has a Zone of Excellence, a set of activities that you do extremely well, typically make good money with and often become quite successful from. The temptation is to stay in this zone because we are addicted to comfortable and easy—and yet it is the Zone of Excellence that causes us to disconnect from our real WHY—living in our genius. By holding ourselves hostage to the Zone of Excellence we cause our genius to stagnate. Our Zone of Genius is the only level at which we ultimately thrive and feel satisfied. By feeding ourselves the story that we can't give it up or make a change, we create tension that eventually causes us to combust.

My business had been built around my Zone of Excellence, and I had been happily pursuing more of that safety. Heck, I made good money in this zone! People eagerly paid me $15,000 to work together for six months! I had several $2,000 programs that I sold over the Internet without batting an eye. Who wouldn't want to make that bigger, right?

Here's the problem with becoming conscious. Anything that is not supporting your greatest expression on this planet must shift so you come into alignment. By getting too comfortable in my Zone of Excellence, I was not willing to look at the signs it was time to make a change. I put my head in the clouds and kept focusing on how to create bigger, more expensive programs so I could be just as wealthy as my friends. My cosmic 2x4 had to intervene and give me a good whack to wake up.

For the first time, I awakened to my truth—not the poor me, victim energy I had been swimming around in. I got it. This wasn't anyone else's fault. All of these situations were a divine intervention to shift me into my genius. My genius had been calling to me for some time. I just didn't understand what it was and quite frankly, I was pretty sure that it was just a distraction. I then began to realize that I had fallen into a trap that had become destructive to my genius with:

- The mantra of "If no one else had made money with it there is a good reason." So I kept following other people's cookie-cutter systems to replicate their success.

- Being accepted into certain circles being so intoxicating I kept drinking their "Kool Aid" of how success should be.

- My old habit of giving my power away, of accepting other people's truth about my business, rather than trusting my intuition.

- My conditioning to take care of everyone else before considering what I needed/wanted. This had led me to build a machine that couldn't be sustained.

I became an incubator—going deep into a discovery process to regain my energy, power and clarity of my purpose on this planet. I scoured through the clues that had been popping up for years. Going back to the basics, I took myself through a process of syncing up to my genius. A fire started to build inside of me.

I felt a bit like Michelangelo as I looked at my work like a slab of marble. I removed, released and shed the parts that weren't meant to evolve with me, creating a space for the work of art to be revealed. I began to feel liberated from constraints that had been holding me hostage.

What became very clear was:

Old paradigm strategies had kept me stuck. In order to thrive in my new era of entrepreneurship, I had to make every decision from my highest state of consciousness.

Other people may or may not "get me" now. It was up to me to choose wisely in whom I would share my vision of a new era of entrepreneurship.

I was NOT alone. As I shared more of authentically about my experience people showed up to say, "Thank you. I felt so alone in my experience." Other leaders revealed similar stories of pain as they had muddled through the awakening in their business. People needed the knowledge and support I could give having gone through such a painful (but highly necessary) evolution.

And so my teachings around New Era Entrepreneurship were born. I'm deliriously happy in my business and equally petrified that I don't have all the answers.

What I know is how to elevate my consciousness to attain any shift I desire. I see how to help my clients shift into theirs. I know how to stop doing what doesn't work to make room for what does. I know now how to make peace with my journey, even when it is painful. I know that it's okay not to know what my business is supposed to look like tomorrow and experience the joy of money flowing in just because I'm so aligned with my truth. I care less what other people think now (okay I'm not 100 percent there yet but it's a work in progress).

I know that if you are still reading, then you are ready for what I now know how to do—to create a business solely based on your terms. It's time. Let's do it before you get whacked with the cosmic 2x4 though okay?

Melanie Benson Strick, The Big Idea Catalyst, helps big-thinking entrepreneurs and thought leaders get liberated from the daily grind while developing a world-impacting, six-figure plus platform. She founded Success Connections in 2001 when she left behind a lucrative corporate job with a Fortune 500 company to pursue her passion in life—transforming the lives of overwhelmed, burned out entrepreneurs—with her secret weapon of leverage.

A licensed spiritual counselor and certified Master NLP therapist, Melanie uses innovative techniques to help people create new levels of success on their terms. With her trademarked systems in team building, leadership and high performance productivity, Melanie has guided many of the leaders in the coaching and information marketing worlds into high six- and seven-figure revenues.

Along the way she's co-authored several books including Entrepreneur.com's *How to Start an Information Marketing Business* and is on faculty with StomperNet, the world's leading e-commerce training center. She currently offers high end coaching, mastermind programs, and personalized training to design your dream team at SuccessConnections.com.

Get a sneak peek into what's possible with this free video series "3 Reasons Why Entrepreneurs With Big Ideas Don't Hit the Pay Day" at www.successconnections.com

Melanie spends her free time in search of the best spas and beaches in the world.

CHAPTER 47

What's the Point If You Can't DANCE?

by Kiva Leatherman

Have you ever just decided to give up on being great? I did—quite purposefully. I was 16 years old and I'd been dancing since—well, forever. My mom came to find her passion for dance later in life and she was going to make sure I didn't have to wait quite so long. I grew up in New York, and so had access to some pretty incredible teachers and schools. And by the time I was 16…I was great.

But that felt like a lot of pressure. And expectation. And auditions! I hated auditions—because I wasn't always the greatest. And so I quit, in my mind at least. I danced for a few more years into college, and then, I quit letting my body dance.

I decided that it would be much more fun to be ordinary—as ordinary as I could make myself, anyway, having been reminded by my mom constantly, that I was actually extraordinary, not just because I danced, but because I was smart, and independent and I could take care of myself. She taught me so well, but I decided, in my infinite wisdom, that she was wrong. I decided that the real key to happiness was to act just like everyone else.

So I worked at being ordinary for a very long time. I did not excel in college. Despite my best efforts at ordinary, I did reasonably well in my career in the mutual fund industry, advancing quickly. Since it was the end of the greatest bull market in history, I did very well financially, too. I was very good at it—I loved the speed of it, and giving presentations. I enjoyed the beginning, especially in that steep curve of learning a whole new language and a whole new world. I enjoyed the journey to becoming an expert.

But after 10 years or so, I was bored. I still did well. But to be honest, I could have done so much more. Always squeaking by and always doing the least amount of work possible, I held on. And I made it look like I was enjoying myself.

The bitter truth is that I was so sad during that time. On the outside, and I'm sure to all of my friends and family looking in, it looked like I'd lived up to my potential, and that I'd fulfilled my mom's promise (and expectation) that I was extraordinary.

But to me, it all felt like a big, fat lie. I guess it was. And eventually, that lie caught up to me. Hating your job does not inspire your best work (as I'm sure many of you can relate) and I got fired.

So I faked being happy that I got fired. I told myself and everyone else that it was ideal, that all I wanted was to be a mommy. I actually had two young children at the time—and I was genuinely grateful to have the opportunity to spend time with them. But I was not fulfilled. They are wonderful—and a huge part of my purpose, but they are just a piece of my puzzle.

I spent a lot of time watching television in those years. I taught myself to crochet. And I got certified to become an aerobics instructor. I started teaching a dance class at my local gym, teaching women simple choreography to amazing music. In that gym, with those women, my heart soared. I mean, I felt elation like I've never felt before in my life… as an aerobics instructor. Wait…I'm supposed to be extraordinary. "Well, this can't be it," I thought, "I can't have been put on this earth to be an aerobics instructor!"

So I thought some more and contemplated my future. I seriously had no idea who I was, or what I was "supposed" to do. I just knew I had to figure it out, because sitting home and watching my children grow up, waiting for the bus to come home and chauffeuring them to soccer and ballet wasn't going to do it for me. I crocheted, and thought some more and watched a ridiculous amount of TV. One day, while doing all of the above, it came to me. Like a bolt of energy that shot down through my brain and into my body, I knew what I had to do. I figured if I could take what I loved about teaching women to dance, and combine it with what I knew about investing and business, that I would be able to have an incredible business teaching women about their money and about living up to their worth.

The amazing thing was that I'd been thinking about how to spend my time when my children were off to school, which was a couple of years away at that point. But I was so excited by my idea that I started right away. I called an old co-worker, my partner Julie, who is an amazing trainer and coach. I knew I lacked expertise in that area. A few weeks later, we signed the incorporation paperwork at a local playground, while our children enjoyed a play date. The Wise Women Network was born.

We started offering local workshops to teach women to succeed with their money, their health and their time. And it went okay., but I realized that I had a lot to learn. I realized that there were no shortcuts to be taken in building a business. And I realized that there was no faking it, no squeaking by, and that hanging up flyers around coffee shops in my community was probably not the most effective marketing plan. I realized with astounding clarity that in order to teach women to live up to their worth and reach their potential that I better start living up to mine.

I dug in, and sought to immerse myself in learning about online marketing, and operations, and information publishing and technology. I read everything I could get my hands on about teaching women, and learning about the challenges that women face in their careers, families and with the competing requirements on their time. I hired a mentor. I became passionate about empowering women in third world countries to learn about entrepreneurship and attended conferences with incredibly amazing women doing incredibly amazing work in the world.

For the first time in my life, I was demanding excellence of myself. I was really busy. And I was spending a lot of money and not making any. Well, except for the $15 an hour that I made teaching my aerobics class.

I started to have a conversation with myself that went something like this:

"Wow, Kiva, you are really busy and you are not making any money."

"Something is not working."

"Maybe it's because all of your creative juices are being used up for your dance class and not for your business."

"Maybe you should quit teaching your dance class."

The next week, in front of 40 women—I blew out my ACL, in a spectacular crash landing out of this spinning jumping thing that I was trying to show-off…which if you know anything about knees, means I was done—dancing—and maybe for good. Ouch.

I knew right away I'd have my knee fixed and go through the rehab, and that I would be back teaching as soon as they let me. I needed to have my passion taken away to learn deep in my heart that I couldn't give it up. For me, I soar when I dance and when I see the women in my class moving and shaking and laughing and sweating and being amazing.

In the time that I had during my recuperation, I did a lot of writing and a lot of working on the marketing and messaging of what I wanted Wise Workshops to be. I knew that I wanted to teach women to be successful with their money, their health and their time. I knew I wanted women to believe that they can be whatever and have whatever they want. I knew that it was vital that women have the education, means and resources to be self-reliant, not to depend on anyone else for their financial, emotional and physical well-being. I knew that I wanted women to know that through engagement and action, they can have an immediate impact on issues in our world. I knew that I wanted women to thrive. And suddenly, it came to me. Wise teaches women to DANCE.

Our process became the acronym D.A.N.C.E.—Decide—Accept—kNow—Commit—Expand, to teach women to achieve their goals—regardless of whether they are financial, emotional, physical or career goals, these are the steps that we teach for success. But the coolest part is that when I'm giving a talk or teaching a workshop, I literally teach the attendees to dance! I've had lunch seminars up and boogie-ing around the table and college women coming together to learn choreography—moving and shaking and laughing and sweating and being amazing and LEARNING.

The crazy thing is—once DANCE became a part of our lexicon and what we do at Wise—everything began to come together in crazy cool ways. Speaking opportunities materialized, partnerships became easy. Even time management came easier, since I know that I am on the right path, I am more present for my family, making sure to have time just for them, no cell phone allowed!

If you can figure out how to design your work so that it is so incredibly rewarding and connected to who you are, and allows you to do things that make your heart soar—suddenly work doesn't feel the same. Things that used to feel tedious have purpose. I like to say that you know that you're on the right path when you do what is necessary, even if it's really, really hard.

I think the key is to stop thinking about the aspects of your life as separate and conflicting demands on your resources and to begin to consider how you can integrate those pieces into your very own beautiful puzzle. As an entrepreneur, you have an incredible opportunity to create whatever you want. There are no rules. There are no limitations. You can become one of the privileged few that get to do exactly what you were made to do. You get to design your life.

So that you can soar, and you can be wise and you can dance.

Kiva Leatherman is the Founder and President of the Wise Women Network, which inspires and teaches women to live up to their worth—emotionally, physically and financially. She is also the host of Web Talk Radio's "A Woman's Worth." As a speaker, Kiva encourages women to know themselves, to know about their money and to stop living vicariously through others—to achieve success and happiness on their terms.

Kiva was formerly a sales vice president with a major investment firm managing a territory that generated over $100 million in sales annually. Although the investment business was definitely a boys club, Kiva found a way to succeed with grace, humor and feminine strength.

Her presentations on women and investing laid the groundwork for what eventually became Wise Workshops and her personal mission to ensure that women are in charge of their own money, their own time and the decisions that they make regarding their nutrition and health.

She teaches women to create a framework for success which gives them the power and freedom to live well.

Kiva graduated with degrees in psychology and performing arts from Washington University in St. Louis. She loves teaching women to get their groove on through dance and is a certified fitness trainer. Kiva lives on the beautiful Seacoast of New Hampshire with her husband, Michael and her young children, Myles and Charlotte.

CHAPTER 48

Follow the CASH Model to Success

by Lisa Larter

As an only child who was raised by a single mom who dropped out of high school at the age of 18—I was destined to work a minimum wage job and struggle for the rest of my life.

Instead, I chose to work hard and believe in my own ability to succeed. It started at the age of 12 when I was hired and let go from my first job because I was not legally old enough to work. At that moment, I knew I needed to find a way to make money if I wanted to have the things I desired in life.

Whether intentionally or not, I have lived my own CASH model since that day and it has served me well.

I have always believed we get to choose how we live our lives, and although that might sound like an idealistic approach, I think I am living proof and my simple model can help you, too.

Anyone who chooses to follow the 4 simple steps outlined in this CASH model can attain success in their lives. It is that easy.

C stands for Courage

This is where most people stop instead of start. Fear prevents most of us from ever taking action—and every person who has acted in spite of fear knows that it was never as bad as you imagined it to be.

It is a myth that successful people do not feel fear. Successful people find courage in the face of fear and act anyway.

At the age of 19 when I was working in retail, I was asked to transfer to Toronto and to become an assistant manager. My first reaction was fear. I made a mental list of all the obstacles: I can't move, I don't know anyone and rent will be more expensive.

I decided to take the opportunity and go in spite of my fears. That started my path in retail where I continued to grow and move into more senior roles up until 2006 when I finally left the retail world to open my own store. I went from making minimum wage in retail to a healthy six-figure income by the time I left.

It took tremendous courage to walk away from the safety and security of that six-figure income and to invest over $200,000 in my first serious business.

Had I not found the courage to act on that first opportunity, the rest never would have happened and who knows what my path would have been.

A stands for Aptitude

If you had a hammer and someone gave you all the materials you needed to build a house, you would never be successful because building a house requires more than one tool.

If you only possess one skill and you are trying to build a successful life—you will face the same challenges.

Aptitude is the constant reminder that if you live life on a quest to learn more skills, you will, in fact, be able to build or create the life of your dreams. Aptitude is the key to inspiration.

When you need to learn something new, act with courage and determination. Often courage is what enables us to learn what we need to get to the next level in our lives. Investing in your self through learning is powerful.

I do not have a high school diploma, nor do I have a university degree. I have, however, read more books than the average person will read in a lifetime and I continue to invest in myself through others to learn what is necessary to have the life I desire.

When I face a challenge in my business, the first thing I do is figure out my aptitude gap. When I opened my store, that gap was cash flow. I do over a million dollars a year in sales which means I buy close to a million dollars in inventory.

Understanding income and expense is one thing. Understanding the timing of when people get paid and how to manage cash flow is a completely different monster.

When I realized I had a cash flow problem, I went on a mad quest to learn as much as I could about this topic. I remember reading in an *Inc.* magazine article that if you couldn't accurately predict how much money your business would have in the bank six months to a year out—you were in trouble.

I asked my bookkeeper to create a model for me to help me stay on track. He created a fancy spreadsheet that allowed me to once and for all understand inflows and outflows in my business. He populated all the data and explained it to me. As soon as he left, I deleted everything and did it all over myself.

Why you might ask? You don't learn how to fly a plane by reading a manual. You have to practice if you want to understand. I knew that cash flow was more important than customer service in my business and I needed to submerge myself in the process in order to fully understand it.

Today, I have no problem letting someone else manage the process—I know I have the aptitude to manage cash flow in any business.

S stands for Self-Confidence
This is where people get things mixed up. You are not born with Self-Confidence—you earn it. Self-Confidence is earned when you find the courage to act in spite of your fear.

I was not born with tremendous Self-Confidence. In fact, I had many events in my life that caused me to doubt myself. I learned to be more confident when I took action. The courage to take action builds life experience and it is those experiences that create Self-Confidence.

I am not confident about every single decision I make—but I am confident about one thing. I will act in spite of fear. I will learn from my mistakes.

One day in 2009, I received a phone call from someone who works for Arielle Ford asking me if I would speak at one of her events about social media. I remember distinctly I was at my cottage and I was a bit awestruck to be invited to speak at such a prestigious event.

I handled that call with the least amount of Self-Confidence one could muster. I asked her if she was sure that I was good enough to speak on that panel. I spoke to this woman for a while and in the end we agreed that I had what it took to be there.

When I got off the phone, my husband was standing there looking at me. He said to me "Don't you ever ask someone again if you are good enough when they call you for something like that. If you weren't good enough, they wouldn't have called."

In this situation I acted in spite of fear. I found the courage to say yes, to fly to San Diego and speak at an event where I was terrified that I would not be good enough in comparison to some of the other speakers.

I got on stage and almost felt sick to my stomach and noticed I was the furthest away from Arielle Ford, which must mean I got to go last. I had time to get my nerves under control.

I was wrong—I was the first person asked a question, and when I began to speak, Arielle stopped me and asked me to repeat what I just said, and in that moment, a switch in my heart flicked on. I had my game. This was my moment and I was no longer afraid.

I sat and listened to what others said and felt validated in many cases as they responded exactly the way I would have.

Had I not found the courage to do this, I never would have found the Self-Confidence to speak at larger events and do so knowing I deserve to be there—I am good enough.

I hope you know, you are good enough, too, and that you own Self-Confidence will only grow when you find your courage and take action in spite of your fear.

The H stands for Habits

Habits are fundamental to success. You cannot accomplish much in life without a set of successful habits.

Habits are boring and under-rated though. We forget about habits we already have like brushing our teeth. We just do it every day without thinking about it because we know it is necessary.

When you create a deliberate set of habits designed around moving your life forward, it is magical what begins to happen.

Habits that have served me well are creating systems in my calendar to get the important things done. My calendar ensures I do things such as working out, reading, client appointments, and more.

For me the most powerful habit I have is utilizing my calendar. It is a simple and effective time management habit. If it does not go into my calendar, if I do not have an appointment—it does not get done.

This habit along with my lifelong habit of writing lists is key to remembering to focus on what is most important.

When I first started my business, I felt guilty that I was not making as much money as I did when I worked in the corporate world. Thus I was not investing in myself as much as I should.

I made an appointment to talk to a personal trainer who specialized in ortho-therapy, nutrition and personal training. That day I invested $4000 in myself to create a healthy habit. I invested at the highest level so I could guarantee myself the habit of taking care of my body.

And I felt so guilty. The little voice in my head said "What are you doing paying someone to get you to work out? You are so lazy. You have a gym in the basement, why don't you just get your lazy ass out of bed and exercise?"

I knew I did not have the self-discipline to do this on my own and that in order to take care of my health—body and mind—so I could take care of my business, I needed to do this.

It's been three years and I still invest in this habit. If I don't have an appointment with my trainer, I am not consistent. I believe this habit is one of the ones that empowers and energizes me to do everything else that I do in my business.

Taking that first step of investing in yourself financially is difficult and once you have done it, it pays back dividends.

These four simple steps have taken me where I am today in life. It all starts with Courage.

Courage is the key to stepping into your power and manifesting the life you want. In my world, Courage is the key to cash and cash empowers you to do what you love to do most in your life.

Lisa Larter is an International Business Consultant, Social Media Strategist and Live Motivator. Her Mastermind Program, which debuted in November of 2010, sold out in just four months. She is a highly recommended and sought-after speaker for corporate events and seminars.

With little more than a determined spirit and the support of her family and friends, she began her career as a retail sales associate and quickly started climbing the corporate ladder. Upon reaching the top, where she was responsible for hundreds of millions of dollars in sales for a Fortune 500 company, she decided that it just wasn't quite enough. In 2006, her entrepreneurial spirit took over and she founded Parlez Wireless, a Telus Mobility store in Ottawa, as well as Lisa Larter Consulting.

Her innovative approach to business is hard-hitting and no-nonsense. She coaches her clients in maximizing their sales and growth through

Social Media, Relationships, Systems and Technology. Lisa has worked with some truly amazing people such as, Deepak Chopra, Arielle Ford and Peggy McColl. She has a true gift for breaking complex ideas down into simple, manageable steps that can easily be executed by small business owners to achieve the success they dream of.

If you are planning an important meeting or conference and are looking for a keynote speaker with substance who can motivate your team to achieve their full potential, look no further! Lisa is dedicated to providing you with the most innovative and current ideas in Social Media, Leadership Development, Strategic Planning, and Sales and Marketing. Her passion for business will ignite your sales force and expand your bottom line!

CHAPTER 49

Share Your Brownies and Step Into Your Big WHY

by Fabienne Fredrickson

As entrepreneurs, we're a strange, different breed from the rest of the people out there. We don't really always fit in. Our family and friends don't always understand us. Some of us, like me, are completely unemployable now that we've 'tasted' self-employment and probably many years before that. And I sometimes wonder what makes us willing to start our own business, when those around us think we're crazy and caution us against such foolishness. *"Why on earth would you walk away from a 'safe' job in corporate to start something that most people fail at, when you could get a regular, steady paycheck working for someone else?"*

I heard this a few times when I was starting out about leaving the "safety" of corporate to do my own thing. And then I saw the Apple "Think Different" commercial and was overwhelmed by a sense of belonging, a sense of acceptance and of doing something that truly mattered. Here is the script from that commercial:

> *"Here's to the crazy ones. The misfits. The rebels. The trouble-makers. The round pegs in the square holes. The ones who see things differently. They're not fond of rules. And they have no respect for the status quo. You can quote them. Disagree with them. Glorify, or vilify them. About the only thing you can't do, is ignore them. Because, they change things. They push the human race forward. And while some may see them as the crazy ones, we see genius. Because the people who are crazy enough to change the world, are the ones who do."*

I never get tired of watching this video, getting tears in my eyes every time I do. And what I've realized is that we're all here for one thing and one thing only. And that's to make the world a better place, in a way only *we* can do it. We all have a purpose and we all have a big WHY.

We're all here to be of service, in our own special way, in a big way. You see, each one of us came here in the world to be of service, to contribute, to serve others. We've each been given specific talents, unique abilities and skills, ways of being and ways of doing things, and life experiences (both good and not so good) that have contributed to who we are today, to the whole package of who we are. And none of this was an accident. It was all for a purpose, one that is much greater than you may be able to see right now.

The thing is, this person you've become, the one who's here to be of service, absolutely must get out there in a big way and serve. If you choose not to, you're essentially wasting the gifts that were divinely given to you.

I call this "Sharing Your Brownies."

Imagine that you're in your kitchen, while the rest of your friends and family are in your living room. Quietly, secretly, you've been baking up a batch of ooey, gooey, chocolatey brownies and, as they're about to come out of the oven, a close friend pokes her head into the kitchen and says, *"Something smells really good! What are you making in there?"* And then imagine that your response is, *"Nothing, I'm not doing anything! Please go back to the living room and I'll be out in a little while."* Puzzled, your friend leaves and as you cut up the brownies into perfect squares and stack them on a platter, you choose to not share them, but instead eat them all by yourself.

Would you consider that being stingy? Greedy?

It's the same thing with your gifts. Remember that you were divinely given all the tools you need to get out there in a big way to make a difference in people's lives, in only the way you can, and instead of doing that, you hoard your divine gifts and keep them all to yourself. Would you consider that being stingy, too? Greedy?

I believe that it's our duty to live our purpose, to get out there in a big way to serve, whether it's through our work or business, through writing a book, through volunteering, teaching, or helping others. Otherwise, we're being stingy and greedy with what God gave us.

Deep down, we're here for one thing. It doesn't matter what we do for a living, what industry we're in, what our strengths and skills are. It is to live a life that matters. And when you realize that it's your divine duty to use these skills, and you do so, you begin changing the world.

This might sound a little grandiose at first. But realize that there are people who you could help right now, as you read this, that toss and turn in the middle of the night, each and every night, worried, overwhelmed, frustrated and not knowing what to do about a particular challenge in their life, and knowing that you currently have the solution to their problems, it's actually imperative that you help them. It's a moral obligation, not really a choice. With each person you serve, "Sharing Your Brownies" in a big way, you change the world one person and sometimes many people at a time.

Now, imagine a placid lake. And then imagine dropping a pebble into that placid lake. Doing so creates a ripple, and that ripple travels farther than the original entry point of the pebble. With each client you help, you not only change their life, but you change the life of those around them; their spouse, their children, their co-workers, their friends and family members. Then all those lives begin to affect other people's lives, just by virtue of you having shared your gifts. Through that one life, you've affected countless, untold numbers of lives, even if just subtly.

And then imagine if you throw a second pebble into the placid lake. More ripples, countless ripples and an even greater ripple effect, and untold lives changed. And then imagine dropping 20 pebbles into the lake. The reverberations, the ripple effect can be endless. And then imagine, 200, 2,000, 20,000, 200,000 pebbles. The bigger you "Share Your Brownies," the more you change the world, and the more handsomely you will be rewarded for it because, as a side note, the more people you serve, the more money you can make for yourself, especially if you're in business for yourself.

In fact, the formula for making a lot more money is simple, and please don't underestimate its simplicity, because it is actually pretty profound:

The formula for abundance:

1) Give a LOT more value to the marketplace than you're adding now
2) Give a LOT more value to a LOT more people

That's when you begin to be handsomely rewarded for it. That's when the Universe rewards you with opportunities, clients, financial rewards you hadn't expected. All because you made the decision to live your big WHY, your purpose in a much bigger way. I know, because when I decided to do just that, to step into my purpose and "Share My Brownies," that's when my business started multiplying at a rapid pace, that's when the most incredible opportunities started coming my way, out of thin air, and that's when I quickly turned my nice little business into a multi-million dollar purpose-filled service vehicle.

I realize that it's not always spoken about in the same sentence: living your purpose and making gobs of money. In fact, talking about money and being rewarded financially for doing good in the world makes many people uncomfortable. But I see it differently.

I believe that when you accept your divine purpose and live fully into it, leaving your comfort zone and being willing to stretch and do things that others aren't willing to do, you're doing "God's Work." And when you align yourself in this way, God (or the Universe) or whatever you choose to call a higher power sees you align in your divine calling, even if it's in your business, it begins to celebrate this and rewards you with everything you need to continue on this path.

So, the opportunities that were not available to you before begin to appear. The happy coincidences start showing up. Even the money starts showing up. At first, you may think it's a coincidence, like I did. But then after a while, you realize that you're being given the tools to continue on this journey, to get this message or service or product out there in a MUCH bigger way.

After buying a few designer pairs of shoes with your newfound money, perhaps a new car and some other luxuries, you realize that you're being giving this "wealth" to use as a tool to throw even more pebbles in that lake, and create even more ripple effects.

So, that means that money is actually a very good thing and it's awaiting you the minute you decide to "Share Your Brownies" with the world in a bigger way. So, going back to that formula, the more you share your brownies (add value), the more people you share those brownies with (your reach), then the more you multiply your income. So, to make even more than you're making now, and to be financially free, you must play bigger than you're playing now.

If it's that easy though, why aren't all entrepreneurs making the money they want to make. What's the problem?

Often, the fear of change is so deep that, instead of playing a bigger game, we desperately cling to the world we know. To avoid discomfort, entrepreneurs make excuses. There are feelings of inadequacy and of not deserving the abundance. Playing too small. Looking at other common entrepreneurs for what your benchmarks should be, instead of listening to the prodding voice inside, encouraging you to go for it.

Self-sabotaging behaviors start to show up. Keeping yourself too busy. Being afraid to invest in yourself. Indecision and waffling. Procrastination. More excuses. Negative self-talk. Fears of what people would think and say. Not enough determination and stick-to-it-ness. Not enough faith. And these are all forms of self-sabotage and they all have to do with your mindset. In fact, your mindset is 90 percent of the reason for your success or lack thereof, in business, in life, in finances, in relationships and in reaching one's willingness to get out there in a big way.

So to play a much bigger game and command more abundance into your life, it's important to work on stretching how you show up in the world and working on that Mindset.

Make the decision to succeed and to go BIG.

You surely know this quote by now:

"Our deepest fear is not that we are inadequate. Our deepest fear is that we are powerful beyond measure... Your playing small does not serve the world. There is nothing enlightened about shrinking so that other people won't feel insecure around you." —Marianne Williamson, *A Return To Love*

This sounds overly simplistic, but you must make the decision to succeed right now. You see, the point at which many people fail to reach their dreams is actually BEFORE it all starts. Most people wait for the opportunity to become successful to land on their laps before making the decision to become successful. But the Universe doesn't work that way. You must make the decision to succeed BEFORE the opportunity will ever land on your lap.

Do you get the distinction? I'll say it again in a different way, just to make sure:

You're waiting for the big opportunity to arrive before you make the decision to live your purpose full out and be successful. But if you understand the game of life and the Universal Success Principles, you probably know that you must FIRST make the decision to do something, before the opportunity you seek will ever arrive.

Success in following your passion and purpose is a decision, not an accident. It is planned, it is pre-meditated and it is on purpose.

And that is one of the major reasons why the masses never reach their full potential. They often bob in the water of life, rudderless, waiting for direction, instead of pointing their boat in a very specific direction and doing whatever it takes to get there.

Now, let's examine some reasons why people never make that decision to succeed on a very big level.

Fear of not being good enough:

Let's be honest. Sometimes you may be scared that you're not good enough or qualified enough to reach that big goal, so you don't even try. In fact, you don't know how "it" would ever happen, you don't "see" it, and therefore, you don't go after it.

Have you ever felt on the verge of something BIG, that the next level is just within your reach, and at the same time, wondering if you have what it takes to make it happen, if you can actually handle it? There was a point in time when I curiously observed this with colleagues, students and clients of mine.

I had wondered, "Why is everyone around me so afraid of the next level? Why don't they just reach out for it and make it happen?" Well, after some reflection, it dawned on me that my clients were essentially holding up a mirror for me, because deep inside I'd been feeling the same fear of leaving my current comfort zone for something much bigger.

You see, things had been going great in this business, and yet, I kept having this nagging feeling that the next big level was about to show up (speaking now, from hindsight, it was right smack in front of me. Duh.) And at the same time, it seemed I was being asked by the Universe to really step up my personal growth. "Healer, heal thyself."

I saw how, to teach others about this 'mindset' stuff on a grand scale, I had to surrender even more to what was possible for me. You'd think this would have been easy, but somehow, it was still a challenge.

Several experiences came up where my "old" ways of being showed up as no longer valid, especially not for a business that was about to grow dramatically (triple its size in one year.) And normally, I take a no-excuses approach to clearing out that kind of stuff. But this time, the stuff was more lodged in than normal.

I questioned whether I was "willing" to do what it takes, whether I had courage to go really big.

And then my good friend Carolyn sent me a copy of the movie "The Moses Code" that same week, saying knowingly, "This is what you need, Fabienne." And within Chapter 5 of the DVD, I broke down and sobbed at my desk. Not from sadness, but for the humbling potential of what is possible for anyone, for my clients, and what was possible for me. The message of the movie for me was simple: we all have a destiny for greatness. And as "The Moses Code" film says, it can be a little scary to tackle an idea so big. The calling for our next stage of evolution (and success) is always upon us. There is a journey that you are being asked to take, something very big.

But what's also pointed out in the movie is that, instead of embracing the journey, we often say to ourselves, "Who am I to do this? I don't have what's required. I'm not enough for that." But the truth is, we must come to the realization that we are all being called to something great, in our businesses or careers, in service to others, in our income and abundance, and that it's okay that we are all not presently the person able to deliver that destiny. The thing is, we grow into it as we say "YES" to the challenge. That's all it takes. Then, everything we need is then given to us.

Whether you use the word "God" in your everyday language or not, here's a quote from the film that really moved me and got me to understand what was going on for me then:

"God does not call the qualified, He qualifies the Called, through the 'yes.'"
—Reverend Michael Beckwith

The important thing I realized is that the person who originally said YES to the call, is not the same person who will reach that destiny. We're constantly evolving and unfolding based on our ability and willingness to say "Yes, I'll go on that journey."

What I got clear that fateful week was that, when you say YES when called and challenged to reach the next level, the thing that called you qualifies you. When you say YES to the next big level in your life, you begin to receive the resources, the skills, the mentor, the employee with the right contacts, the guidance, the money—everything begins to show up. (This is exactly what happened to me.) You then change and grow into the person able to deliver the destiny. So cool.

The struggle is within the ego that steps in and tries to protect the comfort zone that we've been accustomed to. The "old" way of being. And for many, it's mediocrity, struggle and frustration. You'd think, "Why are we so adamant about holding on to mediocrity or frustration if we don't like it?", but if you think about it, if that's what you've been accustomed to for years and years, it's the only thing you know. And anything else involves change. And most people don't like change and they certainly don't like being outside of their comfort zone.

The thing is, to reach that next bigger level of greatness or success in whatever you're striving for, you must be willing to step outside of your comfort zone and be willing to make the changes that seem to threaten your "safe" way of being, knowing that you are always safe anyway.

There is no other way. In fact, if the change is not made, things may become even more difficult, more complicated, and more struggle shows up. Until finally your ego says "Okay then, GO!, do what you have to do, I'm done."

The thing is, you do have what it takes to bring your business to the next level. So, it's a question of courage and the willingness to be without your old, frayed security blanket. And what I know from past experience is that the "fear of change and the unknown" is much greater than the actual discomfort of walking into the fear.

So, it's your choice: Greatness or Mediocrity. Which do you want in your personal and professional life?

Here's what I say: Go Big or Go Home!

"Dream big, hold the dream high enough, consistently enough, and the dream will manifest into form, by law. By universal law, it cannot fail to do so. Do not worry about how. It is all taken care of for you as long as you do your part of thinking, acting, speaking and being in accordance with that dream. Just dream, visualize, and then start doing something. Do the next thing that you feel you should do in accordance with that dream, and keep moving. The little that you do triggers something else you had not foreseen and on and on this goes until it completes." —David Cameron Gikandi

After sharing my personal "Video Vision Board" with my more than 10,000 people recently (you can find it on YouTube by searching "Fabienne Mind Movie"), I received a lot of comments and questions. One of the ones that stood out the most for me was this one:

"Hey Fabienne, just watched the You Tube video. It's awesome. I'm not sure what it is that keeps me from living in the music of possibility. I keep holding myself to something small like "Hoping for another client this month." And here you are on Oprah and making videos with Bono. So cool!! What do I need to drop in order to step in to 'YES' and let go of 'HUH?'"

What I've witnessed is that many people have massive doubt about their ability to do something BIG in this world, including myself up until a few years ago. And because we're doubtful about our ability to accomplish something BIG, we don't allow ourselves the chance to think big, for fear of failing miserably and confirming our own original thoughts. The self-doubt gets hold of us even before we begin to craft our vision. So we keep playing a mediocre game and living a mediocre life as a result (mediocre, in the sense that your life is probably 'good enough' now, but it could be SO much sweeter and richer, if you allowed yourself to play bigger.)

The solution? It's time to drop is the self-doubt and live in faith. (In the word "Faith," I mean, self-assuredness, not necessarily religion.) Most people continue to play small because of feelings of unworthiness or inadequacy. We've all been put down in our lives, especially in our childhood, and sometimes by the people we thought we were the safest with. And we've pushed down our big thinking and play a "beige" existence.

Enough of the beige existence. Enough mediocrity. You are enough. You are not inadequate. In fact, you are powerful beyond measure. There is nothing you cannot accomplish if you believe in yourself. There is nothing you cannot accomplish if you move past the fear of failure or the fear of really being "seen" in a big way. This is your time to shine.

You, me, Bono, Oprah...we're all just people trying to do good things in the world, leaving it a little better than when we arrived. Those you admire still brush their teeth and have indigestion sometimes, like we do. But the difference is that they simply made the DECISION to play big one day. And then they BELIEVED. They were scared, too, and they did it anyway. They, too, didn't know how they were going to fulfill their big dreams (I certainly don't have a thoroughly mapped out plan for how I will reach mine, but I believe they'll happen) but they went for it anyway. That's all.

I recommend you work on your own big vision, starting tonight. Make a list of people you admire greatly and what they've accomplished in the world. Then, get inspired by that and create your own list of what YOU would accomplish if you could do anything. (Hint: you can.) And whenever you start thinking, "What? Me... do this?" then it means it's exactly what you should be shooting for. All you need to do is look for the opportunities and get support to manifest your vision. That is when your life will become even sweeter and richer.

Too many people talk themselves out of their big dreams, goals, passions and living their purpose full out because they can't see how they will ever make money at it. And therefore, they never take the first step. You don't have to worry quite yet about how you'll make money at your passion. That comes later. Just say Yes to it. Don't worry about the How as it relates to how you'll make money at your passion; that's not your job.

Remember, you can't ever "out-think God" around how you'll be able to make money at the thing you're here on earth to do. Surrender that part and just do yours: expand your vision of your purpose here beyond what you're currently doing, and take massive action once the signs are presented to you.

Because if you're going to play anyway, you might as well play BIG.

Fabienne Fredrickson is Founder of ClientAttraction.com, a company devoted to teaching entrepreneurs around the world how to consistently attract ideal, high-paying clients, put their marketing on autopilot and authentically create a highly successful and meaningful business, while working less.

Fabienne created The Client Attraction System®, the proven step-by-step program that shows entrepreneurs exactly how to attract more clients, in record time. Through her workshops, courses, coaching programs, and products, Fabienne shows her students how to create an abundant life they love.

As one of the most influential and highly-acclaimed marketing and success mindset speakers and business mentors in the world, Fabienne's down-to-earth yet powerful presentations have become legendary. She is a sought-after and much-loved coach to thousands of heart-centered entrepreneurs around the globe.

Fabienne's unique ability is getting entrepreneurs who have never experienced real success in their businesses to take immediate marketing action on a systematic basis to produce dramatic results, in record time. She's dedicated her life to helping entrepreneurs and business owners create a legacy of service, adding value to the world in a lasting way and creating breakthrough paradigm shifts in their mindset and their personal income; and then giving back. Her books, newsletters, products, appearances and online reach now inspire nearly 150,000 people each month.

Fabienne's key message—that each of us is here to serve the world in a BIG way and that as a result, we are handsomely rewarded for it—has changed thousands of lives around the globe. She fervently believes in the capacity for each and every one of us to become the full expression of our purpose here on earth, and to do so, we must take a no-excuses approach to growing within. For that to happen, Fabienne teaches her students and clients that any struggle on the outside is a reflection of the struggle on the inside, and once eliminated, that internal struggle gives way to all the abundance, financial and otherwise, that a person deserves and seeks.

Highlights from Fabienne's inspiring career include:

- Crossing the million dollar mark in her business at the age of 38, in an industry where most entrepreneurs barely make $20,000 a year (and doing so with three young children at home)
- Subsequently doubling her business nearly every year to the multi-million dollar level, always making more in the last 12 months, than she's made in the last 12 years combined (both in prosperous times and in a "recession")
- Consistently and repeatedly helping five-figure entrepreneurs cross the six-figure mark, and guiding six-figure business owners to easily move to a seven-figure business, while adding more meaning, purpose and fulfillment to their daily lives
- Creating the world's most verifiable, repeatable Client Attraction System® for entrepreneurs throughout the world
- Conceiving and leading the 'Marketing and Mindset Breakthroughs' Seminar, the first personal and professional devel-

opment seminar for entrepreneurs combining both the pragmatic and practical, with mindset and powerful spiritual principles for success (think Success seminar meets Marketing bootcamp!)

The consistent feedback from hundreds of thousands of Fabienne's students around the world over the years is that it is her authenticity, transparency, vulnerability, "humanness," sincerity and compassion and love for entrepreneurs that separates her from other mentors and is the catalyst to their expansive growth, both personally and otherwise.

To order Fabienne's FREE Audio CD, "How to Attract All the Clients You Need" by mail and receive her weekly marketing success mindset articles on attracting more high-paying clients and dramatically increasing your income, visit
www.clientattraction.com.

Fabienne lives by the sea in beautiful Stamford, Connecticut, with her wonderful husband, Derek, and their three young children.

CHAPTER 50

Branding Yourself *on Purpose*

by Corinna Rogers

I sit in a plush penthouse conference room of a downtown office building. The surroundings are both tasteful and powerful. The room is tense. Our group of C-level executives and high-dollar consultants are positioning solutions, overcoming obstacles and negotiating for change—big change. High-dollar decisions are on the table. Multiple millions and months of company resources will be spent implementing whatever decision is made today. The energy in the room is electric!

Only one thing feels wrong about this day; one woman, seven men. For 15 years, it has been *one woman*. First it was one woman: four men, then one woman: 18 men. During one phase, it was even one woman: 153 men. Ouch. I spent my early career in the IT industry, most of it working with executive teams of very large corporations. I have often reflected on how I made it into that world in which so few women play. Plenty of women have computer and engineering skills. Even more women have executive level educations and leadership skills. Yet in my years of corporate consulting, I rarely crossed paths with women decision makers.

Today I am an entrepreneur. I own a women-centric business which helps next generation women leaders. We work with them to develop the skills and insights they need to accelerate their professional careers. My vision is to see more women thriving in coveted and influential positions. The statistics speak for themselves. Women want successful careers. Currently, more women than men are graduating from college. More women are in the workforce. More women than ever before are launching their own businesses.

When I chose to launch my business, every day was filled with decisions. Big decisions or small ones took up the majority of every day. It seemed overwhelming at times, but more often, I found it to be *exhilarating*. One key decision for me was whether I should brand myself as a business, or brand my business as its own entity. I spoke with many successful entrepreneurs and read everything I could find about branding strategy. Experts seemed to come down on one side or the other; either brand you or brand the business. For strategic reasons, I decided to brand the business. I quickly went about focusing my efforts defining that brand. What did I want customers to feel when they came to my website or my conferences? What message should my logo convey? How should our Facebook or Twitter personality express our business brand? This was actually pretty easy decision-making.

As I worked with other entrepreneurs, I began to notice an interesting trend which made me re-think branding. More and more women entrepreneurs struggled when positioning themselves personally as "the brand." The self-promotion and raw exposure of being "the brand" seemed counter-intuitive to women. Many of us have been socialized to be modest and unassuming, to let our work speak for itself. Today, standing on the merits of great work alone is not enough. These savvy women entrepreneurs could position and market their businesses with expertise and ease. However, they often stalled when it became more personal. Things like getting the perfect headshot, the perfect video clip, or the right tagline seemed daunting. There was nothing clear or easy about these decisions, which seemed more inherently *personal*. To overcome the obstacle, each woman had to comprehend that branding is not about creating someone's idea of perfect, or masking themselves. People like character, *authentic* character. Yes, they needed to present the best of themselves, but they had to make it authentic. They stretched themselves and were rewarded. Exposing some of their human characteristics actually helped engage people quickly and build their trust.

The idea of presenting yourself well or positioning yourself to your best advantage is not new. Your parents have likely been preaching this since your first day of school. Personal branding however is more than just image or self-promotion. It is more than wearing a new outfit, or styling your hair just right. A successful brand also creates a unique and memorable experience; a flash of insight into the consistency and quality of service you offer.

I began to think about how I would brand myself were I to reverse my branding strategy. This was much harder. It was challenging, but necessary. I now realized that this was not really as clear-cut a decision as I originally thought. Brand me vs. brand the business was actually a fallacy. I could choose to lead with my business as the brand, but I still had to brand myself to be successful. Here is why.

When people initially meet you, they probably have no idea what you do or how well you do it. They are introduced to you either in person or digitally. At that time, they immediately form an impression of you. It's just what we humans do. Any time I am speaking for the company (the brand), I still make impressions as a person. Do I want to create and leverage my own brand or do I want to leave control of those first impressions in the hands of others? As you can imagine, there are risks inherent in that second choice. It's a no-brainer, really. There are few things we can completely control, but how we brand ourselves is absolutely one of them.

A brand is powerful. It can connect us with others on a very emotional level. We are stimulated by brands that evoke emotion in us. They can ignite us and move us. We respond and react. We know from research findings that people prefer to do business with people, with *actual individuals*. We make our business or purchasing decisions based on whom we will be working with. We select individuals we like, trust and connect with to engage. Clients, joint venture partners and investors are just a few of those I needed to mobilize with my personal brand.

My brand had to be authentic, consistent, known by and compelling to my audience. I had learned from the experts. Now I needed to transform that knowledge into action! I began the process of self-inspection which would lead to my personal branding. I sought a clear, profound understanding of who I am and what I wanted to be known for. I soon realized this was not an entirely new exercise for me. Similar efforts in my corporate career contributed to how I was able to maneuver my way into increasingly influential positions. During those years, I often thought of business leader Tom Peter's mantra: distinct… or extinct. That one phase drove me to differentiate myself from my peers in the corporate world. The process I used back then involved summarizing my career; characterizing and prioritizing my choices and activities. Each evaluation involved scrutinizing everything I knew about myself and forced me to be explicit. Developing my personal branding was remarkably similar. The only difference was that I had to apply this same activity to my personal life and activities, not my corporate career.

I began by asking myself a series of questions and writing down my answers. Writing it down is an important part of the process for me. Seeing things in writing not only captures the ideas, but it also makes them more tangible. My ideas shift slightly and are transformed as I view them on paper. I am able to explore them more objectively and really fine-tune them. Below are the seven key questions I asked myself.

1. What are my core values?
2. What am I great at doing?
3. What makes me different or better?
4. What brings me joy?
5. What am I most proud of?
6. What is important to me?
7. What do I want to be known for?

These questions seemed a bit general at first but what made them powerful was when I really drilled down and began to illuminate all the parts of myself that I would normally keep private inside; the aspiring me, the competitive me. I had to inspect who my rivals are. What impressions do I get from them? Who exactly do I want to reach? How do I tailor my branding to different audiences and keep the core of it consistent? How much privacy was I willing to trade to be authentic and compelling? Some of these questions were not comfortable, but all were necessary.

I felt somewhat raw after all of this self-discovery, but now I had the data. I just had to compile it into a useful brand. I did so using the following steps.

1. Inspect: My current image, style and communications
2. Compare: Myself to the brand I wanted to share with my audience
3. Identify: Things which needed to be updated or changed

4. Activate: Use my new branding and evaluate the responses I got

At the end of this process, I had crafted my brand. With new focus, I began to spread my message. Networking which had been awkward was now simplified. I used to find myself pitching my business rather allowing people to connect with me. Now I could leverage either my brand or the company's, using whichever was most suited to that situation. People definitely responded to me in a more genuine way once I had clarity about who I am and how I relate to my business. Branding myself helped me engage clients and business partners easily and earn their trust.

I often share this story with women entrepreneurs. I do so to help them understand the value and importance of self-branding. Defining a personal brand can be worthwhile even if their business is the primary brand. People say that entrepreneurs speak for and represent their own business better than any third party could. This is true with a personal brand as well.

Once you have established your brand identity, you will realize this might be an ongoing effort. The core message of your brand may not change, but how you maximize its effectiveness can change over time. Below are my top 5 tips for leveraging Brand-You.

1. *Expedition-You*: Continue exploring what in you is compelling to your audience. This may shift over time.

2. *Mini-You*: Create a concise mini-version of your personal brand statement outlining who you are, what you do, and why you are compelling.

3. *Real-You*: Ask yourself, is your messaging authentic? If not, it will lead to mistrust.

4. *Always-You*: Make sure that your delivery is consistent. Being too variable will undermine your efforts.

5. *Action-You*: Brainstorm new ways to make your personal brand known. Act on those ideas!

When you have a laser-focused brand identity, you can easily share it with others. Instant understanding and connection occurs. Trust is accelerated. People know what you stand for and will want to work with you. The effort really pays off!

Corinna Rogers, an author, speaker and strategist, is the Founder and CEO of She Velocity, Inc. During her years consulting in the IT industry, Corinna was often the only women at the executive table. This experience fueled her desire to help young women advance more rapidly in their chosen profession. Her experiences taught her that women need more focused professional development and skills. They need these earlier in their working lives to move quickly into executive leadership positions. Corinna launched She Velocity to address that gap. The company's bottom line results orientation and new solutions help women ignite their professional success.

She Velocity connects next-generation women leaders with insights, inspiration and connections to accelerate their professional careers.

Corinna has recently co-authored a book with Lisa Nichols, The Breakthrough Specialist and Founder of Motivating the Teen Spirit. The book, *Unbreakable Human Spirit*, will launch in November, 2011.

She Velocity, Inc. is launching the National Institute of Young Women Leaders in late 2011. The Institute will provide teens and college women with life and success skills. These will fast-track their future business results. Connect with Corinna at www.shevelocity.com or directly via email Corinna@shevelocity.com.

CHAPTER 51

How to Double Your Productivity in 5 Days

by Sherry Borsheim

So many people today are so overwhelmed with all the information coming at them from so many sources that their piles of emails and stacks of paper seem to grow on their own overnight. So much for the paperless office! I propose that it's time we go on an "information diet." Sound scary? How many times have you said to yourself, "I'll keep this just in case?" only to find out those years later you never utilized that so called valuable information? Are you aware that the average person wastes 150 hours a year just looking for misplaced, misfiled, or lost information? Just imagine having an extra hour a day. What would you do with that time?

The secret to doubling your productivity is to take some advice from a wise Italian economist, Vilfredo Pareto. In the early 1900s, he used a mathematical formula to demonstrate the distribution of wealth in society—80 percent of the wealth and income was made by 20 percent of the population. This is where the "80/20 Principle" or "Pareto's Law" came from. Pareto's principle has since been applied in many different areas of work and life. For example, 80 percent of the results come from 20 percent of the effort, or 80 percent of the profit comes from 20 percent of the customers. This can also be applied to your clothes closet—you wear 20 percent of your clothes 80 percent of the time. When you think about doubling your productivity, the secret is to discover what is your 20 percent.

Whether you are a seasoned business owner or just launching a new business, it is important to have your foundational organizing systems in place to support you in growing your business for success. I'm going to help you apply the 80/20 principle to your files, your email, your to-do list, your space, and your schedule. I guarantee if you follow the simple organizing systems and processes here, you will dramatically increase productivity and decrease your stress and anxiety. Let's get you organized!

Organizing Strategy #1 — Get laser-focused with your time

Everyone is busy these days, but what are they busy doing? Being busy doesn't mean you are being productive. Busyness is often just an excuse for avoiding the important critical tasks that grow your business. Apply the 80/20 rule to our schedule. Do you ever wonder why some are able to accomplish more than others? Would you like to know their secret? They are clear about their WHY and WHAT they want which allows them to be laser-focused and know that 20 percent of their efforts produce 80 percent of their results. Another way to look at this is 20 percent of an eight hour day is 96 minutes. Just think how much you'd accomplish if you had 96 minutes of uninterrupted time, where you were 100 percent focused on the task at hand to grow your business.

Did you know that every time you are interrupted, it takes 10 to 20 minutes to transition back into the task you were working on, and that doesn't include the time you spent on the interruption? Think about it. You may be the biggest cause of your own interruptions. Focused time means no checking voicemail, email, surfing the web or wasting time on social media sites and turning off all your buzzers and ringers. This could be a challenge for many, but I guarantee if you get laser focused for 20 percent of your day, you will dramatically increase your productivity immediately and be on purpose with growing your business.

Also, beware of multi-tasking. In years past, this was a key skill many put on their resume, but in the 21st Century, beware of how multi-tasking can decrease productivity. For example, have you ever been on the phone and the person you are trying to have a conversation with is checking their email and you find yourself repeating what you've said several times? You could have been finished that call in half the time if both parties were focused! We've all done it. Studies show us that multi-tasking decreases your productivity by 25-50 percent. So, avoid multi-tasking when it takes you away from being focused on the critical task at hand.

Action tip for getting laser-focused — Schedule one to three blocks of time for 96 minutes in your calendar each week. Next, turn off your email notification and ringers. Another suggestion would be to purchase a small kitchen timer and place it at your desk. Set it for 96 minutes and use it during your focused time. Trust me, the timer really works!

Organizing Strategy #2 — Organized efficiency in your space

How organized and productive is your office space? Are you able to function at a highly productive level of efficiency? Using the 80/20 rule, what are the essential items in your office that you need to have at your fingertips? Here are some of my recommendations:

- Wall planner—great organizing tool to keep you focused and on track. Plan out an entire year of launch dates for new products and programs, vacations and other key dates.
- Large magnetic/white board—post your wall planner here, your yearly outcomes, and financial targets. Keeping key information visible keeps you focused and on track. See my favorite organizing products here at www.bizorganizing.com/smartwomenresources
- Action or project files
- Financial files
- Quick reference papers (example—audio training call phone number, code and script)
- Essential office supplies (example—pen, pencil, highlighter, scissors, stapler, tape, label maker, three-hole punch, in tray, recycling bin, and shredder)
- Mailing supplies (thank you cards, return address labels, envelopes, and stamps)

Anything on the top of your desk that is not clearly labelled and part of your office systems needs to go. Remove all clutter and give yourself plenty of clean surfaces to create and do your work. When I'm working with clients, about 80 percent of the stuff on the top of their desk doesn't need to be there and serves no purpose. Yes, that includes all the knick-knacks that are taking up space and distracting you.

A common mistake people make is they position their desk, computer screen, and phone facing the entrance to their office. The ideal layout for a desk is "L" shape or "U" shape. Also, for those who are right-handed, place your phone to the left of your computer screen so when you are on the phone your right hand is free to take notes. Reverse this set up if you are left-handed.

Next, let's look at the floor. How many boxes and files have been piled on the floor for one year, two years, and five years? Let's move them out of the office to storage or simply let them go. One strategy I use with my clients is to label the boxes with today's date and put them in storage. Then we schedule a time in the calendar six months from now to remind them to toss the boxes. If by that time, if you haven't thought about the contents or taken anything from the box, and you don't need to keep it for tax or legal reason…then let it go.

Other areas to look at are bookshelves and walls. Anything that is visual clutter needs to be removed from the space. There is a saying that, "clutter is anything that doesn't enhance your life." Clutter also attracts more clutter. So, be ruthless with yourself and create a highly functional and organized office.

Once the top of your desk and floor is clear of all the clutter, you will notice a different feeling when you walk into your office. When I'm working with my clients, they are always amazed at how great they feel after a *One Day Miracle Organizing* session. My secret is I start with the top of the desk and then organize the rest of the visible clutter. It's a huge stress-reducer, and their thinking becomes clearer. They are able to focus on the key projects and task without all the clutter around them.

Action tip for organizing your space — Remove all the clutter off the top of your desk. Next, place the essential items you need to have at hand in a drawer or contained on your desk or shelf. To minimize interruptions from people passing your office door, position your computer screen and phone so you are not facing the door when you are using them (this keeps you from being distracted by activity outside your office and also discourages people from making eye contact with you as they pass). Next, put any boxes containing extraneous materials into storage. If you have loose papers and files on the floor, put them into a box and sort them as soon as possible. The key is to clear off the top of the desk and the floor.

Organizing Strategy #3 — Go on an Information Diet

Are your filing cabinets bulging to capacity? Are papers overflowing on your shelves? Is your computer desktop covered with hundreds of icons? Have you randomly filed paper and electronic files? Are you wasting time looking for things?

I'm sure there is a lot of information you've filed away and you haven't even looked at in the past two to three years. I know of people who never file any emails away. They take action, read and delete. Now that's what I call clarity. Clarity really is power and the more clear you are on what type of information you need to keep, the more productive you'll be.

Applying the 80/20 rule would mean that 80 percent of the information that you file away you will likely never refer to again. So what is the reason for keeping so much information just in case you may need it someday? It's a really good question to ask yourself.

Highly productive people are selective at keeping the essential information that is relevant to them at the time. They trust themselves that when they need the information in the future that it will be available to them. Besides, information is changing at such a rapid pace, that it becomes old before we even get it filed away.

So trim the fat and fast-forward through your information using this key decision making process and watch your productivity soar on your new information diet. Use the F.A.S.T. Workflow Principle™ and ask yourself what the next action is on any piece of paper, email or piece of information:

File

Act

Schedule

Toss

Note: Download the F.A.S.T. Workflow Principle decision making process chart here www.bizorganizing.com/smartwomenresources

Action tip for going on an information diet — Open up a drawer in your filing cabinet or file boxes, if that's what you use, and do a very quick purge. Quickly glance in the first 10 to 20 files and see if there is any old information you don't need. Be ruthless and practice the **Art of Wastebasketry** with these questions:

- When was the last time you retrieved this information?
- Is the information recent enough to be useful?
- Can you identify a specific use and does it fit into your vision?
- Can you replace or access the information from another source?
- Do you need to keep this information for tax or legal reasons?
- Is the information a permanent record or historical?
- What's worse possible scenario if you let go of this information?

Organizing Strategy #4 — Automate and Batch Tasks

Track your activities for two weeks and notice what tasks can be automated, batched and streamlined. When you automate and batch similar activities and do them at specific times, you will dramatically increase your productivity.

Some batching strategies:

1. schedule a block of time in your calendar to make calls or follow-up on leads.
2. check email at certain times of day
3. pay bills twice a month instead of on random days.
4. If you have questions for your bookkeeper, CPA, assistant or web person, then batch all your questions together by jotting them down in a note on your computer called "Discuss—Bookkeeper," Discuss—CPA, Discuss—Assistant or Discuss—Web Person. When you talk to that person, you'll have all your questions batched together and you won't be calling them multiple times during the week or sending extra emails.

It is vital to look at your tasks and see what you may be procrastinating on doing. One strategy to conquer procrastination is to automate as many tasks as possible or to delegate those tasks.

I have a "Month End Checklist" that lists several tasks I want to complete at month end. For years, I was procrastinating on printing all the receipts from my credit card statement my bookkeeper needed to match the receipt to the statement and enter the expenses into Quickbooks. So I created a recurring "Month End Checklist" that includes hyperlinks and login information for various websites that I to access each month to print the receipt. I accomplished two things by doing this:

1. developed an automated recurring task and
2. batched the printing of receipts

I further freed up time by delegating month-end reconciliation to my bookkeeper so I can focus my time on money-generating activities with a higher return on investment (ROI).

If you want an easy way to batch and streamline your paper actions and tasks, you can set up my Secret Tickler Action File System.

Download instructions here: www.bizorganizing.com/smartwomenre-sources

Action tip for automation and batchin g— Batch and automate as many tasks on your to do list as you can then delegate whenever possible.

Organizing Strategy #5 — Keep a Short To Do List

Ah, the looming to do list with never-ending things to do and never enough time to get it all done. How many items do you currently have on your to do list? Would you like to cut your to do list by 75 percent and double your productivity right now! Well, let's take a look at your to do list.

Look at your to do list and count how many items you "have to" do or "should" do, then count all the items you would "like to" do. I'm sure about 80 percent of the items on your to do list are in the "have to" category, and about 20 percent are in the "like to" category. I'd like to propose that from now on the only items on your to do list are items you would "like to" do, "choose to" do, or "want to" do. Anything that you "have to" or "should" do does not go on your to do list. HOW DO YOU DEAL WITH THE STUFF YOU HAVE TO DO?

Once again, highly-productive people don't do things that they "have to" do. They "chose to" do certain tasks because they are clear on the important tasks that will get them closer to their goals. One of the reasons people procrastinate on completing their to do list is they feel obligated to do something or "have to" do it out of guilt or shame. Hence, the mighty long to do list.

One last comment on to do lists.I If you are really committed to getting things done on your to do list, then schedule the task directly into your calendar and watch your to do list shrink in half! Also, set a time limit for items to be on your to do list. At the end of each month, look at your list and see what you are committed to doing and schedule those tasks right into your calendar. Anything that didn't get done that month will either stay on your to do list or eliminate it all together!

Action tip for keeping a short to do list — Be ruthless with your to do list. Eliminate any items that you "have to" or "should" do. Schedule as many items as you can that you "want to" do and "choose to" do. Add the amount of time you think it will take to complete a task. When you do the task, use your kitchen timer to time yourself. Most of the time we underestimate how long a task actually takes.

Your business systems are key to your success! I've been working with corporate clients, small business owners and families for over 10 years, and what they desire is peace of mind and that they can find what they need when they need it. **Invest time today to create your business organizing systems in our Office Organizing Bootcamp.**

Sherry Borsheim is an international organizational consultant, coach and speaker with an outstanding track record for helping people be organized, stay efficient and streamline their office, home and life so it works for them! Her company, Simply Productive Organizing Association, focuses on teaching and assisting business owners in being organized and maximizing productivity in an information-saturated world. She believes that when businesses are uncluttered and organizing systems and process are in place, businesses run smoother and they are more profitable. She also recognizes that there is no one-size-fits-all solution to being organized and helps each client create customized solutions that work for them. Get free organizing solutions at www.bizorganizing.com/free-kit.

CHAPTER 52

The Power of Choice

by Leona M. La Perriere

In today's competitive world, we are responsible for creating our own opportunities. Yet, so many times, we set ourselves up for failure; it's in the little things we do, or don't do. It's how we communicate with ourselves and others. It's how we put things in perspective. Sometimes we have the best intentions, but don't really know how to go about it. How often do we feel that we might be part of the problem?

I coach people to success, encouraging them to think with the end in mind. Sounds like it should be easy, doesn't it? However, we are captives of our own conditioning, most of it in a negative form, limiting us from achieving our goals. So, how do we transform that negative "stuff" into positive "stuff" and move on to the life we really want for ourselves? How do we go from *instant gratification* to *sustainable gratification*? How do we empower ourselves for success? How do we become part of the solution? Good news! It is more within our control than we realize. It's all about choice…choosing.

Choose to know your strengths and be proud of them.

I find that when my clients feel overwhelmed, they tend to focus on things that are not going right rather than to take a few minutes longer to catch their breath and start to think of other possibilities. They neglect to focus on their strengths to help them be more successful. They've been conditioned to focus on their weaknesses, or what they do not do so well. They've been conditioned to find fault or to blame. They tell me that they feel like they are bragging when they share their talents or strengths with others. I remind them that when they become more comfortable with their strengths and talents and make them an integral part of their being, sharing becomes more natural and non-confrontational and more acceptable to all concerned.

It's really a mindset, not an ego trip. It's how you think about yourself as a parent, a spouse, a community member, and of course, a business person or an entrepreneur. So, take time to look at yourself from another person's perspective and imagine what that person might say. It's okay to recognize your talents. It's taken you quite a few years of time, energy, education, training, and hard work to be the person you are today. Embrace your talents; develop them, share them, use them to help you achieve your goals and dreams. Make a list of your talents and post them in a place that you can easily see as a reminder of how you can make a difference in other people's world—as well as your own. Perhaps you might want to have lists of other people's talents to remind you of all that they have to offer, too.

Choose to discover what is inside you and what motivates you.

Know why you want certain things, how you can get them, when you can get them, and the results you want because of YOUR choices. Stop making excuses. Make decisions based on YOUR talents, YOUR strengths, YOUR life, YOUR job, YOUR passions, and how all this contributes to YOUR goals. This allows you to share the best of you with others. Chances are you will be more energized and will get things done in a more positive manner. One of my secret weapons for success is actually in my hand! I like to think of each finger as one of the five Ws and the palm as the H, using the questions who, what, why, where, when and how. This helps keep me open to other possibilities, more in control, focused, and on track.

I also love tongue-twisters and often suggest that my clients use them as a fun way to jump start their brains when they need a different perspective on things. We have fun making them up together. One of my clients is a Silpada representative and she came up with: She sells sumptuous silver Siplada to savvy sexy senoritas! A tongue-twister that keeps me focused is: Proper Preparation Prevents Poor Performance from Charlie Batch.

Choose to let go of your limiting beliefs.
They look and sound like: BUT this…BUT that… You get it. You can't

get to the top by sitting on your BUT! Find ways to get rid of these limiting beliefs, aka, excuses. One of my clients shared that she really wanted to grow her business but she has little children in school and a husband who worked long hours. After much discussion, she came to realize that people don't want to hear that; they have their own challenges. They want to see what she can do for them. It was okay to set her times for business around HER schedule. Her business hours/appointments are now from 9am to 3pm, Mondays to Thursday. She does not share her family reasons with them. Rather, she tells her clients that she needs time in the day to do quality work on their web designs. She is much happier, more productive, and has more clients!

Another paradigm shift that should be addressed is the use of positive thinking. We need to open our hearts and minds to see how something can be accomplished. In most cases, we have been conditioned to think the opposite. Many times our thoughts and reactions tend to lean on the negative. This negative slant does not have the words NO or NOT in it, but the thought comes out in a negative message. This limits our potential to be successful. It prevents us from truly thinking with the end in mind. It does not allow us to visualize our goal as to appear the way we want it to unfold.

Choose the type of positive thinking that propels actions that empower you to get positive things done.

Choosing to visualize the desired outcome makes it much easier to put a plan into place and act on it. For instance, we may hear ourselves saying, "I hate being late." To hate being late is a good thing. However, it is a negative message and our brain has difficulty thinking in a positive way on how to accomplish this. Since the thought was on being late, the brain tends to want to think of ways to be late. You don't want to hear your brain saying, "How can I be late?" After all, that is not what the goal is. What is the goal? The goal is to be on time. If you restate: "I hate being late," to "I enjoy being on time," or "I respect other people's time," your brain can now work in a positive way in getting you to think of how many ways to be on time. These could include taking a different road, getting up earlier, having an outfit picked out and ready to go for the next day, or having lunches made the night before.

Getting the brain to work in a positive way also ignites some positive internal rewards of being a problem-solver, being in control, showing responsibility, being confident, and experiencing less stress. Some positive external rewards could be a smile on your face or a self-confident walk or driving more carefully since you are not in a rush.

Another example could be: "I hate being fat." Yes, it is a good thing to not want to be fat. What is the goal? Let's turn that around to: "I would enjoy being thinner." "I like having more energy." "I enjoy being healthy." "I love wearing nicer clothes."

Some positive internal rewards to these changes could be more self-confidence, making healthier choices, feeling more empowered, and being proactive. Some positive external rewards could be having a slimmer body, a lighter step, and nicer clothes.

If you start thinking negatively, such as: I hate being late; I hate being fat, remind yourself to think positive and add…because…I enjoy being on time, or I enjoy having more energy. Your brain can certainly work with those positive thoughts better than with the negative ones and will get you to the desired outcomes.

We've also been programmed to emphasize what we don't want rather than what we do want; then, we wonder why we are not getting the desired response. Because people tend to respond to the message they are hearing, the words need to match what you want to happen. The brain visualizes what you say as it acts on the request or statement. For instance, if you tell someone: "Don't slam the door," the door has a great probability of being slammed shut. The brain heard *slam the door*, registered that message, and the result was slamming the door. The chances for the desired outcome would be more achievable if it was phrased like, "Please close the door quietly or gently." The brain hears quietly, gently, registers that message, and chances are, the door will be closed gently or quietly.

Choose to create positive thinking patterns.

State what it is that you want to make happen. For instance, use the word *remember* rather than *don't forget*. Be specific in your statement or request or goal. For example: Rephrase—"Whatever you do, don't be late to the meeting today," to "I know I can count on you to be at the meeting by 4pm today." Simply changing one word in a sentence can pack a powerful punch. Choose to change *but* to *and*; *if* to *when*; *what if I can't* to *what can I do...* Eliminate the word *try* in your sentences. It lessens the intent of the action being attempted and implies the possibility of failure. Replace it with an action word and experience the difference this makes in your outlook and results.

Choose to develop your personal power through the use of affirmations.

Affirmations are basic tools for success, of self-management, through the intentional choice of thoughts and words and actions. They are positive statements that we repeat to ourselves on a daily basis or when we need to give ourselves some encouragement or perspective. The more you reinforce positive thoughts on a conscious level, the more the subconscious begins to pick up on it. AAh! The power of repetition! Positive affirmation statements allow us to strengthen our new attitudes and new habits of thought by changing our mental patterns. Little by little you begin to have more faith in yourself and in your skills and talents. You become a positive thinker looking for solutions. You become more empowered.

Developing a positive, winning attitude requires daily effort. It requires that every day you choose to take the responsibility to put positive input into your mind. Choosing to put some of these basic suggestions into practice should have you feeling a certain sense of control over situations and getting the results that you are wanting or expecting. You might start to notice certain feelings of renewed respect and calm as you are dealing with people and situations.

Success is not for sissies! It is hard work, but you can make it more enjoyable with a positive attitude and support. And remember, you have the power of choice each day.

People are her passion! She loves being with them—talking, laughing, working, playing, volunteering, and coaching. Leona's husband of 38 years, Dan, enjoys saying that she's never met a stranger, and their three children and their spouses can share many funny stories to prove it! Her philosophy is: "Have a positive attitude, be open to new ideas, be true to yourself, and be kind to others."

Leona is a certified personal and business coach, speaker, facilitator, and the published author of: *HEAR APPLAUSE! Choosing Success in 12 Steps or Less*. She also has an audio CD of her book where you can enjoy listening to each of her 18 "guests" speak their own parts in the book! After a wonderful and rewarding career of 28 years in the teaching profession, Leona "kicked it up a notch" and has been a certified coach for the past nine years. Just last year she started her own company, HEAR APPLAUSE! As a coach to hundreds of young professionals and entrepreneurs, she has been told that she excels in motivating, challenging, and guiding people to sustainable success that leads to bold and intentional results…and simply making great things happen.

Leona's enjoyment, belief, and commitment to entrepreneurs and small business owners were rewarded this year as she was selected for the 2011 Small Business Advocate of the Year Award by the Greensboro Chamber of Commerce. An avid networker and volunteer, she is an active participant in all the organizations she belongs to. She is an award-winning Rotarian with the Summit Rotary Club, chairs several of its committees, and is a member of the Board of Directors; an award-winning ambassador with the Greensboro Chamber of Commerce; a consultant and workshop facilitator for the Greensboro Library's Future Cents Project; and is a member of the Board of Directors for The Summit Leadership Initiative. She also belongs to eWomenNetwork.com, Greensboro Merchants Association, Business & Professional Women of the Triad, The League of Women Voters, and the Writers' Group of the Triad.

Leona practices what she preaches: "Be proactive, get out of your comfort zone, challenge yourself to take action on new ideas, and think big and bold." She loves sharing one of her well-hidden secrets of success: "Think with the end in mind."

Leona is a gifted and energetic speaker, coach, facilitator and author. Her mission is to encourage, empower, educate, and entertain people in ways that allow them to—Say NO to excuses and YES to success!—thereby creating their own opportunities to be successful in today's competitive world.

CHAPTER 53

How to Hire a Superstar in Just 3 Days—Yes Really!

by Kiyla Fenell

For the past 22 years, I think the most challenging aspect of owning a business is finding the right staff. Employees can make your business experience a complete dream or they can make your life sheer hell. I have experienced both sides of the coin. I thought many times to myself, if I didn't have to deal with employees, then running a business would be easy. I struggled with high turnover, employee takeovers, disappointments, and betrayal. In fact, early on in my career, I employed someone who was one of America's most wanted and he skipped town with everything in my safe!

My hiring experience started when I was 17. My father made me the manager of five fast food restaurants. I learned how to hire, fire and lead teams. I witnessed firsthand the issues that cause so many business owners pain and sleepless nights.

My dad was a development agent for franchising in several states. It was my job to train all of his franchisees in sales, marketing and building teams. The number one complaint I heard from franchisees was employee-related issues. Every one of them had a difficult time finding good people, hiring the right person and keeping them once they were hired. I felt their pain. I knew all too well the frustration with high turnover. You and I both know that it takes building a strong team to grow your business to new levels. I learned as a teenager...my family was not in the fast food business, we were in the people business. Our business was supported by people who purchased our products and services, and it was run by people who followed our systems and methods.

My father eventually sold his franchises so I went out on my own and started a business. I opened a vacuum cleaner store from my tiny apartment. I had vacuum cleaners stacked to the ceiling. I used my bed as a desk and I would call leads from there. I bought the sweepers for around $500 and sold them for $1600. I started selling a couple of them each day so I was making really good money at a ripe young age. It didn't take me long before I got the calculator out and discovered that if I could train a team of people to do this for me, I could make serious money. So that is what I set out to do.

I tried traditional hiring methods at first and it was a nightmare. For the first time, I was hiring independent contractors for sales positions, and it was challenging. I would be sitting there waiting for my next interviewee to arrive. While watching them get out of their car, I knew immediately I would never hire this person, but out of courtesy I spent 15 minutes interviewing them. I wasted so much time and money on the interviewing process. This process was taking me away from selling, so my revenues began to decline.

I realized quickly that what I was doing wasn't working. I decided to devise a way to reduce my time spent looking for new team members so that I could maintain my normal level of focus on daily operations and sales. I figured why not leverage my time by scheduling interviews all together? Why not schedule a room full of candidates for the same first interview? It was magic! Suddenly, what would normally take me all day was only taking me 30 minutes. I was able to interview 90 people in less than three hours and I was attracting higher quality applicants. This was due to the advertising and phone scripts I created. Everything that I did from that time forward for the hiring process was built around speed and better results. I learned how to filter out all the unqualified quickly and only spend personal time with top quality, cream of the crop candidates.

My sales team sold more vacuum cleaners than any other distributer in the world not once, not twice but eight times. On average, I lead a sales staff of 35 independent contractors. I had a virtual telemarketing room of four phone operators, a secretary and a service person. I was able to build such a successful team because of my unique and fool-proof way of hiring. I have used the exact scripts for hiring in all of my businesses for 18 years.

A unique benefit of using this hiring system is that I made thousands of dollars in sales for most single hires. This hiring process was designed not only to find great staff but to convert applicants into potential customers and/or new client referral sources. It is a company image-builder that turns every applicant into a raving fan of you and your business. I've used this system personally across seven different industries and have helped many business owners around the globe to hire quality staff and generate new business simultaneously.

I have a well-proven, simple method that works so well anyone can do it and you will see results in less than a week! In fact, it's likely that it will only take you three days for around $100 per hire using my five step system.

Here is a brief overview of each of the 5 steps.

Step 1 Have a written job description.
The keyword here is written. Having a written job description makes the selection process so much easier. Writing every task and project to be performed for a position helps you to understand the requirements, skills and personality type you will need to successfully fill a role. This gives you written expectations to hand every applicant so they can identify quickly if they are suited for the position and if it is a good fit for them. It plainly states what your realistic expectations are for every position. Written job descriptions are great tools to delegate everything and anything that you should not and will not be doing in your business. After clearly identifying what type of person you need from the written job description…now it is time to find these people.

Step 2 Attract the superstars.
I like to envision the interviewing process as a big funnel. I call it the Applicant Funnel™. The funnel is obviously big at the top and very small at the bottom. Your goal is to fill the funnel with as many highly qualified leads as possible. As your leads move down the funnel, they will go through a filtering system. The more quality people you can filter through this system, the higher probability of finding that superstar. These filters will help you to select the best possible candidate for the position. There are many ways to fill the funnel with top leads. My favorite approach is to recruit top quality prospects in public.

If you find yourself on the receiving end of great service or you observe someone displaying great attitude and personality, don't just admire their abilities…interview them. A salesman did a fantastic job at convincing my husband to buy a couple of high end pairs of shoes. I hired her the next week and she added an extra $300,000 that year to my revenues. I also recruited a receptionist at a pediatrician's office and she increased my scheduled consultations over 50 percent. It pays to recruit superstars in public.

Step 3 Use a telephone screening process.
Okay so picture having many sources of quality leads filling your funnel. Recruiting in public, newspaper ads, Craigslist, Monster, social media, etc. are working for you to attract top prospects. Now begins the filtering process to find the one right person(s) for the job. Instead of having people email resumes, send letters or have them come to your place of business, have them call. Who wants stacks of resumes and letters sitting on their desk? Resumes are full of fluff with words that are meant to impress you. The telephone screening process quickly weeds out unqualified candidates in one day.

Inform your leads to call in on Monday from 9 to 5. Ask them three qualifying questions. This step is very important to eliminate and "trim the fat" off of the hiring process. I teach many different reasons and methods as to why and how to do this exactly in my system. Since much of what your team says and does is a direct reflection upon you and your company, it is imperative that you look for those callers that have a pleasant disposition, tone and attitude on the phone. Do they communicate clearly? Knowing this, these key characteristics immediately will filter out two-thirds of the prospects. The telephone screening process will take hours, days and weeks off the hiring process.

Step 4 Hold a group interview.
Directly from the telephone screening process the qualified candidates are scheduled for a group interview. This is not to be confused with the group interviews or "cattle-calls" that are being done today. If done right, this one step becomes a great image-builder and turns every applicant into a raving fan of you and your business. This is the step in the process that I made sales and got referrals.

Every attendee fills out an application. Do not accept resumes instead.

Spend less than a minute with each candidate to ask them brief questions about their application facts. Then address the group from the front of the room and introduce yourself, the company, position, pay and opportunity. Tell your story. Share why you started the business and the difference you are making in people's lives because of it. Give them testimonials about your products and services. At the conclusion, ask them 10 questions that will further help you to make a decision about who you will spend a personal interview with. Ask the applicants to call back the same night to see if they have been selected for a second interview for the following day.

Step 5 Conduct second day interviews.
From the group interview, you will make the selection for the second day interviews. During second day interviews, I do in-depth questioning, testing, personality profiling and reference checks. I also give the candidate a comprehensive look at what their duties, assignments and role would be with the company. I have the candidates call back that evening to see if they were selected for the position.

So this is the 3-day hiring timeline.

- Place ad(s) and have all lead sources working to fill the Applicant Funnel ™ by Sunday.
- Do the telephone screening process on Monday.
- Host a group interview Monday evening.
- Conduct second day interviews consecutively on Tuesday.
- Hire a superstar Tuesday evening or Wednesday morning.
- If Monday through Wednesday does not work for your particular business, you may use any three-day span during the week.

I designed this simple hiring process to protect my time, money and energy. Remember good staff can make you, bad staff can break you.

Hiring stellar support staff is usually an entrepreneur's biggest challenge, and a hit-or-miss process. Bad hires can cost you tens of thousands in the end, so hiring right is a must. But how? ...Kiyla's 5-step system is making waves because it WORKS for any type of business. And it's incredibly simple, too!

Hiring consultant Kiyla Fenell teaches companies around the world how to hire superstars in just three days. For two decades, Kiyla's fun and simple methods have been used to build award-winning, record-breaking teams to grow her million dollar businesses. Throughout Kiyla's career, she has created, operated and sold million dollar companies spanning seven different industries.

She lives in Tulsa, Oklahoma with her husband Robert. Together, they homeschool their daughter Milan while traveling and making a difference around the world. To learn more about scripts, templates, forms, and samples in The Ultimate Staffing Success System, please visit www.dreamteamhire.com.

CHAPTER 54

Become the Leader of Your Change

by Catherine Rocheleau

Change is defined as:

1. To become different or undergo alternation
2. To undergo transformation or transition
3. To go from one phase to another, as the moon or seasons.

Reference: Merriam-Webster Online dictionary

Change…such a simple word for a complex set of events and emotions. Some of us enjoy the adventures that come with change; others want a stable routine and resist the transition (good or bad) while others just ride the wave. How do you accept change?

No matter how we accept it, change is one constant in life. Today's business world is changing rapidly and it is important to be able to adapt to it for long-term success. Small businesses have a key advantage to their larger counterparts—they are better able to react quickly to change. Although small businesses are more capable of making changes quickly, they don't always capitalize on these opportunities. Change is not always easy. It takes energy and it doesn't happen overnight. Day-to-day operations, resource limitations and our own blind spots can get in the way.

Leaders Lead Change

Are you ready to move forward? Are you prepared to do what it takes to lead yourself (and your team) outside of your comfort zone and break through your impasse to reach your goals?

Leaders are change agents. They are willing to take risks and go where others dare not. Their vision is stronger than their fear. It's normal to have some reservations or questions as you lead change, but leaders have the internal drive to face these gremlins and do what it takes to push through these barriers to be successful.

Seth Godin, in his book *Tribes* identified 4 key characteristics present in leaders. A leader will:

- Challenge the status quo
- Step to the front of the group
- Create momentum
- Create the change they believe in.

You are the leader of your business. You lead your team and engage them to assist you in making your mark and fulfilling your vision. My vision is to empower professionals and business owners to engage others to achieve sustainable results through leadership development and change strategies.

Our true passions frequently emerge from our life experiences. I realized my passion for assisting others through change about five years ago when I was re-examining my own career path and what I wanted in my future. Since that time, I have been involved in leading numerous change initiatives—changes in organizations I was working with, mentoring and coaching professionals and business owners with their own change needs, as well as undertaking my own significant changes. Although I enjoy change and the opportunities and variety that it provides, I cannot deny that there are times it would be nice for some things to remain the same… I have to admit, I want stability when I'm in a hurry and do not want to think too hard about what I'm doing.

Throughout my career, I have always sought out opportunities where I could build and set things up but soon realized that once I achieved the desired result, I was ready to move on. Each new job stretched my knowledge and skills but the cycle continued for several years as I rose through the ranks in the food service and healthcare industries. When I would be interviewed for new positions, it was very clear that "career-lifers" did not view these frequent changes as a desirable trait in an employee.

Ironically enough, it was my own blind spot and limiting beliefs that held me back and kept me thinking small. My own fear was stopping me from taking the lead in my own career and this presented itself as procrastination and avoidance. It was only when taking time to explore my own "why" that I made my personal breakthrough.

Looking at my WHY

"A philosopher once said, "He who has a why to live can bear almost any how." I would add, "He who has a why to lead can bear almost any trial."
—Leslie Bains, *CEO Modern Asset Management*

I have often wondered what sparked my desire to lead changes in myself and others. For many, their WHY spurs from a bad life experience. My WHY' stems from being a daughter of a naval officer. We moved a lot as I grew up. Before the age of three years, I had moved homes and moved across the country. Once I started school, our moves continued and I changed schools almost every year. I went to seven schools in 12 years. Interestingly enough, the longest I stayed in a school prior to university was three years. After four years of university, I again moved across the country to a city where I knew no one to complete my internship.

As I look back, I realize now that with each change I gained new skills, experiences which have allowed me to be resilient and persistent. It always amazes me when parents today say they don't want to move because their children will have to change schools. I don't view school changes as a bad thing. I believe it offers children some unique opportunities to develop an ability to adapt to change, expand their network and explore the unknown. These are great assets in today's fast-changing world.

Fast forward to my career. I started my career in food and nutrition. I realized before I had even graduated that I had strong interests in business management but I was not able to pursue these interests while studying. University advisors told me "dietitians do not need business courses." (Oh, how wrong they were!)

Although I was very successful, I had my fair share of challenges and failures, too. My career led me into many interesting arenas and strengthened my ability to do what I do today, and I never stopped looking at other ideas and learning new skills. Today I know I have a good fit—I am not avoiding opportunities. I am willing to stretch more than I ever have before and I look at my business as a CEO instead of as a technician. The passion and excitement for life and business has returned, too.

Set Your Intention

I have always believed that if you send out what you want or need, and are open to what comes back, your dreams can be answered. Some call this the law of attraction, others call it luck. No matter what it's called, it works! Your mindset becomes a critical key to unlocking the obstacles within you so that you open your thoughts and heart to the wonderful things you can put into action.

My entrepreneurial journey has involved lots of changes, and more ups and downs than I'd like to think about. No matter what happened, I continued to move forward on the leading edge of the wave. My professional practice was thriving, and I knew entrepreneurship was the right decision for me. Brian Tracy once said "If you fall, fall forward so you are closer to your goal." Without planning to, I did this, more out of fear of failure and a strong desire not to let a setback keep me down.

Clarify Your Purpose

What does success mean to you? What does it look like? How are you going to achieve your vision of success? For me, creating a plan that I could follow was key. A business plan doesn't have to be a long document but it should outline what you will do in your business, how you will get there and what milestones you will use to measure your progress.

I use a mind map for my annual business plan. The mind map provides me with an easy to follow, visual roadmap of what I want to achieve. I incorporate colors, visuals and words. Because I write it by hand, it reinforces my intentions and stimulates innovation. Each quarter, I am able to review the mind map, determine what has been accomplished, what is in progress or what requires adjusting. This is vital for keeping my focus and re-visiting my goals.

Take Action

Once you have a plan in place, you must implement it even if you start small; the key is to move forward. I realized recently that I frequently created great programs and product ideas and then pushed them aside. This blind spot was stopping my success from expanding. What I found was that uncertainty and fear were holding me back.

Successful leaders achieve successes because they have two key qualities when it comes to implementing their plan—dedication and persistence. Leaders are committed to their vision, to each goal and to their accomplishment. These qualities are most important when you encounter obstacles!

Reflect and Adjust

I have been an entrepreneur for a long time. When I hit my own wall a few years ago, I knew I had to make changes. The challenge I had was which path would I take and what destination would I aim for? One thing I knew for sure was that I wanted a better balance between the time and energy I spent on work vs. life.

Looking back, I realized that I had fallen into the traditional trap of most professionals. I was a great technician in my field and I was very successful. I was recognized as a leading expert and I earned a six-figure income. The down side was I worked non-stop. Gradually I started to feel the effects of serious burnout. I was frustrated, unfocused and lacked the sense of passion I had once felt. It was definitely time for a change. Leaving two key contracts was difficult but a necessity. I was putting my heart and soul into my work but lacked the gratification and rejuvenation I once experienced.

In the past year, I made a decision to shift my business yet again and adopt a new business model. The process of this shift has enabled me to gain even greater clarity and reignite my passion because I took the time to work on my WHY. The clarity gained from my new vision also helped me realize that my old goals were no longer realistic, and I had to create new goals in their place.

When change happens, taking time to reflect will allow you to learn more about yourself, your passions and challenges. For many, changing goals are regarded as a failure, but because I took the time to reflect, I was able to explore different perspectives. When you review your progress, you can also re-examine the appropriateness of each goal, its priority ranking and its contribution to your overall strategic plan. In particular, take time to examine the WHY behind the goal itself and the results, (or lack thereof). The WHY can be very telling.

Instead of seeing my past efforts as failure, I was able to recognize that I needed this shift to achieve my ultimate vision. I also saw the change as a new opportunity that would allow me to share my gift with more people. If I viewed my goals as unchangeable, I would miss out on a great opportunity to uplevel my business. I would be sacrificing long-term success for short-sighted results.

There is a lot written on why it's important to set goals. Little is written on why it's important to take time to reflect on the reasons goals are not successful, or dropped from our field of vision. Celebrating our successes is truly motivating and helps propel us forward. When results are less than stellar, it's human nature to push them aside and try to forget we set the goal in the first place. This is a lost opportunity to learn more about ourselves, our dreams, passions and priorities.

Keep On Track

Have you noticed that when you are in the midst of change, you feel like you are in chaos, even when things are going as planned? I know I do. When my clients are experiencing change in their careers or businesses, they frequently want to place things on hold so they can catch their breath. I can certainly relate to this, and I help them see that it is better to live in the chaos and push through it rather than to stall their progress.

Why? Because it is normal for things to feel chaotic when you are making progress. Every time we make a change, we push ourselves out of our comfort zone. In addition, if you are an "A" personality, you like to have control, and change takes some of that control away. This can be scary but it's only temporary.

How to Move Through Change Quickly

Great leaders are known for creating a strong support network to assist them along the way. They also surround themselves with excellence. As a successful professional or business owner, you also need great supporters. Coaches can provide you with the expertise, knowledge, insights and skills you need to accomplish your goals. Other options include creating a board of directors or participating in a mastermind group. Each of these alternatives help you remain focused and moving forward to uplift your business. Remember...

"Alone we can do so little; together we can do so much." —Helen Keller

Catherine Rocheleau is the Founder and CEO of Ignite Leadership International™. Catherine works with business professionals to face their challenges, drill down to identify what is holding them back and create strategies for leadership development and change.

Catherine's career started in the food and nutrition field where she ran multi-unit food service operations and coordinated nutrition services for clients in facilities and in the community. She began her entrepreneurial journey on a part-time basis and soon expanded it to become her full-time career.

Change has been a constant in Catherine's life. As the daughter of a naval officer, she moved schools annually, having spent three years in just one school prior to attending university. The opportunities and determination to succeed gained from these changes early in life have set the stage for the work she does today.

Catherine's business ventures have transitioned many times as new opportunities presented themselves. She ran her professional practice as a Registered Dietitian, and held management consultant contracts for many years prior to reducing her contracts to allow her to lead a registered charity. During this time, she worked with the board of directors to expand the organization's size, scope and revenues, and established new systems to ensure long-term sustainability. Today she runs a successful consulting and coaching business.

Catherine has a Master of Business Administration in Managerial Leadership and Project Management. She maintains her Registered Dietitian designation, and has attained designations as an

Organizational Change Professional, Executive and Business Coach, and Master Coach Trainer. She embraces lifelong learning and enjoys working with motivated professionals to propel their careers and businesses forward.

Catherine is a proven visionary and progressive executive with more than 18 years of leadership and organizational change experience. Her experience as a professional, business owner and former non-profit executive allows her to focus on both the head and heart aspects of business. Her dedication to client success, her experience, insights and SPARK™ System will ignite your solutions for sustainable results.

CHAPTER 55

Generativity & Generosity: Qualities Smart Women Use To Make A Difference

by Dolly M. Garlo

Women have come a long way, baby, and we can change the world for the better in a big way. We are 'generative' beings, possessing not only the 'power to reproduce' (keeping the human race going, and all), but also the 'capacity to produce,' as in "the generative power of the life force." With that life force, we can do many other great things.

Some still work at shattering the glass ceiling, becoming CEOs for large companies and world leaders. More have moved in a new direction, building and operating their own businesses, pursuing success on their own terms. Women are building their own significant wealth. With that comes the capacity to make a big, sustainable difference that benefits the people, places and things they love for generations to come.

Beyond Success—The Next Developmental Stage

Role models like the great industrialist men of history—Andrew Carnegie, John Paul Getty, and John D. and William Rockefeller—don't fit us. Where we lack experience in this arena, though, we merely need guidance and resources. Stories of women making a big difference need to be captured, developed, actualized and shared. They need to be told and re-told to the generations of women who stand on the shoulders of the pioneers who campaigned for women's rights, entered the domains once dominated by men, mastered their crafts, and became leaders in business and government—all while giving birth and nurturing life. As the old saying goes—Ginger Rogers did everything Fred Astaire did, backwards and in high heels.

Advances in healthcare and improved focus on self-care taught us to put our oxygen masks on first and then help those around us. The incredible women of the 21st Century have 20, 30, maybe even 40 more years beyond initial successful careers and child-rearing to make a significant impact. Women with an entrepreneurial spirit are in the best position to do so. My passion is helping do that through the avenue of legacy development.

You may be thinking, "why should I care about that?" Maybe you've never considered it as part of your own life's path. Creating your legacy is not a 'should.' The subject is an opportunity for the ultimate journey of a lifetime.

Many people think of legacy as something beyond them. Or they think of it in the traditional legal sense—who gets my stuff when I die? The concept applies to everyone, and it's not just about assets or inheritance (finances, real property, or family heirlooms).

Legacy development may well be the best part of life planning. It is the pinnacle of self-actualization and individual fulfillment. It is about realizing the blessing you are to the world and the contribution you have to make to some corner of it that you value. Pursuing it may even answer that existential question "why am I here?"

Creating a legacy is about joyfully giving your best self to the world in a way that really adds lasting value. The longer it lasts, the more value it adds. Your legacy is about what means so much to you that you're willing to support it for the benefit of others. It is a way to give your gifts (not just finances, but all the gifts of *who you are* as a unique individual) and make the positive impact only you can—not just for your children and extended family, but for your community, your nation, maybe even the world at large. It can take the form of significant philanthropy, business or another tangible form. You get to choose.

Beyond the traditional legal, *creating your legacy is a living process* that may involve your money and assets; other individuals or institutions; your time, effort and enthusiasm—likely, a combination. Your pursuit may well involve estate, financial and business planning—depending upon the idea and the structure needed to make it sustainable. You develop it while being fully involved. Yet, you build it from the beginning so it will endure long after you step away.

Consider The Elements

First, legacy is about giving your unique gifts in a way that is authentically you. It is about nurturing and giving back—or rather, giving forward.

As successful career women, we've received many gifts on the road to where we are. Consider the Global Rich List (www.globalrichlist.com). That site shows where you fall on a spectrum from richest to poorest, financially speaking. Enter a figure for poverty level annual income in the USA of $12,000 a year—it's in the TOP 12.88 percent of the richest people *in the world...*

If you have a college education and a computer, you are quite likely in the highest wealth category in the world. Bravo! Have as much as you want, but determine what is 'enough' for you. If you don't, no amount of striving or acquiring will ever be fully satisfying. When you know what is enough for you materially, you can focus on what you *really* want personally, emotionally and spiritually, based on your values and interests and how you want to spend your precious life energy. Then you can better see your own the amazing gifts and blessings, with which you can make your unique contribution.

Likely, that involves those things you do so well and so naturally, that you likely think are no big deal—and might even be fun or enjoyable for you. Even better! Somebody needs that from you. Maybe a lot of people. You get to enjoy giving it, and they give you back sincere heart-felt appreciation. Priceless...

Second, designing and living a legacy is a consciously creative process, which can begin at any time. Endowed with idealism, kids and young people engage in it very naturally.

In contrast with the traditional approach of planning to leave things to others when you're done with them, legacy development is about creating and building something now that endures.

Don't think you're creative? Humans have the unique capacity to manifest something from nothing—take a thought or idea and turn it into something tangible. Doing so engages your precious life energy for something you care deeply about. Carrying your creation on after that may well involve your family.

Third, your "legacy creation" can take any number of forms and sizes based on your circumstances. Whatever form, you consciously fashion it to persist in the world after you step away from it, creating a sustainable benefit.

Today, the type and scope of forms for legacy projects is truly endless. In addition to traditional means, there are many alternatives for creating something beneficial to others long term. That's what makes it fun and doable for anyone. Models exist for whatever you choose to create—so you don't have to reinvent the wheel. Yet, yours can be as unique as you.

Your project will likely involve legal, financial, accounting and tax, organizational and operational, people and information management issues. You may utilize some or all of your assets. Designing the structure and right team of appropriate, reliable professionals and others will be needed to navigate through unknown territory where you don't speak the language. Knowing how to work with and get good advice from them is key.

Hiring a trained coach to create your roadmap for this journey can help immensely. Coaching is working with a partner to maximize your personal and professional potential, and find the resources *you* need to get where you want to go—particularly applicable for realizing your unique legacy. When creating my own first legacy project, I longed for a single advisor who could help me pull it all together—rather than doing it all from the seat of my pants while trying to figure out on my own, which was slow and expensive. The experience reinforced my decision to coach and consult in this arena.

Which Legacy Structure Fits You?

The structure simply needs to fit your circumstances. It will be designed from the outset to stand alone and continue on after you step away from direct or active involvement. Consider these three forms:

Financial only legacies with little or no involvement.

This form incorporates traditional estate planning. Some part of that may figure into all legacy structuring so it's good to understand. It addresses things like:

- Wills—which focuses on distributing assets outright to others.
- Trust—which focuses on holding property or assets for later distribution to named recipients called beneficiaries—who can be individuals or organizations.
- Community Funds, philanthropic "Planned Giving," Scholarships or Endowments.
- Charitable foundations or non-profit organizations, and there are different types, depending on what you need or intend to do.

Some of these structures can design in a certain amount of lifetime involvement.

Participation-only legacies with little or no personal financial contribution.

Many legacy projects start with little money. If it's a good and viable idea, the money can be raised and there are known ways to do that and people who can help.

One example is an organization called *Hoops of Hope* (www.hoopsofhope.org). It was started in 2004 by a nine-year-old boy, who didn't know the excuse "I can't," and figured out a way to use what resources he had. A basketball lover, he started a free-throw fundraising event, then connected his project to an existing non-profit, replicated the event-based fundraising method, and built several schools and clinics in Africa for children orphaned by the AIDS epidemic there—all before he even graduated from high school.

Danny Thomas began the *St. Jude Children's Research Hospital* (www.StJude.org), devoted to pediatric cancer research, when he was a struggling young actor still breaking into show business. Rather than money, he had vision, passion, and persistence. He and his wife Rose created one of the most respected health care institutions in the world. Their own children, including actress Marlo Thomas, are now involved in carrying it on.

Participation only legacies can also be simple and small, yet meaningful and helpful to those who benefit from them. These include things that almost anyone can do thanks to the high tech age we live in. A "legacy recording" in the form of a memoir, electronic or self-published book, workbook, training program, blog, audio, or video can preserve precious memories or guidance for others. Just being genuine and honest about who you are and your journey can add value to someone.

Volunteering can also be a good, hands-on way to live your legacy, and to discover what what's wanted and needed in the world, where and by whom. By participating on a board of directors, you can learn more about non-profit operations and volunteer coordination. The information and experience gained from these involvements may help you craft your own standalone project, or attach it to an existing organization to build from there.

Legacies combining financial contributions and personal involvement

This category includes creating social enterprises or corporate social responsibility programs, which may exist independently or be connected to your existing business.

Social enterprises are essentially businesses that incorporate a strong emphasis on social responsibility, and making a positive difference through sound and fair practices. They can be structured as either non-profit or for-profit organizations. They may utilize a very new structure called the Benefit Corporation, which is a for-profit corporation (so it can raise capital from shareholders) that includes in its Articles of Incorporation a stated social mission, and reports both on its profit making as well as the accomplishment of that mission.

Based on your financial situation, these legacy structures depend on whether you will use your own resources for funding, need to raise funds, need current income yourself, want to form your own independent operation, or want to connect your project to another organization like an existing non-profit, for-profit, private or public, academic or even government operation.

Two of my amazing clients provide inspiring examples of this type of legacy.

One is a company called AVANCEN (www.avancen.com), started by Dr.

Sharon Conley who transitioned from the full-time practice of medicine to bring to market a new medical device she invented to help hospitalized patients control their pain. She chose a for-profit corporate structure due to its revenue-generating focus, one that can stand alone or eventually merge with another similar company. It expresses her vision of making a positive difference in the medical industry by "improving patient care at the bedside" with a tangible product that will be used around the world.

The non-profit HealthStart Foundation (healthstartfoundation.org) was founded by Robin Herskowitz, president of her own public policy consulting firm. She loves the firm she's developed, and hopes it will carry on for many years to come. Yet, she realized she needed an eventual exit strategy. She also wanted to act on a desire to give back to her community around her passion for kids and health. Investing her own funds initially, the tax-exempt foundation allows her to pursue charitable donations to fulfill her desire to have something significant live on after she is gone.

Both of these women were successful in their careers, and have used some of their own funds to develop these projects with structures that allowed them to raise the additional operating capital and develop the systems and teams the projects would need. The forms they chose involve a more hands-on, entrepreneurial approach—designed so their projects will successfully endure when they choose to step away.

Why Do It?

Again, designing and living your legacy may be the best part of life planning and an opportunity for the ultimate personal journey in generativity and generosity. It feels good to give back, and it's also good for you.

Women naturally want to contribute to what we care about. Legacy development is an *exercise in significance, consciousness and creativity.* Rather than just hard work, it is great work that is personally creative and gives you the opportunity to discover and actually live your life purpose—to actualize the reason you're on the planet.

Research shows that approaching life from the spirit of giving, generosity and contribution has positive health impacts including improved life-satisfaction, better physical and mental health, and living longer. Making a positive difference is win-win.

So, where to you want to make an impact that changes the world for the better and benefits others for generations?

Dolly M. Garlo, RN, JD, PCC, is President of Thrive!!® Inc. (www.allthrive.com) and Founder of Creating Legacy™ (www.creating-legacy.com). A former health care attorney, her current focus is business development, strategic marketing design, professional career transition, social entrepreneurship, corporate social responsibility cultivation, and legacy development to make a difference that lasts for generations. Her own first legacy project, the Garlo Heritage Nature Preserve, was developed as a collaboration between her family and the Seneca County Ohio Park District.

CHAPTER 56

Ignite Your Business and Transform Your World: How Finding Your Voice, Standing as a Leader and Playing Big Serves the World

by Kelly K. O'Neil

"Never doubt that a small group of thoughtful, committed citizens can change the world. Indeed, it is the only thing that ever has."
—Margaret Mead

Each year, as a professional speaker, best-selling author, award-winning results coach and branding strategist, I have the distinct privilege of working with thousands of women entrepreneurs and small business owners, teaching and inspiring them to ignite their businesses and transform their world.

I believe we all have infinite power, and that when you change your circumstances, the circumstances of the world change. But first, as Ghandi said, "You must be the change you wish to see in the world." It all starts with you.

That is my mission. My big WHY as we call it. My purpose for living is to inspire you to step up as an authentic woman leader in your business, your community and in your life, and to set an example for what is possible for everyone around you.

The world is in a time of massive transformation and evolution. There is a shift in human consciousness occurring even as you read these words. There is quite a bit of evidence of massive breakthroughs occurring: the appearance of stunningly-gifted children in unprecedented numbers, the emergence of innovative and integrated healing modalities, people becoming less "religious" and more "spiritual," and the dawning of new communities and social structures based on servant leadership and other partnership principles. And this is not just being talked about in the metaphysical world.

International leaders are seeking spiritual guidance from healers and intuitives in droves. Even Oprah, our national treasure, regularly speaks about the evolution of consciousness. She hosted Eckhart Tolle and his book *A New Earth: Awakening to Your Life's* Purose on her first-ever webinar series that was attended by millions of individuals ready for a spiritual awakening. As of 2009, over five million copies have been sold.

This trend cannot be ignored. As Tolle says, *"Humanity is now faced with a stark choice: Evolve or die.... If the structures of the human mind remain unchanged, we will always end up re-creating the same world, the same evils, the same dysfunction."*

Conscious Entrepreneurship: Business for the Greater Good

As leaders and entrepreneurs, there has been a Universal call to arms for us to step up in consciousness. The Universe is demanding it because, as human consciousness exponentially increases, Earth will also undergo a significant—and observable—transformation.

In America, with the financial crisis, it's entrepreneurs who are going to save the economy. Entrepreneurs have the power to turn this around. We can change the way that people think about what is possible. We have a clear vision of what is possible for all humans. Entrepreneurship is key to growth and job creation in America. Small companies earn 50 percent of the Gross Domestic Product and provide 50 percent of all jobs.

After being in the personal and business development industries as a thought leader for more than a decade, I see that there have been two predominant schools of thought. There are the die-hard make capitalist entrepreneurs who tend to go to events that are all about making money, and then there are the spiritual events where everyone goes to meditate and love one another.

My work lies at the juxtaposition of those two worlds. I have helped build companies to into multi-million dollar organizations, and I have done work for non-profits. At this point in my career, I am much more passionate about conscious entrepreneurship. A broad definition of a conscious entrepreneur is someone who merges their life purpose with their business to create a livelihood that is spiritually fulfilling, as well as a direct path to freedom.

In 2009, I started a new company called Kelly O'Neil International, Inc., which is a coaching and training company that serves female entrepreneurs who are passionate about the work they are doing in the world. They know it is time to get their message out there so they achieve their biggest goals and transform the lives of the millions of people in the process. But they aren't quite sure how. And frankly, it can be frightening for us to step out into the spotlight in such a big way. So instead, many women have been playing it safe and playing small, hoping no one notices. Not only are they hiding their gifts… their businesses are suffering, too.

Does this sound familiar to you?

I started this company because I hold a very strong belief that it is equally as important to help humanity and serve the world as it is to serve you and your family. There is nothing glorious or enlightened about being poor, but helpful. In fact, I will take that a step further. **I believe it is your *responsibility* as an entrepreneur to build a thriving, profitable business that serves the world in a way that enhances humanity and fosters abundance.**

Now… re-read that last sentence. Notice where you feel that in your body. Is your tummy saying, "HELL YES!" or does it make you want to loose your lunch? Do you feel angry? Do you feel afraid? Do you feel undeserving?

Now notice what you are saying to yourself. "No one will pay me big money." "Making money is not important." "Helping people isn't what my business is for. It is to make money."

Here is why that is a critical exercise. The way you feel about yourself and your business impacts the way you think. The way you think impacts your actions. Your actions impact your results—financially and in your ability to serve the world.

Are you getting the results that you desire? If not, it is time to step up your game.

Our world is at a crossroads. In their book, *Half the Sky: Turning Oppression into Opportunity for Women Worldwide* (Knopf), husband and wife Pulitzer Prize winners, Nicholas Kristof and Sheryl WuDunn, argue that the key to economic progress in the world lies in unleashing women's potential. Education is a key to change. When you educate one young girl or woman, she takes what she learns to her community—and when a community knows better, they do better.

As entrepreneurs, we can no longer be silent. We must stand up and share our voices, share our healing, and support one another in this journey. YOU can no longer be silent.

Your Time Is Now…To Allow Courage to Eclipse Fear

The first step to playing a bigger game is to make a decision to do it, and that takes immense courage. I know that may sound simple, but this is where 95 percent of entrepreneurs get stuck. So often, we take action without making a decision first. That renders any and all action useless.

Several years ago, I read a poem that changed my life. I now read it every single day, and assign this same practice to my coaching students:

"Our deepest fear is not that we are inadequate. Our deepest fear is that we are powerful beyond measure. It is our light, not our darkness that most frightens us. We ask ourselves, who am I to be brilliant, gorgeous, talented, fabulous? Actually, who are you not to be? You are a child of God. Your playing small does not serve the world. There is nothing enlightened about shrinking so that other people won't feel insecure around you. We are all meant to shine, as children do. We were born to manifest the glory of God that is within us. It's not just in some of us; it's in everyone. And as we let our own light shine, we unconsciously give other people permission to do the same. As we are liberated from our own fear, our presence automatically liberates others." —Marianne Williamson, *A Return to Love*

FEAR: False Evidence Appearing Real

I knew that playing small was not acceptable. It was not acceptable for my life, or the life of those individuals I am meant to serve. Was I afraid? Yes, but I had to reach deep and muster the courage to start. Being fearless isn't about being 100 percent unafraid. It is about being terrified, but jumping in anyway. Every day, I jump in anyway. When you share your gift in a profound way and shine your light, you provide your clients with permission to do the same. Each time we face our fear, we gain strength, courage, and confidence.

Your Time Is Now...To Embrace the Leader Within You

Every year, I speak to entrepreneurs on stages all over the world. I have spoken alongside brilliant entrepreneurs like Harvey McKay, Tony Hsieh, Jack Canfield, Mark Victor Hansen, Brian Tracy, and Christopher Howard. More often than not, I am the only female taking the stage. I am part of an exclusive organization of the world's leading speakers and authors. Until a few years ago, I didn't even receive an invitation to attend. When I finally did, out of a room of 125 of the nation's elite, there were 10 women, and five of them were assistants to the big guys. That year, I began my mission, and in 2010, we finally did a woman's panel at that event. It was touted as the best segment of the event. But I couldn't help wondering "where are all the women leaders?"

More than ever before, the world needs women leaders. We are transforming the way business is conducted. I feel passionately about this mission, and in 2011, I announced a new division of my company called The Women's Leadership Academy. I could no longer be silent. An analysis in *Psychology Today* of 45 leadership studies found that the best leaders are inspirational mentors who encourage their followers to develop their abilities and creatively change their own circumstances. Women, on average, are more likely than men to enact this "transformational" style. Previous research has shown the transformational style to be most effective, particularly when companies rely on innovation to stay competitive.

Transformational leadership is a type of leadership style that leads to positive changes in those who follow. Transformational leaders are generally energetic, enthusiastic, and passionate. Not only are these leaders concerned and involved in the process, they are also focused on helping every member of the group succeed as well.

As an example, we offer profit sharing programs at my company. My company is about creating a WIN-WIN-WIN scenario—the customers win, the team wins, and my company wins. It puts every team member in the place to choose their own income and fosters dedication to the vision.

It Isn't Just My Opinion, the Research Shows It All

If that doesn't convince you, consider this research. According to the Center for Women's Business Research, women currently control $14 trillion in assets—a number that is expected to grow to $22 trillion within the next 10 years. Women also make up 43 percent of the North American affluent segment, which isn't necessarily surprising when you consider that women are starting businesses at twice the rate of men (based on Merrill Lynch research). As of 2010, there are over 10.6 million women-owned businesses employing 19.1 million people and generating 2.5 trillion in sales. Women business owners employ 35 percent more people than all the Fortune 500 companies combined (how many of your clients are women-owned businesses?)

According to new data projections from The Guardian Life Small Business Research Institute, future job growth will be created primarily by women-owned small businesses. Guardian's research shows that by 2018, women entrepreneurs will be responsible for creating between 5 million and 5.5 million new jobs nationwide. That's more than half of the 9.7 million new jobs the Bureau of Labor Statistics expects small businesses to create, and about one-third of the total new jobs the BLS projects will be created nationwide in that time frame.

Why are we so successful? It is the way we run businesses. Studies indicate that women entrepreneurs are diligently engaged in the strategic and tactical facets of their businesses. They are proactively customer-focused, likely to incorporate community and environment into their business plans, are receptive to input and guidance from internal and external advisors, and are committed to creating opportunities for others.

When You Lead, You Serve

Leadership is all about service. When you lead, you serve. Those who serve learn an important lesson about leadership. Leadership empowers, lifts, and inspires. When you serve others, you empower, lift, and inspire, and you feel the satisfaction of making a difference if for no other reason than it was the right thing to do.

It is time for you to embrace your inner leader.

Your Time Is Now…To Do Whatever It Takes To Create a Highly Profitable, Conscious Business

Creating profit is not just about living a luxurious lifestyle, although there is absolutely nothing wrong with that. When you create a profitable business, you not only become a leader (as part of the statistics above) where you are creating jobs, but you also then have the financial means to give back. When you follow a conscious business model, you seek to benefit both the external livelihood as well as the internal lives of the company's shareholders and employees.

Every day, I teach clients how to build highly profitable, conscious business models in my Ignite Business Coaching Program. For more information about this program, feel free to visit my website: www.kellyoneil.com. Building the business model is just one step. But for many of us, we can take all the right action in the world, but it is not enough.

If you will take the time to line up your Energy, meaning create a vibration match between your desire and your belief, the Universe will deliver to you amazing circumstances and events toward your physical conclusions. "*However, if you proceed with action before you have aligned your Energies of belief and desire, there is not enough action in the world to make any real difference.*" —Abraham-Hicks

Develop a Love Affair with Money

Many of us, especially women, do not have a healthy relationship with money. We are taught by others that we don't deserve money or it is hard to make money, or that by earning money, you are taking it away from someone else and it isn't spiritual to earn money…blah, blah, blah. These are all false and limiting beliefs that will keep you and your business playing small.

If your bank account is not full, you likely have resistance to receiving abundance.

"When people ask us how long does it take for something to manifest, we say, It takes as long as it takes you to release the RESISTANCE. Could be 30 years, could be 40 years, could be 50 years, could be a week. Could be tomorrow afternoon." —Abraham-Hicks

Your ability to create and retain wealth is determined by your relationship with money. Like everything on this planet, money is a simply a form of energy which is attracted to the energy that is like itself. Your relationship with anything determines how much of that thing you are attracting or repelling. Money does not exist by itself but it is always attached with the energy of the person who relates with it.

It all comes down to values. Wealthy people know that money is very important, that is why they have it. Poor people think money is not important, that is why they lack it. Can you imagine if you kept telling your significant other or your children that they are not important? How long do you think they are going to stay with you? What you appreciate, appreciates in value. What you do not appreciate, depreciates in value.

Here is where most people get trapped. Your motivation for making money is vital. If your motivation for making money comes from fear (lack), anger or the need to prove yourself, then money will never bring you happiness. Anger and the need to prove yourself are also forms of fear. It is a state of being where you feel you don't have something and therefore you need to fight to get it. It is to intend and act from a place of fear. The opposite is to intend and act from a place of love. It is a state of being where you are whole and doing what brings you joy. This is where you have the greatest power to be of service and attract the most money.

There is nothing enlightened about denouncing wealth. The more money you have, the more you can circulate back into society and be a part of the abundance cycle.

Try this money exercise I assign to my clients developed by Louise Hay. Every day for 10 minutes, look yourself in your eyes in the mirror and say:

"I am one with the Power that created me. I am totally open and receptive to the abundant flow of prosperity that the Universe offers. All my needs and desires are met before I even ask. I am Divinely guided and protected, and I make choices that are beneficial for me. I rejoice in other's successes, knowing there is plenty for us all." —Louise Hay

Be Grateful

God gave you a gift of 86,400 seconds today. Have you used one to say "thank you?" —William A. Ward

One of the things that has had the biggest effect on my life is the realization of the power of gratitude. Truly being grateful for everything I have. It has affected everything. It has made me a more positive person. A more productive person. A better friend. A better coach. A happier person.

There's no doubt in my mind that the simple act of being in a state of gratitude on a regular basis will change anyone's life, positively, and immediately. If you look at what you have in life, you'll always have more. If you look at what you don't have in life, you'll never have enough.

This is a value I instill in those around me. In fact, when my friends and family sit down to eat at night, a ritual around our table is to tell everyone one thing that we are grateful for. I often have my team and my clients create a gratitude list of 25 things they are grateful for. At night when I lay my head on the pillow, I thank God for all of the gifts in my life, including the ones that are posing themselves as challenges. In fact, especially the ones that are posing as challenges.

"Life will give you whatever experience is most helpful for the evolution of your consciousness. How do you know this is the experience you need? Because this is the experience you are having at the moment."
—Eckhart Tolle

Living in a state of gratitude is perhaps the most powerful key for a woman to stay in a positive mindset. The reason for that, we now know, is that the part of the brain that is associated with feeling gratitude is not the same part of the brain that experiences fear, and that when one of those is sort of switched on, the other one automatically switches off. The way to be fearless is to start focusing on things for which you are grateful.

Give Back

With this new shift in business, I believe that we are moving away from competition and moving toward collaboration. If you believe in abundance, I mean really believe in abundance, then you know there is more than enough to go around. What would the world be like if we all helped each other lift one another up instead of tearing each other down?

I watched a movie several years ago called *Pay It Forward*. The movie is about a school social studies assignment that leads to social changes that spread from city to city. Assigned to come up with some idea that will improve mankind, a young boy decides that if he can do three good deeds for someone and they, in turn, "pay it forward," positive changes can occur.

From this inspiration, I developed a program called The Impact Model (available on my website). In my company, we provide free content and telecourses for entrepreneurial women who are just starting out.

What are some ways you could pay it forward and give back in your business?

Your Time Is Now…It Is Your Time to Shine

If you are reading this, it is no accident. Think of this chapter as a guardian angel tapping on your shoulder, reminding you of what you already know has been inside you waiting to come out. The world needs you and needs your gifts. It is time for you to step up and shine your light on the world.

Award-winning author, speaker and coach, Kelly O'Neil, is passionate about helping entrepreneurs think big, play bigger and step out into the spotlight to build highly profitable businesses that help create transformation in the world so they may live a truly extraordinary life. Kelly is the author of *Visionary Women Inspiring the World: 12 Paths to Personal Power* (Skyward, 2005). She has given thousands of media interviews to outlets that include *The Wall Street Journal, CNN, Bloomberg, Associated Press, The New York Times, USA Today, Time, Business Week, Forbes, Fortune, and even MTV*. She also appears regularly as a speaker at professional associations, as well as national and international conferences. Known for her devotion to excellence, Kelly's company has won several awards, including the PR Compass Award for Outstanding Public Relations and The ADDY Award for Branding. In addition, her company was named one of the 500 most innovative companies in America by Mega Marketing Guru, Seth Godin. Kelly was personally honored by the presidential council with the National Leadership Award. You can learn more about Kelly O'Neil International at www.kellyoneil.com where you can download our free gift.

CHAPTER 57

Networking? Are You Kidding? I Am Schmoozing!

by Anita Elias

December 10, 2008, Stockholm, Sweden, the lobby of the Grand Hotel. Tuxedos and gowns mingling with Tiaras and medals, where mostly all first names were preceded with the likes of Doctor, Minister, Duke or Countess, and "your Excellency" or two. The cold air outside somehow found its way through the glass and gold trimmed revolving door, prompting the black wool coats and oh so many furs to be hurriedly placed in a nonchalant fashion over dignified shoulders. The Press impeccably dressed as to blend inconspicuously among the ones they elegantly hunted for photo ops and impromptu interviews were on their best behavior. Here I was in the midst of it all, a nice Mexican girl, a proud U,S, citizen and single mother of one. My role: the strategic senior advisor for the 2008 recipient of the Nobel Prize for Medicine, which was to be given this night. I stand in the lobby in complete awe at the brilliant minds around me. And they were all getting ready for the most important night of their lives and the most prestigious event on the planet: The Nobel Prize ceremony hosted by the King and Queen of Sweden with all the "who is who" of the science and political world.

For me, it was the ultimate gig: fundraising for the Professor's Aids Foundation. Getting to know all of the people involved in his entourage was in itself a challenge. So many names and titles to remember! Politics was definitely in "da" house. Aids were a hot topic in political circles and events and this was no exception. Controversy surrounding the Nobel was not new and the scientific community is well known for its fierce cat fights. And so, in that lobby, I was quietly informed of my next assignment that would take place the following night, prior to dinner: to keep a very well-known VIP busy and especially kept away from my

Nobel prize-winning boss. The "whys" are not important, what mattered was that I had to engage this very important person, a total stranger and keep him away and entertained as much as possible. He was—so I was told—a very bright individual who had also a reputation for being extremely difficult and demanding. Nobody wanted to deal with him. He was that strong willed. And so it was up to me, the rookie in the team, to prove my worth. Oy!

"We heard you are a great schmoozer, so now is your chance to prove it," I was told in a serene but forceful way. A great schmoozer! It was not the first time I heard the term applied to me, but certainly the first time it made me shiver with doubt. I had to use my schmoozing skills on purpose? Focused and with a goal in mind?

I have to admit that every time somebody referred to me as a "natural schmoozer" it always made me uncomfortable. The connotations of schmoozing were too disturbing back then. Today the term is better understood and used much more often.

So what is schmoozing? According to the Oxford Dictionary schmooze is, as a verb, to talk intimately and cozily; to gossip. To talk in a cozy or intimate manner to (someone), typically in order to manipulate, flatter, or impress them. As a noun, it is a long and intimate conversation. At the Urban dictionary, you can find the following definition of schmoozing: "Making ingratiating small talk—talk that is business-oriented (note: not always), designed to both provide and solicit personal information but avoids overt pitching. Most often an artifact of "networking." It is more art than science but can be learned. "

This for me was profound in more than one way. First it legitimized for me that who I was—a schmoozer—was not a "bad" thing, as so many columnists and authors go to great lengths to emphasize. I was a natural born conversationalist, who delights in meeting new people and connecting with them. Second, and the most important to me was, that it is a skill that can be learned, which meant it can be taught. If I was considered a good schmoozer, I could teach other people how to do it successfully! Schmoozing is about communicating, connecting, and establishing that magic rapport that can carry two strangers into a new level of connectivity in areas as diverse as the human mind can take them to.

It was that night in Sweden that made me realized the importance of schmoozing with a purpose and with a goal in mind (feel free to substitute the word schmoozing with the word networking at any time!) Some of you might think that it is very calculated and borderline manipulative to approach people with a planned agenda in mind, but let's be brutally honest about the subject: we are constantly interacting and connecting to achieve specific goals: personal or professional. It takes the same effort to build meaningful personal relationships as it is to embark on a business mission. And it should take not only the same effort, but also the same commitment and passion that are supposed to go together inherently. The question is how we approach this planning stage. It is not with visions of macabre potions being brewed in huge cauldrons to be dropped in the unsuspecting victim's drink. It is also not using the illicit powers of seduction and flirtation (in no particular order) just to prove our egos that we can.

The principles of good schmoozing have been established long ago. These principles are constants that do not change. Schmoozing's objectives are connecting, establishing rapport and building productive relationships. Our take or angle in this equation is that besides the fact that we have a focused purpose, our approach to the ritual of schmoozing is from the perspective that we do not see it only as a tool. It is a way of connecting to our fellow humans. It is an attitude towards life, it is how we communicate; it is who we are, when we are at our best!

When reviewing various articles on the art of schmoozing, we encounter the same advice over and over again and for a good reason: they are universal codes of conduct when being true to ourselves! Here are the tenants of good networking, with our guide for effective schmoozing:

Smile: Smiling puts us at ease and improves our mood. Smiling is contagious. Smile sincerely and trust will follow.

Connect: Convey who you are with confidence and a great opening line. Yes, rehearse it. Memorize it and make it memorable. Many times I introduce myself as a "Communications Plumber" and people remember me!

Help: Remember John F. Kennedy: "Ask not what your connections can do for you—ask what you can do for your connections."

Motivate: Research who you are going to meet. Familiarize yourselves with that person's reality. Learn about their passions, achievements or their style. Are you impressed? Go ahead and pay them a sincere compliment. From the heart! Don't know them? No problem, establishing common ground based on the immediate circumstances is easier than you think. Just look around and assess where you are, with whom and why.

Observe: Learn to read their body language. Are they fidgeting? Nervous? Looking you in the eye? Avoiding touch? Facing you? Mirroring you? Be alert and conscious about these signs. They will tell you more than any word coming out of their mouths.

Open: Be approachable and light! Don't take yourself too seriously. We are all here to meet and greet and live and breathe. Remember the non-verbal communication signs for yourself as well. Do not stand in a corner with your arms crossed or checking your smartphone to avoid eye contact.

Zip it! Once the introductions are done, and the flow of conversation gets going, allow the other person to talk! Really! Your job is to listen, and to encourage the other to talk about themselves and what makes them tick. You are there to listen and learn!

Enrich: Nourish your brain, body and soul with anything and everything your heart desires. Follow your passions and hobbies. It will make you a much more interesting and whole person. It also creates a domino effect with those around you.

As for what happened that night in Stockholm with my mission impossible assignment, I must say it was one of the most challenging and memorable nights of my life. I decided to ignore all references to the VIP's character and made a leap of faith in human kind. As I was being introduced to him, I couldn't help notice a very nice medal in his lapel. I was curious. Breaking protocol and with the biggest smile on my face I asked for the reason his wearing a medal. He smiled back and started telling me the story of his medal, his life and his passions. Needless to say, I was totally engaged in conversation with him for the next three hours, sitting together for cocktails and later for dinner. I found him not only intelligent, but full of charisma and he had a great sense of humor! That night, I gained not only a wonderful new friend, but a whole new perspective on the old art of small talk.

Anita Elias is a specialist in business leadership and cross-cultural communications. Her humorous and straight forward approach has been perfected through 15 years of training executives, actors, health-care providers, teachers and business owners at institutions such as New York University, Citibank, The AIDS World Foundation, and The New York City Board of Education.

Since relocating to Florida in 2004, Anita has worked extensively throughout the U.S. as a leadership and career development Coach for JAFRA Cosmetics International, a global cosmetics corporation. Additionally, Anita served as Senior Strategic Advisor for Professor Luc Montagnier and his World Foundation for Medical Prevention and Research. Prof. Montagnier was the 2008 Nobel Prize recipient in medicine for his discovery of the Human Immunodeficiency Virus (HIV). She also joined Influens, Inc., an international training and coaching company, focusing on performance and executive coaching of Fortune 500 companies. These experiences have given her an invaluable inside view of leadership and human performance development. As of January, 2011, Anita launched The Schmooze Guru™, a consulting and training company specializing in interpersonal communications and leadership development.

Born and raised in Mexico City, Anita's credits in her native country include work in theatre and TV, as well as radio appearances as an actor, director and commentator. Anita holds a BFA in Theatre from Tel Aviv University, Tel Aviv, Israel and conducted graduate studies in Interpersonal Communication and Speech at New York University. A true citizen of the world, Anita is trilingual and delivers trainings in fluent English, Hebrew, and Spanish.

Anita currently resides in Miami, Florida with her husband Michael and their kitties Maddie and McKenzie.

Section Six

Resources

Resources for Smart Entrepreneurs

Article Directories (submitting your articles)
www.ezinearticles.com
www.ideamarketers.com
www.goarticles.com

Audio for Websites, Podcasting Syndication, and MP3s
www.smartwomenaudio.com

Blog Services
www.wordpress.org
www.blogger.com
www.wordpress.com
www.typepad.com

Bookkeepers
www.smartwomenteam.com

Bookkeeping Software
quickbooks.intuit.com

Book Printing
www.smartwomeninstitute.com/publishimprint

Business Card Printing
tinyurl.com/overnightprints-com

CD Duplication
www.vervante.com

Clip Art
www.clipart.com

Coaching/Consulting
www.smartwomeninstitute.com

Copyright & Communications Law
www.legalwritepublications.com

www.copyright.gov
www.fcc.gov

Copywriting
www.smartwomenteam.com

Creating a Group (Network, Association or Organization)
www.smartwomeninstitute.com/createnetwork

Creativity Tools
www.visualthesaurus.com
www.visual-mind.com
www.smartdraw.com

Domain Registration and More
www.godaddy.com

Editors
www.smartwomenteam.com

Email Autoresponders
www.practicepaysolutions.com/sherimcconnell
www.aweber.com

Email Publishing & Marketing
www.practicepaysolutions.com/sherimcconnell
www.constantcontact.com

Fax/Voicemail/E-mail/Conference (Includes 800 #)
www.onebox.com

File Sending
www.dropbox.com
www.yousendit.com

Free Telephone Conferencing and More
www.freeconferencecall.com

Free Search Engine Submission
www.dmoz.org

www.about.com
www.yahoo.com

Fulfillment Services
www.vervante.com
www.speakerfulfillmentservices.com

Graphic Facilitation for Meetings
www.makemark.com

Incorporation
www.corporatedirect.com

Legal
www.smartwomeninstitute.com (Faculty)

Logo Design
www.LogoYes.com
www.thelogocompany.net

Marketing
www.smartwomeninstitute.com/products

Merchant Account
www.practicepaysolutions.com/sherimcconnell
www.Paypal.com
www.Clickbank.com

Office Solutions
www.onebox.com
www.volusion.com

Office Supplies
www.officedepot.com
www.wtsmedia.com

Podcast Directory Submission
www.smartwomenaudio.com

Publicity
www.prtakeoff.com

www.anniejenningspr.com
www.publicityhound.com
www.guerrillapublicity.com
www.helpareporter.com

Printing
tinyurl.com/overnightprints-com
www.vistaprint.com
www.mimeo.com

Product Creation, Packaging
www.vervante.com

Product Fulfillment (Mailing Services)
www.vervante.com

Project Management
37signals.com

Publishing Consulting
www.smartwomeninstitute.com

Search Engine Optimization
www.overture.com
www.wordtracker.com
www.accelerateonline.net

Shopping Cart
www.practicepaysolutions.com/sherimcconnell

Small Business Advice
www.smartwomeninstitute.com

Social Networking
www.facebook.com
www.twitter.com
www.linkedin.com
www.ping.fm

Success Strategies for Entrepreneurs
www.smartwomeninstitute.com

Survey Tool
www.surveymonkey.com

Trademark
4trademark.com

Virtual Team Experts/Assistants
www.smartwomenteam.com

Website (Hosting)
www.bluehost.com/track/sherimcconnell

Website (Full Solutions
www.wordpress.org

Website (Statistics)
www.webstat.com
www.google.com/analytics